How Food
Made Histor

HOW
FOOD
MADE
HISTORY

B. W. HIGMAN

⊛WILEY-BLACKWELL

A John Wiley & Sons, Ltd., Publication

Blackwell Publishing was acquired by John Wiley & Sons in February 2007. Blackwell's publishing program has been merged with Wiley's global Scientific, Technical, and Medical business to form Wiley-Blackwell.

Registered Office
John Wiley & Sons Ltd, The Atrium, Southern Gate, Chichester, West Sussex, PO19 8SQ, UK

Editorial Offices
350 Main Street, Malden, MA 02148-5020, USA
9600 Garsington Road, Oxford, OX4 2DQ, UK
The Atrium, Southern Gate, Chichester, West Sussex, PO19 8SQ, UK

For details of our global editorial offices, for customer services, and for information about how to apply for permission to reuse the copyright material in this book please see our website at www.wiley.com/wiley-blackwell.

The right of B. W. Higman to be identified as the author of this work has been asserted in accordance with the UK Copyright, Designs and Patents Act 1988.

Wiley also publishes its books in a variety of electronic formats. Some content that appears in print may not be available in electronic books.

Designations used by companies to distinguish their products are often claimed as trademarks. All brand names and product names used in this book are trade names, service marks, trademarks or registered trademarks of their respective owners. The publisher is not associated with any product or vendor mentioned in this book. This publication is designed to provide accurate and authoritative information in regard to the subject matter covered. It is sold on the understanding that the publisher is not engaged in rendering professional services. If professional advice or other expert assistance is required, the services of a competent professional should be sought.

Library of Congress Cataloging-in-Publication Data

Higman, B. W., 1943–
   How food made history / B. W. Higman. – 1st ed.
     p. cm.
   Includes bibliographical references and index.
   ISBN 978-1-4051-8948-4 (hardback) – ISBN 978-1-4051-8947-7 (paper)
1. Food habits–History.   2. Food–Social aspects–History.   I. Title.
   GT2850.H46 2011
   394.1'209–dc23

                          2011022726

A catalogue record for this book is available from the British Library.

This book is published in the following electronic formats: ePDFs 9781444344646; Wiley Online Library 9781444344677; ePub 9781444344653; Mobi 9781444344660

Set in 10.5/13pt Minion by SPi Publisher Services, Pondicherry, India
Printed in Singapore by Ho Printing Singapore Pte Ltd

1   2012

Contents

Illustrations

Preface

Food history has at least two major strands. One is concerned primarily with the history of food itself, often finding its voice in celebration of the joy of preparing and consuming particular foods – raw or cooked – with a strong emphasis on pleasure. The second strand originates more often with social and economic historians whose concerns typically lie elsewhere and show little evidence of the pleasures associated with food. Indeed, the regular fare of this second variety of food history is found in painful problems rather than pleasure, with an emphasis on deprivation and the role of food in conflict, for example, or, alternatively, studies of production and trade located firmly in the "dismal science" of political economy. Alongside these two main streams in the writing of food history are studies emanating from the disciplines of anthropology, archeology, sociology, geography, and psychology. A further, parallel, division exists between the popular celebration of food – exhibited most clearly in the West in the proliferation of television cooking shows, which had their beginnings with James Beard in 1946 – and the predictions of doomsayers, seeing famine and disaster beginning in the global South and spreading globally.

These two central themes, pleasure and pain, coexist in food history but most often run along separate paths. One of my aims is to bring them together, or to make sure at least that the separate routes criss-cross, because fundamentally the division is a false one. A major reason why it is false is simply that food systems are interconnected and codependent, both internally and externally. Contrasting outcomes are frequently merely two sides of the same coin. I believe these connections need to be confronted and the two strands brought together, however uncomfortably, in a single account.

The subject of this book is vast. My objective has been to provide a broad sketch of the history of food but without imagining that this can be achieved in a genuinely comprehensive manner. It is not possible even to mention all the plants and animals that have been important in the food culture of every region and society, in every period, let alone put the development of food cultures in the context of social, economic, and political change. Rather, my method has been to emphasize the truly large-scale and the truly dramatic and significant. This means picking out some periods and places for special attention. As a result, the past 50 years are given a good deal of space, not simply because they are recent and familiar to readers but because they represent a distinctive period in many ways unlike any that went before. The revolutionary transition to agrarian and urban systems that was clearly articulated by 5000 BP (before the present), though far from universal, also receives close attention, as does the fundamental transformation of world food systems that followed the Old World's discovery of the New. Occasionally, I have focussed on a particular food, because it is especially important or because it represents a type of development. Otherwise, I have selected specific episodes to illustrate the broader trends and processes.

What I seek to do is explain how the history of food, particularly the choices people made about what to eat and how to produce and consume it, has been a fundamental driver of world history in all its aspects. This is a two-way street, an interactive process. Food is both a central driving force and a central part of life that responds and transforms in turn.

For putting me on the path that led to this book, I thank Diane Kirkby and Tim Rowse. The manuscript was written in the School of History of the Research School of Social Sciences at the Australian National University. I thank my colleagues for their comments and suggestions and also the students who took my courses on the history of food. Merle Higman read the entire manuscript, more than once.

Prologue: Questions of choice?

Of the many choices we make in our lives, what to eat is perhaps the most enduring and important. Whereas individual human beings can go through life without participating in political acts and without personal liberty and can survive without forming a family or having sex, none of us can go without food. It is the absolute biological necessity of food that makes it so central to cultural history and so inclusive of all peoples in all times. As Brüssow (2007: 20) puts it, "eat" is "the first commandment of the laws of thermodynamics." Energy cannot be created from nothing; it can only change form. It is food that draws human beings into the web of life. However, unlike other basic human needs driven by biology, the desire to eat can be satisfied in a huge variety of ways, opening the possibility of choice and selectivity, and making the consumption of food a part of culture. It is this necessity and this shared experience that helps make food history so appealing, inducing a kind of intellectual salivation that matches the appeal of reading cookbooks and watching cooking shows.

The question of choice, sometimes called the question of social nutrition, is not the only way of approaching food history but it is perhaps the most fundamental. Tracing the history of choice opens doors on its many consequences and ramifications. Choice affects every one of the major phases of the food system, from acquisition to production, processing, and preservation, to distribution and exchange, and preparation and consumption. Each of these phases is important in itself, with far-reaching consequences for world history, while the different phases can also be articulated in a wide variety of combinations. Thus, any attempt to understand systems of food production and consumption requires close attention to the global pattern of

How Food Made History, First Edition. B. W. Higman.
© 2012 B. W. Higman. Published 2012 by Blackwell Publishing Ltd.

resources and human perceptions, changing patterns of availability and seasonality, the diffusion of plants and animals, human migration and colonization, warfare and domination, as well as social attitudes and religious prohibitions, the concept of taste, health and nutrition, and the politics of distribution. For many people, and for many long periods, the search for food has been a central preoccupation and a vital driver of social, cultural, economic, and political development. Only in very recent times have some societies enjoyed food security and year-long abundance. How this transition came about, and why it occurred in different ways in different regions of the world, is a fundamental question not just for food history but for world history on the grandest scale.

How much choice do we really have? How has the ability to choose changed over the long term? The notion of abstract freedom is at base a dubious assumption to apply to the living of daily life, because humans are creatures of habit. As social beings, we find it difficult to surrender long-held practices and attitudes shared with a community, and difficult to offend or contradict others. Communities and societies quickly build hierarchies of power and command, so that the ability to choose is regularly surrendered to individuals or small groups who take advantage of their authority to make decisions for the population. Further, and more broadly, it can be argued that it is climate and soil that play a determining role in ordering the world, creating patterns of production and consumption that essentially remain intact in spite of the great forces of imperialism, migration and globalization (Becker and Sieber, 2010).

However it may be produced, distributed, and exchanged, food serves as one of the most vital means by which power relations are expressed. Thus, those agents who hold the reins of the political economy, and those who possess the authority to control consumption by law and custom, have great power to shape societies. Such domination is not confined to the power of nation-states but has been exercised also by chiefdoms, warlords, religious institutions, global trading companies, multinational corporations, and social modelers. Further, the hegemonic power derived from the control of food has not been limited to the satisfaction of material, bodily needs, but has also been mediated through ritual and symbolic meals, in which food is deployed as a means of connecting the physical with the spiritual, this world with other universes.

Why do we eat what we eat and why have different cultures and societies at different times eaten other things? These questions put the idea of choice at the center of the narrative and thus open up connections with the broader context and the implications of specific decisions.

A simple model of food choice would look something like the following. People choose first from the environment around them, selecting from the plants and animals that may be ingested directly, fresh, without ill effect, and, hopefully, taste good. Plucking a ripe fruit dangling tantalizingly from a tree, for example, may appear seductive but may equally prove a deadly choice. Deciding to swallow something new represents a vital moment, answering an expectation of pleasure and satisfaction but matched by fear.

This association of pleasure and pain created what Rozin and Rozin (1981: 12) were first to term "the omnivore's dilemma," a dilemma which confronts modern humans and affects their willingness to sample unknown foods but was much more threatening for those who were the original testers (Pollan, 2006). Further risky experimentation was essential to demonstrate that some plants and animals have ill effects if consumed fresh but are safe and nutritious once processed in special ways, by squeezing out toxic elements, for example. Cooking, the application of heat, offers the next stage in the chain of choice, making certain plants and animals edible or better tasting, as achieved by the roasting of yam or kangaroo meat, for example. Regardless of particular methods of preparation and cooking, these technologies helped introduce to the human diet plants and animals that would not otherwise have been eaten.

From the thousands of possible plant and animal species that might be eaten by humans, only a small proportion is in fact consumed. A further narrowing is associated with the self-conscious manipulation of nature, through cultivation and management, that privileges certain plants and animals over others. Domestication carries the process to a new stage, through the selection of particular species and varieties, and the selective breeding of seeds and animals. It is a process dominated by choices, whether decisively or less consciously made. This process can be carried to a high level of scientific sophistication, as in genetic modification or superdomestication. On the other hand, knowledge of the foods, plants, and animals natural to the world beyond the boundaries of a particular region or locality creates the potential for choices about what to adopt and adapt, with the outcome generally expanding the locally available range of possible food choices, though sometimes with quite different long-term consequences. All of these choices involve selective acquisition from nature.

The next stage in the model relates to preservation, processing, and distribution. Being able to stretch food supplies over long periods is important, especially where acquisition and production are highly seasonal or uncertain, with abundance followed by scarcity. Preserved foods not only contribute to improved food security for local communities but also enable exchange and long-distance trade. Spinach grown in India can be frozen and shipped to markets across the world, for example, and, long before the invention of freezing, fish could be made viable by drying, smoking, salting, or pickling. Rapid transport, by steamship or airplane, created trade in exotic fresh fruits, making available bananas and mangoes grown in the tropics and sold in temperate zone markets. Canning had a similar effect but required prior processing. Thus, preservation, processing, and transportation technologies determine choices about what can be consumed out of season, what can be consumed in exotic places (which do not themselves have the conditions necessary to produce an item), and what can be acquired cheaply by trade. The choices made can create very short or very long food-chains.

Choices about distribution depend not only on technologies. Trade and exchange are controlled equally by decisions made about preferred market partners and what we wish to offer and accept. Such choices are often as much about politics and social relations as they are about price. There are many levels of choice here, ranging from distribution between households and local markets, to distribution between nation-states, governed by theories of the benefits of trade and agreements brokered by the World Trade Organization. Individuals may seem to have little choice under some of these arrangements and even at the household level distribution may be quite closely controlled by custom, with rules about who gets the biggest and best portions based on gender, age, and social rank.

Overlapping and adding to some of the choices already introduced to the model, the next stage in the food system relates to preparation. Where people in the past depended on a single basic element, like whale meat among the Inuit or potatoes among the Incas, the possible ways of preparing food were inevitably limited. Where modern systems of supply make available almost any ingredient in any season of the year, the choices appear much greater. Outcomes will depend on particular cooks, whether poor people cooking for themselves at home or chefs employed as professionals in the kitchens of expensive restaurants, and their knowledge and experience. The combination of ingredients in single dishes depends on cooking technologies and fuel, as well as the availability of cooking media: oils, fats, ovens, spit-roasts, and so on. As well as these choices based on knowledge, resources, and technologies, it is necessary to decide whether to do one's own cooking, to appoint a cook from within the household (typically a wife or mother, or perhaps a servant), or to eat the food cooked by commercial establishments such as restaurants or takeaways.

Finally, choices are made about how to consume food, be it raw or cooked. When to eat and with whom to share. Whether to eat alone or communally, whether to eat inside the house or out, whether to dip from a common pot, and whether to use utensils or the hand. Whether to organize a meal into courses, and how to decide their order. All of these matters may be surrounded by tight social rules and rituals.

Even the simple model outlined here suggests the numerous and multilayered choices that are made by individuals, communities, and states in the process of deciding what to eat. Not only are the choices significant in their direct consequences for the development of global agrarian systems and patterns of trade, but they may also be seen as additive. This is one reason why the trajectory of world history or so-called big history can be seen to speed up as we approach the present. Broadly, we can regard the last 50 years, the time in which we now live, as a unique period of momentous change, equivalent in many ways with the global transformation that occupied the previous 500 years, the centuries since Columbus. These fundamental shifts match changes that had their origins five to ten thousand years ago, derived from the growth of agriculture, urbanism, and writing, which marked the true beginnings of the modern world food system. This rough periodization does not fit every large region of the world equally well, but it can be deployed as a guide to megatrends that not only had implications for food history but were also very often themselves the product of dynamics within the food system itself.

A central feature, and apparent paradox, in the long-term development of world food systems has been a parallel trend toward both uniformity and diversity. On the one hand, modern human migrations and the associated redistribution of plants and animals have given a substantial portion of the world's people access to a wider range of foods than they knew five or ten thousand years ago. This means that people can now choose between a much extended range of possibilities but, at the same time, their experience is repeated across the globe to a significant extent. It is also repeated across seasons and climatic zones, thanks particularly to rapid and cheap transportation technologies and methods of preservation. There are still significant regional and ethnic variations in food cultures, but many items have come to be naturalized to such an extent that they are no longer thought of as having their origins far away in different places.

References

Becker, J. and Sieber, A. (2010) Is the spatial distribution of mankind's most basic economic traits determined by climate and soil alone? *PLoS ONE* 5: e10416.

Brüssow, H. (2007) *The Quest for Food: The Natural History of Eating.* New York: Springer.

Pollan, M. (2006) *The Omnivore's Dilemma: A Natural History of Four Meals.* New York: Penguin Books.

Rozin, E. and Rozin, P. (1981) Culinary themes and variations. *Natural History* 90: 6–14.

CHAPTER ONE

The Creation of Food Worlds

Although the modern food system has come to appear almost normal, many of its fundamental features are in fact very recent. Only recently have people lived in a world in which most food has been consumed by a dominant urban-industrial population, heavily dependent on resources transported over great distances, from quite different environments and regions – the modern world in which "food miles" can add up to a worrying degree. Only in recent times have consumers in some countries come to think of food as a packaged good, to be obtained almost exclusively by purchase, and come to regard anything taken directly from the wild as potentially dangerous.

Only in the past ten thousand years have human beings moved decisively toward living in sedentary settlements, using agricultural, horticultural, and pastoral techniques to produce food from domesticated plants and animals. Over the great length of human history, beginning with the emergence of *Homo erectus* in Africa two million years ago, some 90 per cent of hominin[1] species have lived by hunting and gathering. The experience for anatomically modern humans (*Homo sapiens*) is strikingly different, though covering little more than 200 000 years. The greater part of this period belonged to hunter-gatherers, and as late as the time of Columbus fully one-quarter of the world remained hunter-gatherer, but the massive and accelerating growth in population over the past two hundred years placed the weight of numbers within an agricultural realm.

[1] *Hominin* is preferred to *hominid* in identifying modern humans and their immediate bipedal relatives and ancestors. In the light of recent genetic findings, the term used previously to describe human-like primates – *hominid* – is now used to include also gorillas, chimpanzees, and bonobos (Barham and Mitchell, 2008: 1 and 476).

How Food Made History, First Edition. B. W. Higman.
© 2012 B. W. Higman. Published 2012 by Blackwell Publishing Ltd.

Settled, domesticated life associated with "civilization" comes late in the course of human history, marking a new relationship between people, plants, and animals. The transition became possible only with the end of the last Ice Age, which brought to a close the Pleistocene and ushered in the modern post-glacial epoch, the Holocene, an era of global warming. Sea levels were lower at the Last Glacial Maximum around 20 000 BP (before the present) than at any time over the previous 100 000 years, but then rose rapidly to the modern maximum with the melting of the northern glaciers and ice sheets. These changed environmental conditions enabled not only the transition to agriculture and urban life but also new modes of hunting and gathering. They created the conditions for the transition from a relatively uniform global food system to a world characterized by large-scale regional diversity and strongly contrasted modes of feeding a growing population.

Making the ancient world food map

The creation of unique and separate food worlds occurred in at least two ways. Most obviously, the rising sea levels associated with the melting of the massive glacial caps altered the balance between land and sea. Land which had long been dry and available as a pathway for human and other animals was inundated, creating formidable barriers. The most significant of these barriers was the Bering Sea, which cut off terrestrial movement between Asia and the Americas, thus establishing the basis for long-term independent development in the world's supercontinents, the so-called Old World of Eurasia and Africa and the New World of the Americas.

The result was two essentially separate food worlds, cut off from one another for millennia. This was something new in world history because, although there had been a series of transitions between glacial and interglacial conditions since the emergence of hominins, it was the first time human beings had been living in all the world's continents (except Antarctica) and the first time anatomically modern *Homo sapiens* had experienced such massive changes (Manning, 2006).

The rise in sea levels also created new island and archipelagic environments. In southeastern Asia, the Indonesian archipelago was brought into being and its islands cut off from New Guinea. The northern tip of Australia was separated from New Guinea and to the south Tasmania was similarly divided from the mainland. In the Caribbean, islands such as Cuba and Trinidad were separated from the Central and South American mainland. The possibilities of settlement and colonization by plants and animals became more difficult than they had been when land bridges existed. The animal life of islands, before the coming of humans, exhibited high levels of diversity and endemism, but large mammals, including carnivores, that might have been used for food or motive power were generally rare.

A second, quite different, consequence of the end of the last Ice Age was the warming of the planet, which ultimately created the conditions for revolutionary change in the human exploitation of plants and animals for food, the transition to domestication and agriculture. Early hunter-gatherers typically depended on food resources within a limited territorial range. Their choices were constrained by what was available within that zone. They were food takers rather than food makers. If the resources became depleted, there were good reasons to move on, to look for fresh sites with similar plants and animals or to new places with a different mix of potential foods.

Over millennia, the process of seeking out fresh food resources contributed fundamentally to the migration of people and the first colonization of the world. This initial colonization consisted principally of people finding new sites, empty of people, where they could exploit the available resources, in a manner parallel to the spread of plants and animals into new niches. The entry of people, as well as of plants and animals, changed the ecological balance, and people learned how to manipulate aspects of the ecosystem in order to ensure their supplies of food. However, before domestication, people rarely carried seeds or animals with them in their migrations. Their objective was to exploit whatever existing stock they found in a new region, not to transform it.

Because the initial colonization of the world was achieved by hunter-gatherers, it took a long time to complete. Although human beings with all the skeletal characteristics of their modern descendants, *Homo sapiens*, inhabited Africa from about 200 000 BP, they did not leave the continent for many millennia. The great migration that spread human beings across the world commenced about 70 000 years ago and continued to 10 000 BP, during which long period resources were often limited by environmental conditions. As in much human migration, people were impelled to move on because they felt that they would starve if they stayed where they were and could only hope that where they went would be a better place. They were pushed rather than pulled. They possessed only limited knowledge about what lay ahead, but observed the movement of animals, much as sea-voyagers later took the flight paths of birds as an indication that land lay ahead unseen, beyond the horizon. These anatomically modern humans out of Africa also encountered populations of archaic *Homo* species in Eurasia – Neanderthals in Europe and the recently identified "Denisovans" of southern Siberia – with whom they sometimes mated, exchanging genetic material and, no doubt, knowledge (Reich *et al.*, 2010).

So long as the total human population remained small, there was little pressure to move on quickly. Probably, the desire to satisfy curiosity about what lay across the next ridge or river accounted for a good deal of incremental migration, as much as any search for fresh food resources. In the Ice Age, however, the meager potential food resources in many regions meant that meat-eating humans often had little choice but to actively pursue their food when it moved ahead of them. Until the ice sheets and glaciers began to retreat, much of the arctic north was inhospitable and virtually uninhabitable because of the lack of food for animals as well as humans. Thus, the momentous movement of people across the Bering Sea land bridge, from Siberia to Alaska, that initiated the peopling of the Americas, commenced only toward the end of the Ice Age around 15 000 BP when the sea level was 300 ft (90 m) lower than it is today.

Most important in driving the pattern of migration was the fact that the people were hunter-gatherers, not looking for well-watered fertile sites where they could plant introduced crops and raise livestock, but always assessing the survivability of a place in terms of the observed stock of animals and plants that existed naturally in that environment. They devoted energy to digging for roots and tubers, and to the grinding or pounding of these materials using mortar and pestle, but for these omnivorous hunters what made a place attractive was above all the presence of animals which could be efficiently killed, cooked, and consumed. They were dedicated meat-eaters, obtaining more than half their calories from flesh and willing to tackle animals much larger than themselves. It was a dangerous business, with sabre-tooth tigers and other, now extinct, savage beasts competing for the same game.

It has long been claimed that it was the eating of meat that contributed most to the development of *Homo erectus*, separating human beings from the other primates, with a bigger brain and the capacity to construct language, itself arguably a product of the need for cooperation in early hunting and scavenging and meat distribution within groups (Bickerton, 2009: 121). Alternatively, because there were many hazards to depending on a meat diet, not only from the uncertainty of supply and the fierceness of prey and competitors but also from parasites, it may be that early humans used their new-found tools to dig up the roots and tubers that grew in secure abundance rather than to stalk wild animals or even to scavenge (Eisenstein, 2010). Tubers could have provided the brain boost needed for human development but only if they were first cooked, by roasting or boiling/steaming.

This necessity led recently to the hypothesis advanced by the biological anthropologist Richard Wrangham that cooking, using fire as a tool, is at the center of these developments. Heat transforms meat (and other food) not only by making proteins and starches more digestible, and safer by warding off parasites, but also by increasing the amount of energy it delivers. The virtue of cooking is not a recent discovery. Rather, argues Wrangham (2009: 14), it occurred at the beginning of human evolution with the emergence of *Homo erectus* and had anatomical consequences, so that we are creatures of our "adapted diet of cooked food, and the results pervade our lives, from our bodies to our minds." Raw-food diets can prove viable and have modern advocates but cooked food is the norm for almost all humans. It is cooked food that the starving dream of.

Fire was not only essential to cooking; it served as the most important tool of early transitions toward the manipulation of the environment and the behavior of wild animals within these ecosystems, practiced as early as 50 000 BP in southern Africa and Australia (Wrangham and Carmody, 2010). Down to about 10 000 BP, however, the essential cultures of hunting and gathering, fire and cooking, were effectively universal, and for this reason contributed little to the making of a diversified and regionalized ancient world food map. Until the end of the Ice Age, the pattern was essentially the same everywhere, though nuanced in terms of the specific plants and animals that were consumed in direct response to the biodiversity and environment of particular regions. This was not a closely interconnected world but one in which relatively isolated small communities existed within their particular ecological niches. It was the transition from hunting and gathering to agriculture, beginning around ten thousand years ago, and based on domestication and cultivation, that represented a true revolution in the global pattern of food systems.

The origins of domestication, agriculture, and urbanization

By 10 000 BP *Homo sapiens* had effectively settled in most regions of the world. Of the continental landmasses, the major exceptions were Antarctica, the coldest parts of the Arctic, and the icy northern two-thirds of mainland Eurasia. The peopling of these regions depended on the development of effective technologies for the hunting of large mammals, as well as more effective clothing and shelter. Antarctica never became attractive. Many islands also remained unsettled, particularly those of the Caribbean and the Pacific, because they were not stepping-stones to other places and lay beyond the accessible horizon. The islands of Remote Oceania, making up most of the Pacific, remained uninhabited even at 5000 BP, their peopling delayed by the need to develop ocean-crossing technologies and navigational skills. The food resources of such distant, isolated islands was impossible to predict and potentially hazardous.

Movement out of Africa into the tropical zones of Asia was relatively rapid once it began, with people settled all the way to Australia by 50 000 BP or earlier. The migration followed the water's edge around the tropical rim of the Indian Ocean and its often dense borderline of bamboo, subsisting on fish, crustaceans, and plant food, and into the mainland and islands of eastern and southeastern Asia, as far as New Guinea. It was the warmer, southern regions of mainland Asia and the islands of southeastern Asia that were most densely peopled and it was there that the transformation of food production occurred first. Early migrations of *Homo sapiens* out of Africa to parts of eastern Europe proved fragile, and the establishment of a permanent population, interacting with other varieties of *Homo*, was not firmly established throughout Europe until about 30 000 BP. The human settlement of the Americas also moved rapidly once it was begun, around 15 000 BP, spreading speedily down the western spine before spilling out into the eastern vastness.

Hunter-gatherers moved conservatively, unwilling to risk more than necessary in a world still clothed in thick forest and grassland, in which lurked wild animals and unknown potentially deadly plants. Even where human beings had lived for millennia, the density of population remained sparse in 10 000 BP. The total for the world was not much more than five million. There seemed to be plenty of food for these few people. It had only to be collected or killed.

Five thousand years on, the world's population was ten times larger, reaching about 50 million by 5000 BP. The rapid acceleration that occurred in these millennia was not evenly spread across the world, however, but confined largely to those few regions where domestication provided the foundation for an agricultural revolution, in fewer than ten independent sites known across the globe. It was this revolution that made possible the new mode of sedentary living and the beginnings of an urban revolution and a completely new system of food supply. Even though the first farming technologies were crude and domestication limited, together these innovations were able to support as much as 100 times the population that hunting-gathering could efficiently feed. The origins of the agricultural revolution are disputed but generally attributed to the impact of changing combinations of complex interactions between overpopulation, overexploitation, settlement patterns, climate change, and temporary climate reversals (Dow, Reed and Olewiler, 2009; Barker, 2006; Bellwood, 2005; Cohen, 1977).

Whatever the causes of the agricultural and urban revolutions, a key feature of the transformation was that they occurred independently at a widely separated series of sites spread across the world rather than diffusing from a single cultural hearth. This strongly suggests that the transformation was rooted in fundamental changes in the relationship between human beings and the natural world, associated with the transition from the Pleistocene to the Holocene. It is equally clear that the new ways of obtaining food did not quickly dominate everywhere and that not all peoples embraced the new ways, even when they became aware of these practices. This is an historical understanding not always shared by earlier interpretations of the transition.

Indeed, the scholar who invented the central terms of the debate, the Australian archeologist V. G. Childe, thought of the Neolithic Revolution and the Urban Revolution as confined largely to Southwest Asia and the Nile valley.

Childe's achievement, first set out in his book *Man Makes Himself* (1936), was to shift the study of prehistory away from the previously dominant three-age system with its emphasis on inorganic materials and tools – the Stone, Bronze, and Iron Ages – to a way of thinking about the past that introduced organic materials, particularly people and their food, as central drivers of change. The Neolithic Revolution – literally the New Stone Age, contrasted to the Old Stone Age of the Pleistocene – did not completely escape the traditional model but Childe used the term to distinguish its peoples from the "food gatherers" who had come before. He argued that this revolution transformed human economy by giving people control over their food supply. The Urban Revolution depended on the availability of surpluses and a diversified agriculture that could cope with seasonal variations in cropping patterns.

These changes were closely connected with innovations in knowledge and technology – from the plow to irrigation, writing and numeric notation, magic and religion – which Childe considered more significant than anything that had come before or was to come after. His revolutions were effectively complete by 5000 BP. Scholars have come to call Childe's Neolithic Revolution an Agricultural Revolution, which better identifies the core of his concept and points to its organic and biological underpinnings, but the fundamentals of his ideas remain secure and ensure a central role for food in long-term human development. The transition is undoubtedly one of the great turning points in history.

Research over the past half-century, particularly the use of new techniques for establishing ancient chronologies and tracing genetic heritages, has enabled a richer, more nuanced and more diverse view of the past than Childe's model was capable of capturing. Not only is it accepted that there were multiple, independent Agricultural and Urban Revolutions scattered around the world but it is also now recognized that the very meaning of "agriculture" and of "farming" need to be freshly conceptualized. Similarly, the notion that hunter-gatherers can be defined in simple opposition, by their merely not being farmers, has been challenged.

Most definitions of hunter-gatherer or forager societies refer to the distinctiveness of their patterns of subsistence, notably their hunting of wild animals, their collecting of wild plants, and their fishing, all without control over the reproduction of these food resources and without recourse to domestication. However, between the hunter-gatherer peoples who depended exclusively on wild plants and animals, at one extreme, and those farmers who relied heavily on the managed production of domesticated species at the other, there existed a vast and varied population that picked and chose from resource and technology options in ways that are not neatly classified and are

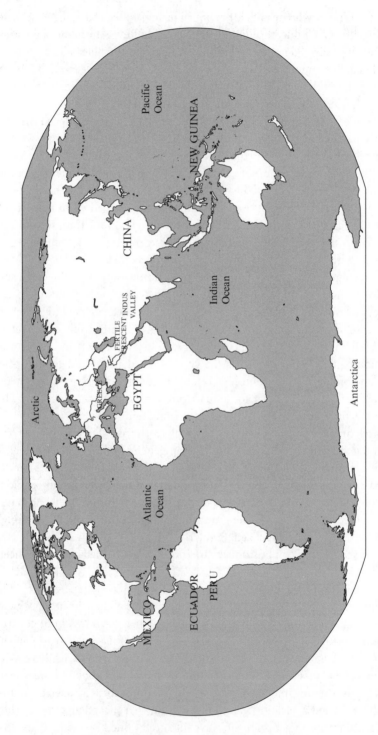

Figure 1.1 Sites of early agriculture, circa 5000 BP.

hard to map. The existence of this middle group demonstrates that there is nothing fundamentally incompatible about foraging and farming, and that the transition from one to the other need not be swift and sure. Low-level food production can exist with or without domesticated plants and animals, and with or without the application of land management technologies such as fire (Smith, 2001).

Thus, rather than seeing a sharp break between hunting/gathering and agriculture, it is possible to conceive a continuum, stretching from strict forms of hunting and collecting from nature all the way to the mechanized industrial agriculture of domesticated plants and animals. Along this continuum, the manipulation of soil, water, and microclimate is gradually intensified but the nature of the choices made about what to eat and what to grow remain essentially the same. Change might be extended over generations or even millennia. Thus, it can be argued that the behavior of those hunters and gatherers who did not invent or adopt agriculture was not unaffected by the transition from the Pleistocene to the Holocene but simply took different forms. In some cases they went only part of the way toward domestication. Some embraced the agrarian way of life only to reject it. But every choice, every selection, of what to consume from nature and what to avoid had its genetic consequences and its impact on the dispersion of plants and animals.

The outcome of these changes was a world of contrasting regions of food production and consumption, setting up the potential in the long term for exchange as well as competition and conflict for territory and resources. Previously, there had been significant contrasts between regions in terms of the particular foods that were consumed, since they all depended on what was available locally, but modes of exploitation had been more uniform. Now, there were contrasts not only in what was consumed as food but also in how it was produced, distributed, and prepared. It was a revolutionary and long-lasting difference but one observed only by those who lived in a few widely scattered sites. Those who looked on from the perspective of hunting and gathering were not always impressed by what they saw, thinking the life of the farmer much inferior to their own in terms of the amount of time and effort required to produce foods which were no better than third-rate. Vast regions of the world remained dominated by peoples more or less happy to depend on hunting, fishing, and gathering.

Food worlds at 5000 BP

The map of global food systems in about 5000 BP was more complex than any that had gone before but displayed no more than scattered suggestions of what it might become (Figure 1.1). It was characterized by "islands" of agriculture, either beacons lighting the way or alternatively vulnerable experiments that might falter and fade, in the midst of a still overwhelming world of hunter-gatherer economies. The domestication of the most important crop plants, including rice, wheat, and maize, was already almost at an end, completed within the years between 10 000 BP and 4000 BP. However, the proportion of the world's population living in urban places at 5000 BP was small and none of these settlements was individually substantial in modern terms. Not all of them would survive. What would happen next was far from a foregone conclusion.

Although in 5000 BP vast regions of North and South America still waited for their transitions, as did much of mainland and island Asia, and most of sub-Saharan Africa, Australasia, and the Pacific, the world food map was much more diverse than it had been five thousand years before. The transition to agriculture probably occurred first in Southwest Asia by 10 000 BP and from there diffused to the Indus valley of what is now Pakistan by 9000 BP, Greece by 8500 BP, and to the lower Nile by 7000 BP. The initial spread of agriculture into eastern and central Europe, around 8000 BP, followed the migration of people from Southwest Asia. Widely separated, but strikingly contemporaneous, independent examples of the shift occurred in New Guinea (10 000–7000 BP), Central Mexico (by 9000 BP), China (8500 BP), and northern South America (7000 BP). Almost all of Europe made the transition by 5000 BP, as did several additional regions in mainland eastern and southeastern Asia (Putterman, 2008: 745–6; Denham, 2007: 16).

Beyond the boundaries of those few scattered cultures that embraced the Agricultural and Urban Revolutions in the fullest degree, hunter-gatherers experimented with new ways of finding their food and at least implicitly faced hard decisions about whether to continue in the old paths or to adopt elements of sedentism and the hard labor of cultivation. Generally, people could make these decisions on their own terms. With the exception of some special cases, this was not a time of great empires or military conquest. Nor was it a time of powerful state systems or organized religion. People found their gods among the plants and animals with whom they shared the world. Although in some places, for example Central Europe, the first farmers were not descended from local hunter-gatherer populations but rather from people who had immigrated in the early Holocene, it is not clear how far this may have involved invasive colonization (Bramanti *et al.*, 2009).

In some cases, there is evidence that first farmers expanded their populations and spread into nearby regions, imposing their genes, languages and cultures on hunter-gatherer communities, but cultural diffusion and a process of gradual absorption of farming and food systems seems to have been more important in the long term. Rather than being forced to adopt or participate in any particular system of resource exploitation, in ways that would dominate much of the history of the world in the millennia to come, most people had to base these decisions on their perceptions of the environments in which they lived and their relationship to other living things. They were relatively free to make their choices on the basis of their local knowledge, including the observation of farmers and town-dwellers if such communities existed within their range.

Hunter-gatherer peoples occupied the widest range of environments. Their food sources and their technologies varied in direct response to differences in the environments in which they found themselves or chose to inhabit by migration and colonization. For individual groups and communities, choice was effectively bounded by their immediate environmental sites and by the biodiversity of those sites. The world beyond those boundaries was typically hostile and its resources potentially hazardous. Thus, the hunter-gatherer peoples of 5000 BP could do no better than choose to eat from what lived around them, whatever those resources might be. In doing so, human beings proved themselves highly adaptable omnivores, selecting from widely different ranges of foods in different places. However, in spite of these strong contrasts, hunter-gatherers lived according to a relatively uniform set of principles, in a pact with nature which was both respectful and fearful. A central feature of hunter-gatherer societies in 5000 BP was the eating of meat. In some regions, where plants could not prosper, meat-eating was a necessity. This was most obviously the case where climatic extremes of heat and cold, and wet and dry, created deserts and ice fields, which were parsimonious in their supply of edible plant life suited to the human digestive system but supported a relative bounty of land and sea animals.

What exactly did people choose to eat around 5000 BP? In part, the contrasts around the world reflected differences in a population's location along the tangled continuum that stretched from strict foraging to strict agriculture, but they also had to do with geographical location, rooted in local differences in biodiversity and topography, climate and soil. There were limits to the range of environments in which *Homo sapiens* could survive, but beyond the extremes people seemed able to find food almost everywhere on earth. The species proved highly adaptable. The plants and animals which made up the food of human beings were significantly less adaptable, flourishing in some environmental niches but not in others. Further, their dispersal by diffusion was less universal than that of humans.

Africa

Within Africa, the birthplace of *Homo sapiens*, people diffused first from their original home in the continent's eastern and southern grassland ecosystems to occupy the great zone of savanna stretching from Ethiopia to Senegal (Figure 1.2). The region was, however, subject to some of the most extreme

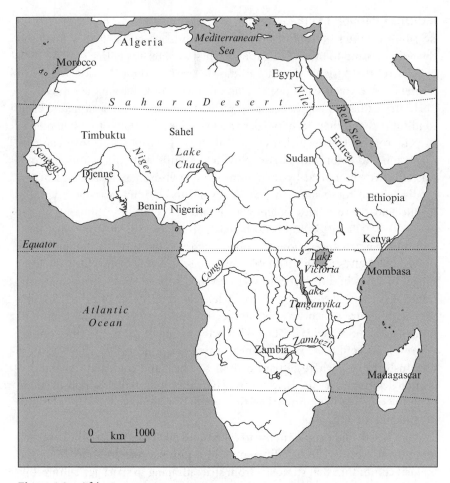

Figure 1.2   Africa.

fluctuations in climate experienced anywhere during the Holocene. Hunter-gatherers prospered on the grassy savannas from about 9000 BP, until severe aridification drove the early pastoral peoples from most parts of the Saharan desert around 6000 BP, often for as long as a thousand years. New groups of humans began to enter the region around 5000 BP, taking advantage of lakeside sites that offered fish, clams, and crocodiles that could be used to supplement the now scarce land animals.

Away from the lakes, there was intensified herding of domesticated cattle, and of domesticated sheep and goats introduced from the Levant which did better under drought by more efficiently exploiting the diminished vegetation, for a more diversified diet. The rapid desertification of the Sahara around 5000 BP made livestock increasingly important, by providing a relatively dependable supply of milk and meat, and perhaps blood. At the same time, the expanding mobile pastoralist peoples pushed into moister grassland regions to the south and east, and continued to practice hunting and gathering, including the collection of fruits, tubers, and wild grains (Barham and Mitchell, 2008: 359–62; Shaw *et al.*, 1993; Phillipson, 1985: 113–47). Here then was a perfect example of the continuum from foraging to farming, of the long-term coexistence of pastoralists and foragers, and of the potential for exchange between food producers.

These forces of change led to an expansion of food production systems into sub-Saharan Africa, which eventually saw the combination of herding with cultivated crops come to occupy almost the entire continent. This system was not derived from the experience of Egypt, which had the advantage of unusual ecological conditions. The domestication and cultivation of grain crops to the south exploited different plants, all of them indigenous, such as pearl millet and sorghum. Much of this process did not begin until about 4000 BP, and active cultivation rather than the occasional collecting of seed took even longer. Dating of the transition to farming throughout the rainforest remains poorly understood. The range of combinations of systems of food production and acquisition were complex, with the potential for repeated independent invention. It is most likely that sub-Saharan Africa, throughout the equatorial rainforest and beyond, remained the domain of hunters and gatherers.

At 5000 BP, the sole example of settled, agricultural society in Africa was that found on the lower Nile. Small villages of farming people had appeared first in the delta two thousand year before, cultivating barley and emmer wheat, with granaries for storage, and keeping domesticated cattle, sheep, goats, and pigs, but still practicing fishing and hunting, and foraging wild plant food. These settlements expanded substantially during the long period down to the unification of the Egyptian state and the establishment of the first of the numbered Egyptian dynasties, with their pharaohs and deities, in about 5000 BP. It was at this time that a new crop complex was introduced to Egypt, combining wheat, barley, and legumes. Oxen were harnessed for the first time, to pull plows through the wet, heavy soil, but much of the tillage continued to be the work of hand-hoes. This crop-combination was successful in the conditions of the lower Nile, where the annual flood washed away excess salts and fertilized the fields, but it failed to spread much further, even where irrigation was attempted, as for example at oases in the Sahara and in the uplands of Ethiopia and Eritrea (Wenke, 2009: 56–65).

In ancient Egypt, wheat and barley were used to bake bread and brew a thick, dark beer, but sometimes the grains were boiled whole or made into a kind of porridge, or roughly ground and baked as flat pancakes. These cereal

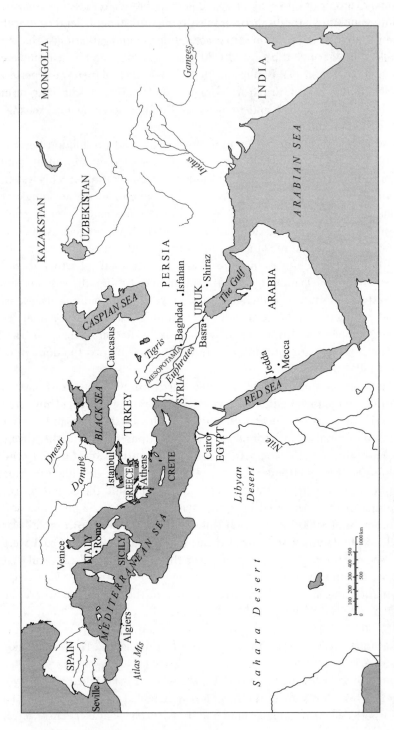

Figure 1.3 The Middle East and the Mediterranean.

foods were eaten together with legumes, such as peas and beans, and vegetables, including onions, garlic, leeks, lettuce, radishes, and melons. The meat of pigs was relatively common but the consumption of beef depended on wealth. Camels were used neither for transport nor food at this time. Fish, including the Nile perch, tilapia, and catfish, were plentiful, especially in the delta but also taken from ponds and preserved by drying and salting. Birds, including pigeon, quail, duck, and geese, were abundant in the delta and often domesticated, serving to recycle household waste and producing eggs as well as meat. Goats were equally useful as recyclers, providing both milk and meat, while pigs were valued strictly for their flesh. Salt was readily available but other seasonings and herbs were more limited. Small birds were sometimes eaten raw, for breakfast. Fruit came from orchards. Some of this fruit, including both dates and grapes, was used to make sweet wine, laid down to age in pottery jars.

Eurasia

The two most influential transitions to the new modes of food production, precursors of what was to happen in Egypt, occurred independently in Southwest Asia and China. It is significant that the first and best-known of these transitions occurred at the interface of Africa with Eurasia, running through the narrow Levantine corridor to the west of the Syrian Desert and curving in an arc through the Tigris and Euphrates river valleys (modern Iraq) to form the so-called Fertile Crescent (Figure 1.3). The transition did not simply mark the movement of humans out of Africa into a new environment but had to wait many millennia for the climate change, and the short-lived climate reversals, of the early Holocene. It was here that wheat and barley were domesticated from wild cereal varieties, and sheep and goats brought into the fold, in some of the earliest domestications (Brown *et al.*, 2009: 103–9). Not only was this small region of southwestern Asia significant for its agricultural revolution; it also formed the focus of influential cultural movements and saw the birth of some of the world's great religions, each with its particular food rituals and taboos.

By 5000 BP the people of the Fertile Crescent had added domesticated legumes such as lentils, broad beans, peas, and chickpeas to wheat, barley, and rye, and pigs and cattle to the sheep and goats. Technologies were developed to store grains and meat, to help provide food throughout the year. Animals were exploited in new ways, notably by harnessing them to provide motive power in the work of agriculture, increasing productivity through their capacity to pull heavy plows, and by using their manure as fertilizer. Cows, goats, and sheep were also milked, providing new food products, such as cheese, ghee, and yoghurt. These new ways of using animals in the food system not only were important within the agricultural zone of Southwest Asia but also enabled the

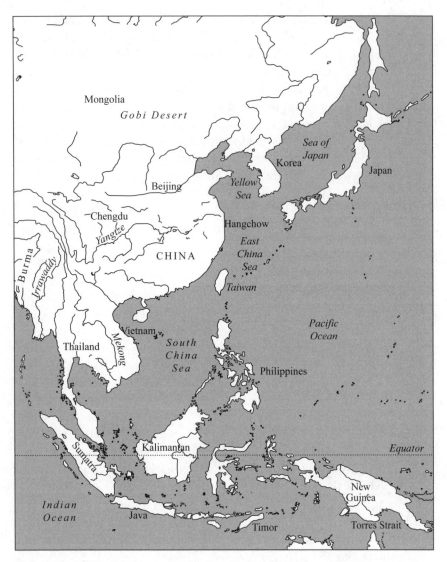

Figure 1.4   China and Southeast Asia.

development of efficient nomadic pastoral economies which spread beyond the region into the Russian steppes, where agriculture did not follow (Kohl, 2007:158–66).

Irrigation and drainage systems enabled the intensive settlement of fertile lowland valleys, where the first urbanized states of Mesopotamia were created. Grains were ground to make flour, and bread was baked. Pottery was used to make storage jars and to cook over fires and in clay-baked ovens. Most cooking involved boiling, steaming, roasting, or baking, effectively extending the range of what was palatable. Fermentation, in ceramic jars, was used to make beer and wine and domesticated olives were cured to make oil. Orchard fruits, such as date, fig, pomegranate, and apple, also became common around 5000 BP. By this time, domesticated animals had largely supplanted their wild relatives and the collecting of wild grain was no longer a profitable use of time. The food system of southwestern Asia had taken on a familiar character. A cuisine, a gastronomy, was taking form.

The second most significant center of domestication and agricultural transition was in China, where rice was domesticated by about 9000 BP on the Yangtze River (Figure 1.4). By 5000 BP large-scale wet-rice farming was firmly established and had spread recently into southern and southwestern China and to Taiwan (Chi and Hung, 2010; Zheng *et al.*, 2009). This development was associated with substantial human migration and population growth. New fields were opened up by the burning of marshes and the reclamation of land, and the soil was tilled using wooden spades and harvested with sickles made of bone. Plows, drawn by water buffalo, were not known. In the north, millet varieties were domesticated on the Yellow River by 8000 BP, and these found their way south, where they joined rice and tubers (yams and taro), and a long list of vegetables from leeks to lotus roots (Bettinger, Barton and Morgan, 2010).

Hunting, fishing, and gathering remained important in China, particularly in the Yangtze valley and in marginal areas, including for buffalo, deer, rhinoceros, elephant, alligator, and tortoise; carp; waterfowl such as cormorant, egret, duck, and heron; and wild fruits such as peaches, plums, acorns, and nuts (Jing, Flad and Yunbing, 2008). It was an eclectic mix of foods. These activities remained vital throughout mainland and island southeastern Asia, where tropical environments offered an abundance and the tubers were much more important in the diet. Cattle, sheep, and goats were domesticated, valued for their meat and fat, not their milk. Rice cultivation, associated with domesticated and transportable animals, notably pigs, had already made a firm imprint but remained to gain regional hegemony. As in Mesopotamia, a cuisine was still in the making, lacking texts and cookbooks.

Outside these two influential centers, southwestern Asia and China, new food production systems emerged through diffusion and, to some degree, local invention. The spread of the "Neolithic package," made up of cereals, cattle, pigs, and sheep, was sometimes the work of farmer-colonists but more often the result of adoption and adaptation, with many discontinuities where the package was not initially accepted in whole or in part (Barker, 2006: 364–6). This pattern of acculturation was true of most of Europe, where the elements of the package were all exotics with their roots in a semi-arid region and required time to acclimatize to an ecosystem barely recovered from deglaciation. Farming began spreading along the Mediterranean coastline by about 7500 BP, adjusting fairly easily. On the other hand, although domesticated cereal crops and cattle had reached as far as Scandinavia by 5000 BP, hunting and gathering remained economically and culturally important.

To the east, a shifting frontier developed between the cultures of wheat and the cultures of rice. Caught in the middle, generally unawares, early sedentary hunter-gatherers across much of Asia exploited wild plants and animals but shifted slowly into small-scale horticulture and rudimentary herding. At 5000 BP the Indus valley was on the verge of urbanism, with an elaborated agriculture of millet and wheat, together with an awareness of rice that was still to develop in water-fed cultivation (Wright, 2010). Similarly, rice was still finding its place in much of the Indian subcontinent, including the Ganges valley. Regions to the north demonstrated a growing commitment to pastoralism and varieties of mixed farming.

Korea and Japan were both following the Chinese path by 5000 BP, though with greater emphasis on fish and shellfish. In the rainforests of mainland and island southeastern Asia, which had been connected landmasses in the Last Glacial Maximum, minimal manipulation by hunter-gatherers was sufficient to enhance the productivity of plants such as bananas, sago, pandanus, swamp taro, and wild rice. These were gathered while meat was obtained from wild cattle and water buffalo, deer, rhinoceros, turtles, tortoises, crabs, fish, and shellfish. By 5000 BP, when the present-day coastline was already clearly demarcated, wet-rice farming was just beginning to get a foothold, in the islands as well as the mainland of southeastern Asia. A number of significant early domestications occurred in the region, however, notably the chicken from the wild red junglefowl nearly ten thousand years ago (Sawai *et al.*, 2010).

Although New Guinea is formally included among the islands of the Pacific, its experience is more closely associated with that of the islands of southeastern Asia. During the Pleistocene, lower sea levels enabled relatively easy movement throughout the region, though Wallace's Line (passing between Bali and Lombok) marks a significant biological boundary where the persistent sea divided the Asian flora and fauna from that of Australia and New Guinea. Down to 8000 BP New Guinea had been connected with Australia by an isthmus across the Arafura plain, and its hills remained above sea level three thousand years later as the Torres Strait islands. However, New Guinea did not share the languages of the wider region but had its own, which effectively set it apart. Equally important, settlement in the coastal lands of New Guinea developed slowly, whereas the interior highlands had been peopled as early as 30000 BP when open grasslands, good for hunting, flourished. Warming in the early Holocene took forest higher into the mountains, and it was in these elevated valleys that early farming emerged, independently, in response to the changing ecology or the need for a more reliable food resource throughout the seasons of the year.

This early farming was based on the cultivation of locally domesticated taro, deliberately moved into the highlands, and later the banana, which was also first domesticated in New Guinea. Agriculture began to replace foraging-cum-horticulture perhaps as early as 10 000 BP. By 5000 BP intensified cultivation was based on irrigation and drainage ditches, with plantings in mounds or raised beds (Denham and Haberle, 2008). Other important crops included yams, sugar cane, sago, and pandanus. Pigs, already domesticated in Indonesia and perhaps ultimately China, were introduced to the food system, though probably eaten only at feasts. This example of early agriculture, without substantial urbanism, is important in emphasizing the role of stress – the need to adapt to a changing environment in a specific niche – in the transition from hunting and gathering. The transition was not complete or universal, with significant regional and chronological contrasts in patterns of plant exploitation. Around 5000 BP most of New Guinea's peoples remained seasonally or wholly dependent on the food they could find in forest, stream, and sea. It was not obvious to everyone that farming stood in binary opposition to hunting and gathering or that it was the way of the future.

Australia

By 5000 BP, the first people of Australia had already accumulated 50 000 years of knowledge of the unique food resources of the land and surrounding seas. This long and close association with the land and its resources had not, however, led to the creation of agrarian societies similar to those in the other continents. Rather, in common with most regions of the world, Australia was the home of people who remained at core successful hunter-gatherers. Archeological evidence of intensification, incipient agriculture, and domestication exists but is almost all confined to the last millennium and to particular regions of the continent (Gerritsen, 2008). More significant in the longer term was aboriginal use of fire – the primal force in the manipulation and management of the landscape and food resources – employed as a variety of "firestick farming," highly effective for its purposes.

Managed burning of the Australian bush facilitated hunting by creating small areas of open grassland which attracted wild animals and exposed them to the weapons of the people. The land animals were largely endemics and often unusual, as a result of the long isolation of the continent and its separate evolution. The same was true of the plants. Broadly, plant foods provided a majority of the diet, together with large game and fish, but varying from region to region and season to season. Desert people probably ate the smallest proportion of meat.

Around 5000 BP the Australian climate was becoming drier and more variable, increasing the amount of land in desert and scrubland, making life harder for hunter-gatherers by reducing wild marsupial and reptile populations

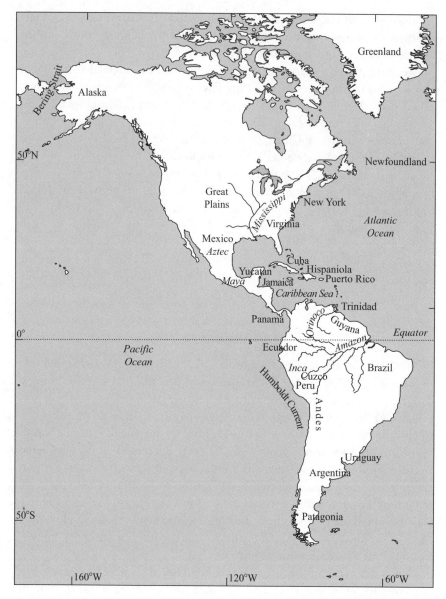

Figure 1.5   The Americas.

and requiring that more of the plant food had to be obtained by digging up roots, rhizomes and tubers, with seasonal fruit such as the bush tomato and quandong (Hiscock, 2008; Keen, 2004; Lourandos, 1997). Temperate and alpine zones saw the use of plants, including cycad seeds (zamia) which require detoxification to be made edible, tree ferns and bracken, grasses and warrigal greens, as well as freshwater fish and eels, yabbies and waterfowl, macropods (kangaroos and wallabies), emus, and insects such as sugar ants and Bogong moths that swarmed seasonally. Coastal economies depended on fish, mollusks, crabs, dugong, seals, and turtle eggs, but often also relied on more seasonal resources like yams, fruits, and berries, and on kangaroos and wallabies. The tropical north offered greater abundance.

The Americas

The people of the Americas, the New World for later Europeans, were relatively recent arrivals, though some scholars argue for dates significantly earlier than the 15 000 BP accepted here. Once they had established a foothold, however, the hunters and fishers who crossed the Bering Strait moved rapidly along the 7500 miles (12 000 km) western edge from Alaska to Patagonia, encountering a great range of ecosystems along the way (Figure 1.5). They spread more slowly eastward through the great mountains and plains, crossing the Mississippi, into the eastern woodlands of the north, and in the south venturing into the Amazon rainforest. The resource-rich islands of the Caribbean remained unpeopled as late as 7000 BP and some of them much longer.

The food resources of these strongly contrasted regions were varied but down to 5000 BP typically exploited by hunting, fishing, and gathering. Hunting dominated in North America and was often highly specialized. In the far north – the tundra and the boreal forests – caribou, moose, and deer were the primary prey. On the northeastern Atlantic seaboard, caribou and beaver were hunted, but less important in the diet than walrus, whale, and seal. On the plains, bulky bison were ambushed and stampeded, people stalking the migratory herds over great distances. In the eastern woodlands, hunting and gathering became more generalized, with an emphasis on acorns and hickory nuts, seed-grasses, bottle gourds, and squashes, the latter among the earliest cultivated plants. By 5000 BP people were beginning to manage and manipulate seed plants, such as sunflower and marsh elder, to induce larger seeds with thinner coats, but no significant seed domestications occurred in North America. Maize was still to come, from the south. In the dry southwest, small game such as rabbits predominated, along with a much larger proportion of plant foods, including the fruit of the prickly pear and mesquite.

Domestication began early in the dry highlands of Central America (Mexico), and by 5000 BP there is evidence of cultivation of maize, beans, chili peppers, avocadoes, bottle gourds, squash, and amaranth. However, the cultivators of these plants remained basically hunter-gatherers and the transition to farming and village settlement did not occur until about 3500 BP. The tropical lowlands of Central and South America were relatively dry in the early Holocene, covered by scrub and savanna rather than rainforest, so that the emphasis was once again on hunting and fishing. Large mammals, such as sloths, peccaries, and llamas were hunted, along with rodents, birds, snakes, tortoises, and turtles. Tree fruits and nuts, fish and shellfish, legumes and other plants also contributed to the diet in early Central and South America. In the tropical forest, a wide range of smaller animals was hunted. Hunter-gatherers used fire to open up niches where grazing animals might be attracted and roots and tubers allowed to prosper. It was here that they learned how to make toxic plants, notably cassava and zamia, safe for humans to eat, by leaching out the bitter juices. This remained a low-level food production system down to 5000 BP, however, not fully appropriated to domestication or the refined agricultural technologies that were soon to emerge.

In the Caribbean islands of Cuba, Hispaniola, and Puerto Rico, first colonized between 6000 and 5300 BP, the few large land animals, including sloths of up to 550 lb (250 kg), insect-eaters, rodents, and flightless owls, were hunted, together with manatee, monk seal, and turtle. The sloths were extinct by 4000 BP. Fish and shellfish were also important in the diet of these fast-moving hunter-gatherers. At first, they moved along the coasts, where progress was easiest, but by 5000 BP they were beginning to burn the forest, to help in the hunt, and planting fruit trees brought from Yucatan in the niches they had opened up, hinting at the first stages of an incipient agriculture.

The only agricultural economies claimed for the Americas at 5000 BP were located on the arid coast of Ecuador and northern Peru, and in the high Andes. Although lacking maize, a system of domestication and cultivation was associated with sedentary settlement, pottery-making, and monument-building, beginning to emerge no earlier than 6000 BP. However, these first farmers depended heavily on the sea for their subsistence, taking advantage of the rich resources delivered by the Humboldt Current, hunting sea mammals, fishing, and collecting shellfish. Domesticated plants included squashes and gourds, lima and jack beans, guava, and tubers such as cassava, sweet potatoes, and potatoes, suggesting early contact with the high Andes where the ancestors of the Inca Empire combined plant husbandry with the domestication of animals.

In the high Andes, disturbed niches created by the herding and corralling of llamas, and fertilized by their manure, encouraged the growth of weedy plants, including the herb quinoa – valued for its leaves and more importantly its seeds, which were vital to the making of soups, stews and porridges – and also primitive forms of potatoes and yams, which were selected for growth and edibility characteristics. On the dry coastal plains, irrigation was just beginning to become important by 5000 BP, but terracing and irrigation were still unknown in the highlands (Heggarty and Beresford-Jones, 2010; Denevan, 2001). These faltering early stages of agricultural development were soon to be followed by remarkable transformations that created complex societies and powerful agrarian states.

Seven claims

A number of claims can be made for the fundamental role of food in the early development of human biological and cultural history. Some of these arguments are directly related to the kinds of foods that were eaten and to technologies of food production, while others are mediated by environmental factors. All of the claims have been influential but have had to compete with alternative hypotheses, such as those which attribute causation directly to ecological factors and long-term environmental change.

The first and most influential claim is that changes in the availability of food resources in the late Pleistocene help account for the emergence of early hominins, specifically their upright stance, bipedalism, bigger and better brains, and stone tool-making. This argument is generally linked with the "savanna hypothesis," which represents these developments as responses or adaptations to the emergence of the dry savanna as a habitat type in east Africa in the late Pleistocene (Rotilio and Marchese, 2010). Transformation of the ecosystem and the landscape had consequences both for the kinds of potential food sources available to hominins and for the technologies appropriate to its hunting and gathering. The shift from wetter forest habitats, suited to "apelike" species finding their food safely above ground, to the challenging open landscape of savanna with its many wild animals had dietary and hence anatomical consequences. Critics of this influential hypothesis have in recent times advanced an alternative in which hominins evolved in enclosed woodland habitats rather than as hunters in exposed landscapes (Bobe and Behrensmeyer, 2004; Potts, 1998). Other interpretations see the two habitats and food systems as combined rather than mutually exclusive.

A second claim is that the development of meat-eating had a direct impact on human anatomy, including increased body size and increased ability to run and to throw, and on cognitive capacity. This argument is closely associated with the savanna hypothesis since the lack of fruited forests meant a changed diet in which meat played a much larger role. Human beings remained omnivores, however, merely choosing to increase the proportion of meat in their diets, following patterns determined by shortages and seasonality. Attempting to be pure carnivores was too dangerous, because of the unreliability of supply and because humans had to compete with mammalian carnivores, notably lions and spotted hyenas, that were strong and dedicated. The physical changes in *Homo* derived from the demands of the hunt, the need to defend carcasses from other predators, and to themselves scavenge meat from animals killed by their carnivorous competitors. An alternative solution for early hominins seeking protein was to rely on small, easily killed animals, notably invertebrates such as insects, but doing so demanded a cost-benefit analysis which weighed the energy derived against the energy required to obtain an adequate quantity of such small animals.

The third claim is that it is not so much meat in itself that matters but rather the act of cooking. The application of heat, supplied by fire, not only made meat more palatable but also increased the amount of energy derived from its consumption. Cooking and the emergence of *Homo erectus* went together, with consequences for human development much the same as those associated with meat-eating. Cooking also made hard-to-chew and hard-to-swallow plant food, particularly roots and tubers, more edible.

The fourth and closely related claim is that the diet shift associated with the emergence of agriculture about 10 000 BP instigated dramatic changes in the continuing process of human evolution. In particular, the shift to grains, legumes, and dairy products, and the production of fermented food and drink, placed selective pressure on genetic variation and induced rapid polygenic adaptation. Populations evolved genes to cope with tubers and alcohol, for example. Parallel genetic change, as recent as 3000 BP, occurred when people moved into high-altitude regions, such as Tibet, and had to cope with reduced oxygen in the atmosphere (Peng *et al.*, 2010).

The fifth claim sees the origins of language in the cooperative communication essential to hunting and scavenging and the associated distribution of meat, and interprets the dispersals of the great language families of the world as a product of the adoption and diffusion of agriculture. The importance of this claim is that it sees the replacement of languages as the outcome of a combination of demographic, social, cultural, and political forces, all of them having their roots in food production systems. Old World language families such as Indo-European began their expansion between nine and six thousand years ago, suggesting a close association with the origins of agriculture (Heggarty and Beresford-Jones, 2010).

The sixth and most comprehensive claim is that the transformation of food production systems beginning about 10 000 BP – the central element in the Neolithic Revolution – is the most profound transition in human cultural history, as argued, for example, by Susan Foster McCarter (2007: 1). Rather than being at the mercy of the natural environment and its wild resources, humans gained control of their food, manipulating the seasonal cycle of availability and climatic uncertainty. In order to more efficiently cook, store, and consume food, first farmers enthusiastically embraced ceramic technologies, which became markers of their cultural development. Cooking in a ceramic vessel had many advantages compared to roasting or boiling over an open flame, or using hot rocks, the only methods available before pottery. Increased food supplies enabled rapid population growth, sedentary settlement, long-term decline in the economic role of food production, the development of specialization and exchange, and the growth of other sectors of economic activity. These changes led directly to hierarchy, stratified social organization, and social complexity.

The seventh claim, growing out of the sixth, contends that the technologies of agrarian systems created the necessity for state-organized societies and the conditions for the development of "civilization." Central to this cultural shift were concepts of non-communal property, the need for boundaries, fences and walls, for numeracy and measurement, and hence for written records and maps of landholdings. The need to regulate water, both for drainage and irrigation, led to the central management of resources and to state systems. Sedentary settlements and urban living created a need for exchange, markets, prices, and money. They also placed great pressure on natural resources, resulting in environmental depredation and degradation (Crowe 2000: 231–6). Inequality followed inevitably, along with conflict, conquest, and war. So did the flowering of art, philosophy, and literature. All of these characteristics of civilized society – good and bad – can be traced back to the new system of producing and distributing food.

These last two claims give a greater role to human agency and individual choice than do the first five. It is no surprise then that the last two, both of them founded on the transition from hunting, fishing, and gathering to agriculture, are the ones to have been subjected to the most critique and questioning. Although radical thought may see *Homo sapiens* as the prime agent in the world's modern environmental crisis, the evolution of the species is understood as unstoppable, and much the same applies to meat-eating, cooking, and the development of language. It is fair to argue that without a cognitively developed *Homo sapiens* there would have been no agriculture, but it is more common to claim that the transformation of food production is the true cause of the planet's problems or, more optimistically, the source of the world's cultural creativity, however short-lived it may be. For good or ill, the working out of these developments formed the centerpiece of the era from 5000 BP, and throughout these millennia the central driver was almost always food.

References

Barham, L. and Mitchell, P. (2008) *The First Africans: African Archaeology from the Earliest Tool Makers to Most Recent Foragers.* Cambridge: Cambridge University Press.

Barker, G. (2006) *The Agricultural Revolution in Prehistory: Why did Foragers become Farmers?* Oxford: Oxford University Press.

Bellwood, P. (2005) *First Farmers: The Origins of Agricultural Societies.* Oxford: Blackwell Publishing.

Bettinger, R. L., Barton, L. and Morgan, C. (2010) The origins of food production in north China: A different kind of agricultural revolution. *Evolutionary Anthropology* 19: 9–21.

Bickerton, D. (2009) *Adam's Tongue: How Humans Made Language and How Language Made Humans*. New York: Hill and Wang.

Bobe, R. and Behrensmeyer, A.K. (2004) The expansion of grassland ecosytems in Africa in relation to mammalian evolution and the origin of the genus Homo. *Palaeogeography, Palaeoclimatology, Palaeoecology* 207: 399–420.

Bramanti, B., Thomas, M.G., Haak, W. *et al.* (2009) Genetic discontinuity between local hunter-gatherers and central Europe's first farmers. *Science* 326 (2 October): 137–40.

Brown, T.A., Jones, M.K., Powel, W. and Allaby, R.G. (2009) The complex origins of domesticated crops in the fertile crescent. *Trends in Ecology and Evolution* 24: 103–109.

Chi, Z. and Hung, H.C. (2010) The emergence of agriculture in south China. *Antiquity* 84: 11–25.

Childe, V.G. (1936) *Man Makes Himself.* London: Watts.

Cohen, M.N. (1977) *The Food Crisis in Prehistory: Overpopulation and the Origins of Agriculture.* New Haven: Yale University Press.

Crowe, I. (2000) *The Quest for Food: Its Role in Human Evolution and Migration.* Stroud: Tempus.

Denevan, W.M. (2001) *Cultivated Landscapes of Native Amazonia and the Andes.* Oxford: Oxford University Press.

Denham, T. (2007) *The Emergence of Agriculture: A Global View.* London: Routledge.

Denham, T. and Haberle, S. (2008) Agricultural emergence and transformation in the Upper Wahgi Valley, Papua New Guinea: Theory, method and practice. *The Holocene* 18: 481–96.

Dow, G.K., Reed, C.R. and Olewiler, N. (2009) Climate reversals and the transition to agriculture. *Journal of Economic Growth* 14: 27–53.

Eisenstein, M. (2010) Evolution: The first supper. *Nature* 468 (23/30 December): S8–S9.

Gerritsen, R. (2008) *Australia and the Origins of Agriculture.* Oxford: Archaeopress, BAR International Series 1874.

Heggarty, P. and Beresford-Jones, D. (2010) Agriculture and language dispersals: Limitations, refinements, and an Andean exception? *Current Anthropology* 51: 163–91.

Hiscock, P. (2008) *Archaeology of Ancient Australia.* London: Routledge.

Jing, Y., Flad, R. and Yunbing, L. (2008) Meat-acquisition patterns in the Neolithic Yangzi River valley, China. *Antiquity* 82: 351–66.

Keen, I. (2004) *Aboriginal Economy and Society: Australia at the Threshold of Colonisation.* Oxford: Oxford University Press.

Kohl, P.L. (2007) *The Making of Bronze Age Eurasia.* Cambridge: Cambridge University Press.

Lourandos, H. (1997) *Continent of Hunter-Gatherers: New Perspectives in Australian Prehistory.* Cambridge: Cambridge University Press.

Manning, P. (2006) *Homo sapiens* populates the earth: A provisional synthesis, privileging linguistic evidence. *Journal of World History* 17: 115–58.

McCarter, S.F. (2007) *Neolithic.* London: Routledge.

Peng, Y., Shi, H. Qi, X. *et al.* (2010) The ADH1BArg47His polymorphism in East Asian populations and expansion of rice domestication in history. *BMC Evolutionary Biology* 10: 15.

Phillipson, D.W. (1985) *African Archaeology.* Cambridge: Cambridge University Press.

Potts, R. (1998) Environmental hypotheses of hominin evolution. *Yearbook of Physical Anthropology* 41: 93–136.

Putterman, L. (2008) Agriculture, diffusion and development: Ripple effects of the Neolithic Revolution. *Economica* 75: 729–48.

Reich, D., Green, R.E., Kircher, M. *et al.* (2010) Genetic history of an archaic hominin group from Denisova Cave in Siberia. *Nature* 468 (23/30 December): 1053–60.

Rotilio, G. and Marchese, E. (2010) Nutritional factors in human dispersals. *Annals of Human Biology* 37: 312–24.

Sawai, H., Kim, H.L., Kuno, K. *et al.* (2010) The origin and genetic variation of domestic chickens with special reference to junglefowls Gallus g. gallus and G. varius. *PLoS ONE* 5(5): e10639. doi: 10.1371/journal.pone.0010639.

Shaw, T., Sinclair, P., Andah, B. and Okpoko, A. (eds) (1993) T*he Archaeology of Africa: Food, Metals and Towns.* London: Routledge.

Smith, B.D. (2001) Low-level food production. *Journal of Archaeological Research* 9: 1–43.

Wenke, R.J. (2009) *The Ancient Egyptian State: The Origins of Egyptian Culture (c.8000–2000 BC).* Cambridge: Cambridge University Press.

Wrangham, R. (2009) *Catching Fire: How Cooking Made Us Human.* London: Profile Books.

Wrangham, R. and Carmody, R. (2010) Human adaptation and the control of fire. *Evolutionary Anthropology* 19: 187–99.

Wright, R.P. (2010) *The Ancient Indus: Urbanism, Economy, and Society.* Cambridge: Cambridge University Press.

Zheng, Y., Sun, Q., Qin, L. *et al.* (2009) Rice fields and modes of rice cultivation between 5000 and 2500 BC in East China. *Journal of Archaeological Science* 36: 2609–16.

CHAPTER TWO

Genetics and Geography

For millions of years, plants and animals evolved through processes of natural selection. As they changed their biological characteristics, and as the earth's surface and climate experienced dramatic cycles and reshaping, plants and animals changed their geographical locations and dominance through natural migration. By their own means, they found their way from place to place, colonizing and invading, across the globe. The speed with which they could move and their success in achieving dominant status within a niche or region was limited only by their own evolving biological characteristics and by the changing physical conditions in the world around them. Ice and fire, meteor strikes, and massive hurricanes not only created hazards and barriers but also opened opportunities. Different species had different chances. A coconut could float across an ocean and strike root when it washed up on a sandy shore. A crocodile might swim immense distances. Appropriately equipped birds, insects, and seeds might fly or float through the air. But a potato or a breadfruit could not long remain viable in saltwater and a pig needed to feel something solid underfoot.

The rules of the game changed with domestication. Only then did human beings begin to play a major role in deciding what would grow where. Only after domestication did the world see a self-conscious "artificial selection" and an active redistribution of plants and animals. Rather than depending on whatever food resources a new place, near or far, might have to offer, migrant groups now carried with them food resources they were familiar with, and had already domesticated, in expectation of planting or raising these plants and animals in new environments. For the first time, biogeographical change followed in the wake of human population movements. The choices

How Food Made History, First Edition. B. W. Higman.
© 2012 B. W. Higman. Published 2012 by Blackwell Publishing Ltd.

that were made had dramatic consequences for the global geographical distribution of plants and animals.

The outcome of this redistribution was both increased diversity in the range of foods people could choose to consume and at the same time competition with indigenous plants and animals. The reason behind this apparent conflict was that after 5000 BP the spread of plants and animals was closely associated with invasive human colonization and imperialism, a process carried to a greater intensity after 1492 and the "Columbian exchange." No longer were people always able to decide on a local level what was good to eat and how to produce their food. Now they had very often to do the bidding of imperial masters or dynastic rulers or dictators, whose choices might be based on quite different principles. Independent invention and diffusion continued to be important in making the world map of biodiversity after 5000 BP but the spread of the new food production systems identified with domestication and agriculture came to be closely associated with the expansion of states and empires.

This was a world created by domestication and its progeny the agrarian system, with implications for the control and regulation of resources and society. The outcome was a new global distribution of peoples and staple foods and in the very long term a tendency toward dependence on a small number of domesticates (wheat, rice and maize, cattle, pigs, sheep and chickens) that came to dominate the world food system. The domestication of all these globally dominant plants and animals was effectively complete soon after 5000 BP.

Paradoxically perhaps, the development of complex societies founded on domestication, agriculture and exchange, went together with the emergence of food exclusions and prohibitions. Things which had been considered good to eat were removed from the list of acceptable foods. These exclusions became firmly installed in social systems and established as food taboos, and often attributed to divine commandment or moral duty. Those who chose not to respect such injunctions could expect only retribution or social rejection. In this way, food taboos helped to narrow the range of potential foods. Why did societies make such choices and why did they impose them as rules rather than permitting free choice?

This chapter deals with three important choices that people made regarding their food sources: what in nature was desirable to domesticate or genetically engineer, what should be prohibited, and what was good to move from place to place.

Genetic modification, ancient and modern

Although domestication entails the purposeful manipulation of plants and animals by selective breeding and culling, with the intention of inducing superior qualities, the question why people in different places first chose to domesticate particular species is impossible to answer in terms of individual human agency. Until very recently, the genetic basis of life was not understood. Darwin had to construct his theory of evolution in the absence of knowledge of genes. Mendel, experimenting with hybrid peas in the 1860s, could do no more than show that traits are inherited separately and can therefore seem to disappear for a generation or two then reappear. His work was ignored at first but by the 1890s fed into the breeding of improved wheat and other seeds. Later researchers showed that genes exist as regions within DNA (deoxyribonucleic acid), but the "double helix" structure of DNA was not established until 1953. These fundamental developments came long after the initial process of selection and domestication was effectively complete.

The first breeders of plants and animals – the people who made the greatest and longest-lasting choices – had little notion of the science of what they were doing. Explanations of their activities and their achievements must be sought in the broader ecological milieu of food production. They must also be understood in the context of the complex overlapping of domestication with the limited artificial selection that was always a part of hunting and collecting. Choices about the scattering of seed and the feeding of animals were at first inadvertent. Wild plants were cultivated and wild animals tamed before they were fully domesticated. The process was slow and sometimes incomplete. It involved many generations of people and extended over many changing generations of the plants and animals that were being domesticated. And it occurred in parallel with human manipulation of their own populations, through selective infanticide and mating avoidances, and continuing natural selection that enabled populations to evolve genetically in response to specific local environments.

Why attempt to improve on nature? Why domesticate at all? These are questions which make sense only after the event, in the presence of the concepts and the evidence. At the very beginning, the process was not only inadvertent but perhaps also reciprocal, when wolves, the ancestors of all domestic dogs, first stole food from humans, then were fed and encouraged for their ability to warn of approaching danger. There was a food connection in this relationship but the first animal to be domesticated as a specialist food producer, several millennia later, around 10 000 BP, was probably the goat.

The origins of plant domestication with an intention of improving food production seem much less self-conscious. The initiation of domestication in plants most likely began with the burning or clearing of forest to enable hunting, thus creating habitats in which some plants flourished better than others, leading to the collection of seeds and the active sowing of some of these. Once this had been started, conscious selection for favored characteristics could proceed, leading to crop improvement. None of this required cultivation of the soil or manipulation of water resources. For both plants and animals, the first wave of domesticates developed not only as a product of human decisions but also through the powerful selection process that followed from adaptation to new environments. Human choices were fundamental but they did not overrule continuing natural selection and adjustment.

Domestication always meant selection for particular characteristics of form and behavior, and the active modification of these characteristics in order to produce varieties with superior qualities for human use, not only for consumption as food but also for clothing, shelter, tools, companionship, and motive power. In some cases, a single plant or animal could be exploited for more than one of these purposes, but frequently the process of domestication was directed at specialized use, as, for example, the fruits, seeds, leaves, or tubers of a plant. The objective in selection is to obtain larger fruits, seeds, or tubers, on stronger growing plants, in which seed dormancy and natural seed dispersal are suppressed.

These benefits are, however, often achieved only as a trade-off. In most domesticated cereal grains, for example, protein content is only half that of their wild progenitors, this loss balanced by increased yield. The cost of selection for specific characteristics was also a reduction of genetic diversity, most particularly in the genes controlling these particular features. This process is seen clearly in the case of maize in which the cultivated plant has a single strong stalk, with multiple short branches tipped by large ears of naked grain, compared to its progenitor (the highly branched wild grass teosinte), which enclosed its smaller grain (technically a fruit) in a tough triangular casing. These selected mutant characteristics, regulated by genes and amino acid substitutions, were present in maize by 7000 BP, though genetic manipulation continued much longer directed at increasing cob size and improving kernel quality (Fuller, Allaby and Stevens, 2010; Doebley, Gaut and Smith, 2006).

In some cases, the process of artificial selection central to domestication led to the breeding of multiple varieties from a single original species. The wild cabbage, for example, was known as an ancient vegetable of the Mediterranean coast, used first only for its stem (Maggioni *et al.*, 2010). By about 2500 BP, selection had given it a larger and rounder head. Later encouragement of particular characteristics and specialized plant organs created numerous varieties (the "cole crops"), some of the best known being kale (perhaps the first cultivated cabbage, lacking a head), Brussels sprouts (developed in northern Europe around AD 500 or perhaps later), head cabbages (cultivated in Germany by about AD 1200), broccoli and cauliflower (close relatives, developed in Italy in the late Middle Ages, valued for their inflorescences), collard greens (a form of kale, adapted to tropical and subtropical conditions), and kohlrabi (appreciated for its swollen stem base rather than its leaves; Purugganan, Boyles and, Suddith, 2000). A similar process occurred in China, where the cabbage has many varieties, from bok choy to pe-tsai.

Both maize and cauliflower eventually became so highly modified that they could no longer propagate naturally. Thus, the interactive, symbiotic relationships developed between humans and plants and animals sometimes lead to complete dependence. Less fully modified plants, like lettuce and carrot, on the other hand, easily revert or become self-propagating weeds.

How to choose what to domesticate? Not all plants and animals are suitable. Some plants are toxic and others not adapted to the human digestive system. Thus trees that do not bear edible fruit are unlikely candidates, and poisonous plants must be avoided unless their toxicity can be countered by processing. Some animals are too small or require too much effort to produce useful quantities of nutritious food, while others are too large and too aggressive. It is only at the extremes that these factors create absolute exclusions. The bark of trees can be eaten in extremis. Although bitter cassava contains cyanide, the poison can be leached out in order to make the tubers edible.

The domestication of animals was in many ways similar to that of plants, directed at increasing their production of milk or the quality of their flesh. However, because animals display varied temperaments and behavioral patterns, some were more susceptible to domestication than others. The valued natural characteristics were gregariousness, which meant such animals accepted being herded and bunched up together in a pen; acceptance of social hierarchy, allowing humans to take a dominant role; and placidity, meaning they are not strongly territorial or aggressive in defense of their space. These are predisposing factors, determining which particular animals were chosen. Wild cattle and buffalo are aggressive but domestication has bred out most of this behavior, whereas bison have proved less willing partners in modern food production, particularly when forced into systems based on feedlots. The gazelle, the favorite meat animal of ancient hunters in southwestern Asia, was not successfully domesticated, because it is highly territorial and nervous, runs away when threatened, and may die of shock or battering when penned. On the other hand, the gazelle was so much favored that its over-exploitation, including the killing of younger animals, is cited as a significant cause of the shift to agriculture and domestication in the Levant (Sapir-Hen *et al.*, 2009; Munro, 2004). Hunting of gazelle persisted alongside farming regimes and has continued into the present in places such as northern India, Tibet, and southern Africa.

However much early farmers savored the meat of gazelle, they chose instead to domesticate sheep and goats, or cattle and pigs. Even for these select few, domestication was directed at accentuating desired behaviors as much as improving the quality and quantity of milk and meat. Aggression, escape behaviors, and intelligence were bred out, whereas animals were selected positively for overall smallness and docility, for smaller jaws and teeth, and smaller, shorter horns. Domesticated animals have more fat than their wild progenitors, producing meat much favored by human consumers of beef and pork, such as the modern Japanese variety of Wagyu beef – tender marbled meat with a high proportion of unsaturated fat – from placid cattle, fed beer and regularly massaged.

In almost all cases, domestication was not confined to a single plant or animal but rather involved a number of things, enabling them to function together in a food production system. In the primary centers of domestication, relatively small numbers of elements made up the foundations of the package. As discussed in Chapter 1, in southwestern Asia these were the plants wheat, barley, peas, and lentils, and the animals sheep, goat, cattle, and pig. In China the foundation elements were rice, millet, beans, tubers, fruits, pig, and chicken.

There was often a long gap between the initial domestication of plants and animals and the emergence of agricultural economies based on sedentary settlement in villages. In the case of Mesoamerica, for example, the domestication of maize, beans, and peppers began about 10 000 BP but the development of agricultural communities with a high level of reliance on domesticated plants and animals did not occur until 4500 BP. Thus, although domestication and agricultural food production systems went hand in hand, it was entirely possible for nonagricultural societies with limited dependence on domesticates to persist over millennia, surviving as successfully as the hunter-gatherers who went before and as well as the agriculturalists who followed them. It is wrong, therefore, to see domestication as leading rapidly and inevitably to agriculture. Many other varieties of stable and efficient systems of food production existed and enabled stable social and political arrangements. Cultivation can occur in the absence of the genetic markers of domestication and, on the other hand, genetic changes can occur as a product of habitat modification unrelated to any intended cultivation.

The first plant-breeders did not always wish to become cultivators of gardens or fields but were satisfied to benefit from the modifications they had made to the ecosystem. Indeed, not all attempts at domestication or management and manipulation were followed to a successful conclusion, and many were abandoned. Some of these attempts were taken up much later, with positive results, but others fell more definitively on stony ground. However, in spite of these alternative paths, the modern food world has come to depend almost completely on domesticates and on agriculture, making the continuing efficient production of these plants and animals essential to human survival. The global failure of crops as important as wheat or maize would prove catastrophic.

Some regions of the world proved resistant to domestication in the very long run. In Australia, for example, "firestick farming" persisted as an efficient system of landscape modification down to the invasion by European farming peoples in the eighteenth century, but it did not depend on the behavioral or genetic modification of kangaroos or other game. Although intensified agricultural systems were found on the most northern of the Torres Strait islands, where Australia verged on New Guinea, these quickly petered out to the south or simply took on forms that were less striking to observers because they seemed to blend into the landscape. Evidence of incipient agriculture can be found in the seed-gathering and -planting activities of some groups, as well as tillage and husbandry, over the last thousand years (Gerritsen, 2008). But even after the invasion of Europeans and the introduction of competitive domesticated large mammals, the domestication of native fauna such as kangaroos was not achieved and rarely attempted (Craw, 2008).

Knowledge of domestication as a principle did not mean a continuous process of artificial selection in which more and more plants and animals were modified and manipulated. Generally, once the basic packages were in place, little was added. There were, however, some significant domestications in Africa in the millennium following 5000 BP, though the precise dating of some of these is difficult. White yam and yellow yam were probably domesticated independently, at distant sites across western Africa, as was African rice. Sorghum had its origin in the region between tropical western Africa and the headwaters of the Nile, spreading to the west and the east around 3000 BP, and then to India about 2000 BP. Other plants domesticated in western Africa in this broad period included the oil palm (which can be eaten raw, boiled, or roasted), groundnut (peanut), and the vegetable okra (Barker, 2006: 281–3; Harlan, 1975: 152–60).

Whereas the domestication of new species of plants and animals was limited after 5000 BP, a good deal of effort was devoted to improving the yield and quality of the few plants and animals that had been placed at the center of the new food production systems. For millennia, this process was little more than the outcome of picking the best of the bunch, without awareness of the biology of heredity involved. Such poorly understood genetic modification went together with changes in agricultural and processing techniques, thought of as crop improvement and selective breeding rather than as the fundamental manipulation of life forms. Methodical breeding by practical farmers hardly existed before the eighteenth century. Beginning in the nineteenth century, scientific experimentation stations worked hard to select for desirable qualities, with only limited success. Yields improved but more often as a result of changes in production technology than in the qualities of the crops and animals that were farmed. Little of this changed the range of choices available to consumers.

This long history of practical genetic modification has been transformed in recent times by the development of processes commonly known as "biotechnology" and "genetic engineering," the latter sometimes labeled "superdomestication." Biotechnology covers broadly the use of living organisms to make or modify products (as in the brewing of beer, for example, known from ancient times), the improvement of plants and animals (as in breeding to increase yields), and the development of microorganisms for specific uses (a recent innovation). Whereas traditional breeding methods depended on the uncontrolled or random hybridization of parent cells, genetic engineering manipulates the DNA of selected cells to induce desired traits in an original genetic sequence. Because they can bypass sexual reproduction, these techniques are therefore capable of moving genes between organisms that are unrelated.

Beginning in the 1970s, the production of recombinant DNA, the artificial sequence created by the combining of two DNA sequences, led quickly to the creation of genetically modified organisms, including "designer" plants and animals, and hence foods. Genetic engineering goes beyond traditional methods of hybridization or breeding and enables the making of organisms that would not have existed without human intervention, thus "outdoing evolution" (Kloppenburg, 1988: 2). This process is not disconnected from ancient domestication and in some cases knowledge of the genes in ancient or "heritage" plants and animals that contributed to early modifications is applied in modern breeding projects.

Genetic engineering has roused much doubt and uncertainty about the risks involved in creating transgenic organisms, as well as posing new questions in science, law, ethics, and society. Genetically modified (GM) crops have many advantages for agricultural productivity but equally create concern about their implications for food chains. Formerly, it was assumed that known foods were safe to ingest, however much they had been manipulated, because they were made up of natural products. Genetic engineering challenged this assumption, locating such "Frankenstein foods" among the drugs categories which had much longer been regarded as potentially dangerous. Cloned sheep seemed bad enough to many, while fluorescent pigs created alarming visions of green ham and eggs. Color and shape are the first things observed by consumers of food, the first clues that something may not be safe to eat (Lawrence, 2007). The first commercially marketed food derived from transgenic animals was salmon, with the principal advantage of accelerated growth in aquaculture rather than any visible physical oddity.

An understanding of genomic sequences, beginning in the late twentieth century, permitted cloning for favored agronomic characteristics, and this also involves a search for superior qualities in wild relatives and unimproved varieties which had not been selected in the long process of artificial domestication. It is expected that this process can lead to the development of new crops and novel varieties. For example, although classic breeding techniques enabled the improvement of sorghum and millet, the most significant cereal crops of Africa, recombinant DNA technology allows the transfer of genes between species, thus creating crops with superior protein quality, minerals, and vitamins, delivering greater nutrition and digestibility. Transgenic maize can be manipulated to improve its content of lysine, an essential amino acid that occurs in proteins and is important in human nutrition, but is naturally the most limited in cereal seeds. Similarly, the gene that controls the development of thick long cobs of naked corn in maize could be applied through engineering to produce wheat and barley "on the cob" (Goodwin, 2009; Doebley, Gaut and Smith, 2006: 1319; O'Kennedy, Grootboom and Shewry, 2006).

These developments are important and will probably lead in the future to novel plants and animals as part of the food production system, but thus far most of the manipulation and engineering has been applied to the limited range of organisms that were domesticated and introduced to agriculture thousands of years ago. It remains an interesting question why so few new plants and animals have been domesticated in recent centuries and why so much attention has been applied to the modification of those already domesticated (Cassidy and Mullin, 2007). Why is it easier to add an animal or plant to the prohibited list than to gain acceptance for one not already eaten?

Prohibitions and taboos

The origins and functions of food taboos are ancient and closely associated with the emergence of the great religious and philosophical traditions. In most communities, fads and fashions, and group preferences for particular foods, have long been common, in addition to individual aversions, allergies, and choices. However, these never had global significance in the way cultural prohibitions were to do once dominant belief systems gained large and widespread adherence. Understood as moral requirements or the directives of gods, food prohibitions took on a powerful status. Those who disobeyed might expect punishment for their evil behavior, something more than simply becoming sick. However, the rules sometimes appear arbitrary. As with philosophy and religion, ideas about what is good to eat and what should be avoided are widely different and often contradictory across cultures: "One man's meat is another man's poison."

The list of prohibited items is extensive, stretching from liquid to solid foods, as well as cold to hot and wet to dry, and includes plants along with animals. The seemingly arbitrary pattern of prohibitions makes these food choices difficult to explain. It is equally striking that prohibitions and taboos grew up alongside the development of domestication and agrarian food production systems, as elements of social complexity and of the development of ideology and self-conscious group-identification. The more complex the distribution and marketing networks associated with food supply chains, the more choices became available to consumers. Paradoxically, the greater the choice, the more easily could consumers reject potential foods, which in other circumstances could only be welcomed. In this way it can be argued that it was the food production system of the Neolithic that created and enabled belief systems which otherwise were an impossible luxury. Notably, although the ancient agricultural revolution marked the transformation of ideas about the proper relationship between humans and other animals, including their exploitation and slaughter, taboos were not confined to the eating of meat.

Food taboos are not the only significant prohibitions raised up by ideology and identity-making, but they are probably the most persistent and widespread, and are followed faithfully even by those who do not display their beliefs in what they wear or how they behave on special days. This stems from the central role of food in defining and creating cultural and national identity, long after nutritional or medical justifications are abandoned or forgotten. The origins of food taboos have been traced by some to utilitarian motives, ideas of moral compassion, or to magico-religious sources. Others have found in these prohibitions a means of conserving the resources of a community as well as the health of its members (Meyer-Rochow, 2009: 5; Whitehead, 2000: 111–14; Simoons, 1994; Harris, 1985: 14–16). Where the ultimate taboo, the eating of human flesh, has been broken, the individuals consumed are typically demonized in some manner to make them other than self-like beings.

Because taboos can be applied differentially within a community, it is also argued that they are sometimes used to secure particular foods for dominant groups, often adult men, and to deny them to weaker people, such as children or invalids, and feared individuals, such as pregnant or menstruating women. This is not so much a matter of securing the best-tasting food for elites as the preservation of their wellbeing. For example, Harriet Whitehead (2000: ix) argues that in highland New Guinea, until recent times, food taboos practiced at feasts performed "a strategic allocation of the flesh of hunted game species," and that "selective taboos – some meats are for women and children only, some for initiated men only, etc. – may have the effect of matching the average expectable yield of meat from any given creature with an appropriately sized unit of feasters." Seasonal taboos may have similar effects but also exist to preserve food stores in hard times, the taboos being maintained even in the absence of such necessity as a means of symbolizing cultural identity.

Early prohibitions derived from the multiple uses of animals in agrarian societies and marked the transition from hunting and gathering. In ancient Egypt, for example, the eating of beef was avoided in order to preserve the cat- tle that had become essential to the agricultural production system, though this avoidance was apparently only partial. Something similar can be argued in the case of horsemeat, but it was eaten more commonly in ancient than modern times, when the horse lost much of its utility as a beast of burden and its role in warfare. Horsemeat is unusual in that attempts were made in recent centuries to restore its place in food systems, though generally with little success. Once established, taboos are very difficult to overcome, whereas they are resilient in the face of changing necessity or utilitarian value. Examples of taboos associated originally with a need to preserve food resources include the total ban on food and drink practiced in the Jewish annual Yom Kippur and the Catholic prohibition of meat, though allowing fish, in the weeks of Lent. These forms of self-sacrifice survive well in the midst of plenty, marking the distinctiveness of a community. On the other hand, the removal of a meat taboo can be used to establish fresh boundaries, as in St Paul's apparent repeal of rules which enabled early Christians to distinguish themselves from Jews and other non-Christians (Rosenblum, 2010: 76).

The prohibition of foods based on their potential to cause illness or death can be traced to direct observation. It was therefore an evolving process, though similarly rooted in conditions that have not necessarily persisted over time or geographical space. For example, the common prohibition of pork probably has to do with the parasites that pigs harbor and harmful substances contained in their meat, but may also be explained by the competition between pigs and humans for water and food in dry lands. An early prohibition of pork occurred in Egypt even before 5000 BP, but adherence to this rule waxed and waned with alternations in the worship of the god Seth, with whom pigs were associated, and his evil brother Osiris. In this case, ideology seems to have been the main driver, rather than any fear of parasites or the pig's love of mud and muck.

A clear distinction between "clean" and "unclean" foods developed over time in the Judaic tradition. In the beginning, all things were considered clean and appropriate as human food. Only gradually were the clean distinguished from prohibited items such as the meat of pigs, camels, rabbits, shellfish, and fish lacking scales or fins; then blood, fat, and sinew; and later, seed contaminated by association with dead animals. These assessments of the inherent qualities of potential foods overlapped with prohibitions and taboos related to preparation, cooking, and storage. Varieties of ritual (kosher) slaughter, designed to remove the blood, are similarly rooted in ancient conditions of sanitation, achieved through a religious regulation of butchers and butchery. Much the same applies to the Jewish prohibition of the mixing of meat and milk products, meaning that they should not be prepared, cooked, eaten, or stored together.

Early Christians, creating an alternative religious tradition, at first chose to reject the rules of the Jewish dietary regime. They returned to the initial position of the Old Testament, declaring all creatures good, coming from the hand of God. This omnivorous approach, interrupted only symbolically by Lent and sometimes a preference for fish over meat on Fridays, persisted until recently. A partial return to central ideas of the Jewish tradition appeared in the nineteenth century, when Seventh Day Adventists, seeking to restore a true Christian church and reviving Saturday as the Sabbath, not only returned to kosher laws and prohibited pork and shellfish, alcohol and hot peppers but also promoted vegetarianism. Soon after, Jehovah's Witnesses followed a similar path. In the 1930s, Rastafarians in Jamaica, tracing their heritage to Ethiopia and the Babylonian slavery of the ancient children of Israel, placed their faith in living, organic foods, as opposed to the "dead" meat of unclean animals, notably the pig but also scavengers such as goats and poultry, and of salt as a seasoning, a dead thing to be replaced with fresh hot peppers and other herbs.

These tendencies, taken together, indicate elements of continuity, perhaps based in common observation of consequences. They equally indicate the continuity of contradiction and diversity, showing clearly the way food choices might ramify through the elements of a system and how they served also to underpin notions of identity and lineage. Christianity is now the world's largest religion, giving its omnivorous dietary ideas a major role in determining the choices of the modern world about what and what not to eat.

The world's second largest religion is Islam. The *Koran* of the early seventh century distinguished between *halal* (allowed, pure) and *haram* (forbidden) foods. Parallel to kosher practices, halal required the ritual slaughter of allowed animals, the killing sanctified by the saying of a prayer. Divine prohibitions recorded in the *Koran* included many of the usual suspects: pork, blood, carrion (the flesh of animals found dead), shellfish, wine, intoxicating drugs, and foods that had been offered to idols. Later Muslim writers added further prohibitions, as, for example, the medieval admonition that milk should not be consumed in combination with fish, in fear of leprosy.

Separate from these traditions with their roots firmly planted in the same small region that gave birth to the Neolithic and the ancient agricultural revolution was the world's oldest religion, Hinduism, with its origins in northern Iron Age India *c.*3500 BP. Early Hindu texts emphasized the dietary significance of distinguishing between plants and animals, and the importance of respect for animals. Pork was prohibited as unclean and beef because the cow was considered sacred. Vegetarianism is regarded as a sign of spirituality. Fasting is a further sign. Buddhism, another major religion with its origins in India *c.*2500 BP, similarly saw vegetarianism as indicating respect for life and typically promoted fasting for the first half of each day, but their monks did not insist on avoiding meat.

Confucianism, which originated in China at about the same time as Buddhism appeared in India, emphasized wellbeing and wholeness, associated with an ascetic, largely vegetarian, diet, in the absence of strong prohibitions. Avoidance of overindulgence was a moral good, and a practical solution to limited supplies of certain foods, but this ideal existed alongside a willingness to consume a wide range of animals and plants, extending to dogs and animals rarely considered in the other traditions. Indeed, extending the range was a means of overcoming shortage. Rather than following those who prohibited pork, ancient and modern Chinese demonstrated a great enthusiasm for pig meat.

Geographical redistribution

The global spread and redistribution of food plants and animals by human agents commenced, largely inadvertently, before domestication and before the emergence of religious prohibitions and taboos. The development of agricultural technologies greatly enhanced the process, however, by means of trade, colonization, and migration. Some things were simply adopted by neighbors through the exchange or gifting of planting materials or breeding animals; others spread by the inadvertent dispersion of seeds disposed of from foods such as fruit as part of local or long-distance trade. Voyagers also contributed to the spread, without necessarily engaging in trade or colonization.

Classical modes of colonization, in which people from one place invaded and settled the lands of another society, were much more hegemonic, imposing new plants and animals on a place together with the systems of food production worked out by the colonists in their homelands. Imperial settlement and invasion brought with it whole cultures, including the people's prohibitions and taboos. These rules, perhaps no longer functional in the way they had been at first, affected attitudes and engendered food prejudices in the colonized populations. Thus, the process worked not only to spread plants and animals around the world but also to spread attitudes about what was and was not good to eat. Sometimes, independent of aggressive colonization, the spread of the great religions and philosophies had a similar effect, encouraging people to add new items to their prohibited lists or, especially where Christianity dominated, to become increasingly omnivorous.

Successful, popular domesticates spread widely though not necessarily rapidly by diffusion. Individuals and communities observed the activities of their near neighbors and, if they liked what they saw and tasted, embraced new food sources and modified their cultural practices. They exchanged products and gifts, and perhaps seed. They learned by the mistakes of others. It was a slow process, with many retreats and many failures, gradually creeping across the landscape.

Maize, for example, spread slowly from its original sites in southern Mexico (see Figure 1.5), where it was domesticated by 7000 BP, to reach Ecuador and southern Peru, in elevated sites that saw the domestication of the potato, by about 3500 BP (Perry *et al.*, 2006: 76–9). To the north, maize reached the region now identified as the southwestern United States by 3000 BP and the eastern regions of North America by 2100 BP, but did not become an important crop there for another thousand years (Fussell, 1992). It also failed to prosper in the early Caribbean, reaching Hispaniola only about 1000 BP. This failure had something to do with soil and climate but was essentially a cultural outcome. The second wave of colonizers into the Caribbean, beginning around 2500 BP, came from the tropical forests of the Orinoco, where they had developed agriculture and pottery, and adopted a sedentary settlement pattern. In particular they had built their system of food production on the cultivation of cassava, a tuber domesticated in the rainforests of the Amazon around 4000 BP. These migrants took cassava with them when they sailed north, taking it to eat on the voyage and to plant on the islands they might find. They also carried peanuts, another domesticate of the Amazon, taking the crop as far as Cuba.

In Asia, many important domesticated plants and animals began their westward diffusion long before Arab and European imperialism. Asian rice first spread south from the Yangtze, then crossed the sea to Taiwan by 4800 BP and the northern Philippines by 4000 BP (see Figure 1.4). By the same date rice had spread west to the Chengdu Plain, and reached as far south as Vietnam and Thailand. This dispersal was slow and erratic at first but, once the agricultural systems of the Yangtze had become highly developed, rice cultivation spread rapidly, the grain traveling together with people, knowledge, technology, and culture (Chi and Hung, 2010: 18–22). Although local domestication may have occurred in Japan, it is generally considered that the islands imported rice cultivation together with domestic pigs and metallurgy from the mainland, through Korea, between 2500 and 1700 BP.

Asian rice and the coconut, carried across the Indian Ocean and used as voyaging foods, were known on the Red Sea coast as early as the first century and on the east coast of Africa by the eleventh century. African rice, on the other hand, was much less successful in expanding its geographical scope, with movement across the continent facing substantial land barriers. In eastern Africa, the islands off Tanzania had developed an economy founded on pearl millet, known as a domesticate as early as 3900 BP, but shifted to Asian rice (and coconut) after the eleventh century (Walshaw, 2010: 137–54). Specialization in rice was part of a process of Islamization that responded to social and political demands but carried with it risks because the region lacked the rainfall needed to ensure reliable crops. Rice has production and processing advantages over millet but millet is superior to both rice and wheat in nutritional terms. The adoption of rice led in turn to new ways in preparation and cooking, part of a larger cultural package.

The coconut existed in wild form around the Indian and Pacific Oceans and was domesticated in southeastern Asia. It arrived in many of the Pacific islands ahead of human migrants and it was on the west coast of Panama before Columbus, perhaps having floated there. The first Pacific colonists took domesticated coconuts with them, recognizing their value as a voyaging food (the younger "water" fruit forming perfect natural containers of refreshing drink). Although the coconut had reached the east coast of Africa by the eleventh century, it was extensively cultivated in western Africa only after 1520, following Portuguese and Spanish voyaging in the Pacific and Indian Oceans, when it was also found on the Atlantic islands (Lewicki, 1974: 20).

The rapid and extensive introduction of the coconut to the Americas came after 1500, when Spanish colonial voyaging in the Pacific enabled access to fresh planting stock. In spite of the narrowness of the isthmus, coconuts intro-duced to the Atlantic coast of the American mainland came from the east – Cape Verde and the Caribbean islands, and ultimately from eastern Africa and the Indian Ocean – whereas the west coast received its coconuts from the Solomon Islands and the Philippines (Zizumbo-Villarreal, 1996). There was also some flow back into the Caribbean, from the mainland, in the early sev-enteenth century. This pattern of diffusion resulted in genetic flow between coconut varieties with different regional origins, as well as hybridization between wild and domesticated plants.

Some plants, including the coconut, are strongly colonial, invading open space and pushing aside weaker species, taking advantage of their capacity to remain viable over long distances and dormant for long periods. Other plants are completely dependent on human beings and have been spread around the world only because of their important roles in food production systems. Two outstanding examples of the latter type are the banana and the plantain.

The banana and its close relative the plantain is a giant herb. Unlike those in the wild, the cultivated varieties are sterile and seedless, requiring neither pol-lination nor fertilization (Heslop-Harrison and Schwarzacher, 2007; De Langhe and de Maret, 1999). Most of these varieties derive from naturally occurring mutants, which were collected by farmers and then multiplied and distributed by vegetative propagation using suckers. The domesticated fruit were full of edible pulp, without the hard stony seeds that had characterized their progenitors. Each plant produces only a single stem or bunch of fruit, made up of about five hands with a dozen fingers in each hand.

Plantain and banana domestication began in the rainforest gardens of New Guinea and eastern Indonesia as early as 4500 BP, and from there spread into mainland southeastern Asia. By about 3500 BP pioneer voyagers set out across the Indian Ocean to southern India and eastern Africa, depending on plantain, taro, and yam to sustain them. Plantain and banana reached western Africa before the arrival of Europeans. At the same time, beginning around 3500 BP, they were taken into the Pacific by the voyagers who chose to head east, where they encountered in some islands bananas derived from even earlier colonizations. Both bananas and plantains got to Spain by the tenth century and from there they were taken to the Americas at the beginning of the sixteenth century.

Although migrants and colonists were often self-conscious agents in the global redistribution of food sources, initially the impact of many of them was inadvertent rather than part of a systematic project of imperial domination. Potential colonists tended to select for transfer only those things they had already domesticated and found fruitful. Frequently, however, these plants and, to a lesser extent, animals were part of the voyaging enterprise, carried by travelers to sustain them along the way, in just the same way that traders traveled, rather than necessarily being designed for agricultural production at an expected destination. Ancient voyagers were frequently more at home on the sea, in their vessels, than on land in potentially hostile territory, but they might leave behind seeds or cuttings that came to life after they had sailed on. In the sixteenth-century Caribbean, European buccaneers left behind pigs and cattle that became feral but reproduced strongly so that later voyagers found ready supplies of meat in islands that had previously had no significant mammal populations. It was here the barbecue was born.

The significance of the European encounter with the Americas, following the voyages of Columbus, was that the long-term westward spread of plants and animals, all of them having their origins and domestications within Eurasia and Africa, was counterbalanced by an exchange between two essentially unique and separate biospheres. The exchange that took place between 1500 and 1800 formed a central watershed in world food history. By 1800, and even earlier in some cases, many of the plants that had been transferred eastward from the Americas had become naturalized in their new geographic homes, to such an extent that they seemed almost indigenous elements in their adoptive food systems.

Thus the tomato of Mesoamerica quickly came to seem at home in the Italian agricultural landscape and the potato became known (even in the Americas) as the "Irish" variety. Similarly, the yams of Africa and southeastern Asia and the mangoes of India blended into the forests of the neotropics, creating a "creole" botanical formation, parallel to the emergence of creole societies in the colonial Americas. Of the major cereal plants of the modern world, Eurasian wheat spread across the temperate plains of North and South America, whereas the production of rice in the Americas never came near to rivaling the output of Asia. Other important crops of the Americas included the sugar cane (domesticated in New Guinea) and citrus (eastern and southeastern Asia). Moving in the opposite direction, cassava and maize did become major crops in Africa and Eurasia, the latter increasingly essential to the feeding of animals raised exclusively as sources of human food. However, the domesticated animals of the Americas did not enter the food systems of Eurasia and Africa, whereas the cattle, pigs, goats, and sheep of the Old World quickly became dominant in the pastures and pens of the New. The same applies to birds, the most important of which was, in the long run, the chicken, domesticated in southeastern Asia. Freshwater fish were rarely transferred until recent times, while the fish of the sea had their own environment.

In very broad terms, then, it may be argued that the Columbian exchange saw the food system of the Americas more dramatically transformed than that of Eurasia. This contrast can be attributed directly to the role of westward human migration and invasive colonization that affected the Americas from Alaska to Patagonia. In the long term, the movement of people across the Atlantic was essentially a one-way flow, dominated until the end of the eighteenth century by the forced migration of Africans through the slave trade, and then by Europeans. The native peoples of the Americas were far more likely to die by disease and genocide than to journey to the other side of the Atlantic. The European colonizers of the Americas did not, however, confine themselves to transferring to the Americas the plants and animals they knew from their own region; they also accessed Asia, Africa, and the Pacific. In some cases they did this in order to provide food for the people they forced to labor, as, for example, in the bringing of the breadfruit from Tahiti to the West Indies in 1793, intended as a food for enslaved Africans on sugar plantations. In other cases, such as the introduction to the Americas of African rice and the ackee, enslaved people may have been active agents in the transfer from western Africa, concealing seeds in their hair, or the seeds may have come from food fed to the enslaved in the Middle Passage (Fields-Black, 2008; Eltis, Morgan and Richardson, 2007; Carney, 2001).

This transfer was part of a large-scale imperial world-system designed not only to improve the food resources of the colonized American territories and make them more attractive to European settlers, in the manner of the Roman Empire, but intended also to enable the production of crops that could not be grown in temperate Europe, notably tropical crops such as sugar and coffee. It went together with the establishment of botanical gardens and experiment stations, beginning in the eighteenth century, set up to test the suitability of exotics and later used to develop hybrids. A similar process occurred in Australia and New Zealand, from the early nineteenth century, but none of the unique food sources of those places had been domesticated and none of them entered the world system. Although colonial settler migration had a slighter long-term impact on the population of Africa, the continent received from the Americas plants that proved highly influential, notably cassava and maize.

Of the dominant cereal crops, wheat and rice were the most imperial, often driving out traditional roots and tubers and dramatically changing foodways. Although the spread of rice culture was not as closely identified with formal (European) imperialism as was the spread of wheat, there exists a strong "rizification hypothesis," which asserts that, throughout Asia, rice has been displacing alternative foods for many centuries. Counter to this interpretation is the argument that in at least some regions of southeastern Asia, such as Indonesia, the traditional tubers taro and yam first gave way to sweet potatoes and then to cassava, rather than succumbing immediately to rice. The sweet potato and cassava were introduced from the Americas by the Spanish, Portuguese, and Dutch after 1500, and sometimes brought in also by Chinese people. By the late seventeenth century the sweet potato had been effectively naturalized. Cassava was not significant until the nineteenth century but then expanded so rapidly that it was said to have initiated a "cassava revolution." The introduced tubers were efficiently intercropped with the traditional food plants, so long as they were part of the subsistence of semi-sedentary communities and the ecological conditions were suitable.

Tubers competed successfully with rice down to the middle of the twentieth century. This resulted in part from the limited amount of land suited to irrigation in some areas, though dryland cultivation remained relatively more common than wet-rice paddy in Indonesia, as well as the Philippines and Thailand, until the late nineteenth century. Rice was essentially a commodity of market culture, and its significance declined in regions dominated by small islands with good access to fish and shellfish, as was typical of the vast area stretching from eastern Indonesia into the Pacific. However, when rice was combined with maize (introduced to Indonesia in the sixteenth century), the two together proved hard to withstand (Boomgaard, 2003, 2005).

Intense local struggles of this sort, between introduced and indigenous crops and animals, continue to be played out globally, and food plants and animals continue to be moved around the world and tried in new ecological niches. However, the greater part of the global transfer that created the present pattern of geographical distribution was virtually in place by the end of the eighteenth century, well in advance of the global redistribution of the human population. The rapidity of the change was dramatic, creating a map strongly contrasted with that of 1490. Although change had been substantial in the millennia before Columbus, it was the interchange between the Americas and the rest of the world that formed the foundation of the modern geographical distribution of food plants and animals. Soil and climate remain the bedrock – coconuts do not grow in Iceland and wheat fails in Java – but within these limits the great redistribution of plants and animals enabled significant increases in food production that were essential to the growth of population and the making of the modern industrial world. Growth in agricultural yields, for food and industrial raw materials, was not simply a product of the moving around of plants and animals, however. It depended also on changes in the way these resources were manipulated, within systems of food production that were themselves evolving.

Three claims

First, before domestication, human migration and colonization had little impact on the global distribution of food plants and animals. Typically, people chose their food from the resources they found where they moved. Domestication and agriculture marked a different attitude to nature and the emergence of an enthusiasm for imposing learned cultures on new places. The migration of people and the diffusion of plants and animals that followed transformed the global food landscape gradually at first but much more dramatically in the period of invasive colonization initiated by Europeans in the fifteenth century. This redistribution of resources fundamentally changed the world food map.

A second claim is that domestication and geographical redistribution pushed biodiversity and the range of food choices in two, seemingly opposite, directions. On the one hand, the plants and animals that had been domesticated and introduced to agrarian systems were scattered widely across the world, increasing choice. At the same time, domestication and agriculture narrowed the range of food sources by specializing in the genetic improvement and production of a small number of major plants and animals, placing pressure on local biodiversity. Once the system was in place, few new domestications occurred, even when migrant peoples encountered species previously unknown to them.

Third, taboos and prohibitions on the consumption of particular foods, though eaten with impunity by other people, flourished together with the growth of the world's major religions and philosophies. The origins of these taboos are difficult to pin down, and the range of prohibited foods varies significantly across belief systems, but generally it was easier to add new items to the prohibited list than to encourage people to consume new foods. The outcome was a further narrowing of the spectrum of potential resources, demonstrating the central role of culture in food systems.

REFERENCES

Barker, G. (2006) *The Agricultural Revolution in Prehistory: Why did Foragers become Farmers?* Oxford: Oxford University Press.

Boomgaard, P. (2003) In the shadow of rice: Roots and tubers in Indonesian history, 1500–1950. *Agricultural History* 77: 582–610.

Boomgaard, P. (2005) Resources and people of the sea in and around the Indonesian Archipelago, 900–1900. In P. Boomgaard, D. Henley and M. Osseweijer (eds)

Muddied Waters: Historical and Contemporary Perspectives on Management of Forests and Fisheries in Island Southeast Asia, pp. 97–119. Leiden: KITLV.

Carney, J.A. (2001) *Black Rice: The African Origins of Rice Cultivation in the Americas*. Cambridge, MA: Harvard University Press.

Cassidy, R. and Mullin, M. (eds) (2007) *Where the Wild Things Are Now: Domestication Reconsidered*. Oxford: Berg.

Chi, Z. and Hung, H. (2010) The emergence of agriculture in South China. *Antiquity* 84: 11–25.

Craw, C. (2008) The ecology of emblem eating: Environmentalism, nationalism and the framing of kangaroo consumption. *Media International Australia* 127: 82–95.

De Langhe, E. and de Maret, P. (1999) Tracking the banana: Its significance in early agriculture. In C. Gosden and J. Hather (eds) *The Prehistory of Food: Appetites for Change*, pp. 377–96. London: Routledge.

Doebley, J.F., Gaut, B.S. and Smith, B.D. (2006) The molecular genetics of crop domestication. *Cell* 127: 1309–21.

Eltis, D., Morgan, P. and Richardson, D. (2007) Agency and diaspora in Atlantic history: Reassessing the African contribution to rice cultivation in the Americas. *American Historical Review* 112: 1329–58.

Fields-Black, E.L. (2008) Untangling the many roots of West African mangrove rice farming: Rice technology in the Rio Nunez region, Earliest Times to c.1800. *Journal of African History* 49: 1–21.

Fuller, D.Q., Allaby, R.G. and Stevens, C. (2010) Domestication as innovation: The entanglement of techniques, technology and chance in the domestication of cereal crops. *World Archaeology* 42: 13–28.

Fussell, B. (1992) *The Story of Corn*. Albuquerque, NM: University of New Mexico Press.

Gerritsen, R. (2008) *Australia and the Origins of Agriculture*. Oxford: Archaeopress, BAR International Series 1874.

Goodwin, I.D., Williams, S.B., Pandit, P.S. and Laidlaw, H.K.C. (2009) Multifunctional grains for the future: Genetic engineering for enhanced and novel cereal quality. *In Vitro Cellular Development Biology – Plant* 45: 383–99.

Harlan, J.R. (1975) *Crops and Man*. Madison: American Society of Agronomy.

Harris, M. (1985) *Good to Eat: Riddles of Food and Culture*. New York: Simon & Schuster.

Heslop-Harrison, J.S. and Schwarzacher, T. (2007) Domestication, genomics and the future of the banana. *Annals of Botany* 100: 1073–84.

Kloppenburg, J.R. Jr. (1988) First the Seed: *The Political Economy of Plant Biotechnology, 1492–2000*. Cambridge: Cambridge University Press.

Lawrence, S. (2007) What would you do with a fluorescent green pig? How novel transgenic products reveal flaws in the foundational assumptions for regulation of biotechnology. *Ecology Law Quarterly* 34: 201–290.

Lewicki, T. (1974) *West African Food in the Middle Ages*. Cambridge: Cambridge University Press.

Maggioni, L., von Bothmer, R, Poulsen, G. and Branca, F. (2010) Origin and domestication of cole crops (*Brassica oleracea L.*): Linguistic and literary considerations. *Economic Botany* 64: 109–123.

Meyer-Rochow, V.B. (2009) Food taboos: Their origins and purposes. *Journal of Ethnobiology and Ethnomedicine* 5: 5.

Munro, N.D. (2004) Zooarchaeological measures of hunting pressure and occupation intensity in the Natufian. *Current Anthropology* 45: S5–S33.

O'Kennedy, M.M., Grootboom, A. and Shewry, P.R. (2006) Harnessing sorghum and millet biotechnology for food and health. *Journal of Cereal Science* 44: 224–35.

Perry, L., Sandweiss, D.H., Piperno, D.R. *et al.*, (2006) Early maize agriculture and interzonal interaction in southern Peru. *Nature* 440 (2 March): 76–79.

Purugganan, M.D., Boyles, A.L. and Suddith, J.I. (2000) Variation and selection at the CAULIFLOWER floral homeotic gene accompanying the evolution of domesticated *Brassica oleracea*. *Genetics* 155: 855–62.

Rosenblum, J.D. (2010) *Food and Identity in Early Rabbinic Judaism*. Cambridge: Cambridge University Press.

Sapir-Hen, L., Bar-Oz, G., Khalaily, H. and Dayan, T. (2009) Gazelle exploitation in the Early Neolithic site of Motza, Israel: The last of the gazelle hunters in the Southern Levant. *Journal of Archaeological Research* 36: 1538–46.

Simoons, F. J. (1994) *Eat Not This Flesh: Food Avoidances from Prehistory to the Present*. Madison: University of Wisconsin Press, second edition.

Walshaw, S.C. (2010) Converting to rice: Urbanization, Islamization and crops on Pemba Island, Tanzania, AD 700–1500. *World Archaeology* 42: 137–54.

Whitehead, H. (2000) *Food Rules: Hunting, Sharing, and Tabooing Game in Papua New Guinea*. Ann Arbor: University of Michigan Press.

Zizumbo-Villarreal, D. (1996) History of coconut (*Cocos nucifera L.*) in Mexico, 1539–1810. *Genetic Resources and Crop Evolution* 43: 505–15.

CHAPTER THREE

Forest, Farm, Factory

The driving force behind the human redistribution of plants and animals was a desire to increase choice. Even without the complementary movement of people, new plants and animals were introduced to existing systems of food production and allowed to compete for space with indigenous resources. This process was in many cases slow and cumulative but in the long term had a significant effect on regional food systems.

By contrast, where the people who did the moving of food plants and animals were themselves colonists or the directors of imperial projects, the pattern of change was both more rapid and more likely to involve long-distance transfers. In either case, the intention was to enable a wider range of choice about what to plant and what to raise, and where to do it. Increasing choice about what to produce and where to produce it was not simply, or even necessarily, a means of improving variety. It was above all a vital contributor to increasing both the quantity and the quality of food, and to improving yields and reducing costs. Ironically, the result was often a narrowing rather than a widening of commonly consumed food types, both locally and globally.

In addition to the redistribution of living things, a further set of choices had to be made about the way the selected plants and animals should be produced, the technologies that could be applied, the structure of the agrarian system, and how the product should be distributed. These were essentially choices about the way the environment should be manipulated in order to provide food for human societies but they had wide-ranging implications for environmental change, the depletion of natural resources, land tenure and labor, government, and social structure. Decisions about all of these things influenced in turn the varied systems of production that were applied to the

How Food Made History, First Edition. B. W. Higman.
© 2012 B. W. Higman. Published 2012 by Blackwell Publishing Ltd.

extraction of food from nature. They also reflected changing attitudes to the natural world and the relationship of human beings with the things they consumed. Food was at the root of most of these changes. Only in the last hundred years or so did the production and distribution of food cease to be the dominant component of the world's economy. Even then, much of the mining and manufacturing, communications, and finance that absorbed the world's energy ultimately found its way into the culture and economy of world food and foodways.

Forest gardens

At 5000 BP a large proportion of the world was covered by forest. The humans who lived within these environments were mostly hunter-gatherers but, as already argued, they had their own impact on what would grow successfully and what they in turn could choose to eat. Small groups of people were still able to live in this way at the beginning of the twenty-first century but they were by then widely regarded as an endangered species. Why did these peoples hold out against agriculture so long and how did they go about obtaining their food?

Whereas tropical forest ecosystems can be seen as a rich resource for modern food production, some of these foods require processing by industrial technologies that were not available to traditional hunter-gatherers lacking iron tools. Many food plants are too high in the canopy, or toxic, or otherwise unsuited to the human digestive system, or too scarce to sustain human populations, however well suited they might be to animal herbivores. Extracting food value from plants was hard work for little return, often delivering little more than snack food. Other resources such as wild honey, sometimes used to soak boiled tubers and roots, were unreliable. Thus, forest dwellers had to depend on meat and, where available, fish to fill the gaps in the accessible plant food (Figure 3.1). Animal fat served as a substitute for the carbohydrates supplied inadequately by wild tubers, but it was unreliable because the fatness of animals varied with environmental conditions. For the last five hundred years, there is evidence that forest dwellers regularly exchanged goods with nearby farmers in order to secure adequate food supplies (Hladik *et al.*, 1993; Headland, 1987). Probably this association and interdependence is an ancient rather than a recent phenomenon. Where such exchange was not possible, forest peoples lived poor lives or, more creatively, transformed their habitats into "forest gardens."

The great rainforest of the Amazon seems to have been empty of people until about 5000 BP and from the beginning communities undertook varieties of farming as well as hunting, fishing, and gathering. It was the discovery around 4000 BP that domesticated bitter cassava could be processed and

Figure 3.1 Tropical forest, South America.

detoxified that made possible sedentary Amazonian agriculture, as noted in the previous chapter. In some regions of the Amazon early farmers constructed large-scale raised-field systems, designed to ensure well-drained soils, in which they grew crops such as maize and squash as well as cassava. Canals and ponds were also excavated. This manipulation of the land had long-term consequences for the ecosystems, particularly their soils, even when the fields were abandoned and allowed to return to forest. These ecosystems are now regarded as unsuited to agriculture. Thus, although the rainforest of the Amazon may appear pristine, it contains elements, their extent hotly debated, which are the product of past agriculture and constitute artifact forest gardens (McKey *et al.*, 2010).

The best-known forest garden in the Americas is that invented by the Maya. The ancestral Maya of the Archaic period, 8000–4000 BP, lived in a period of stable climatic conditions which saw tropical forest expand across the tropical Yucatan lowland. The Maya modified the landscape to ensure their subsistence but, faced by climatic chaos, turned to a more settled agriculture which built on the earlier modification to create a closely managed and highly productive ecosystem, the Maya Forest Garden. This intensive system of agroforestry, combined in some places with raised fields watered by clay-lined canals, and terraced hillsides, proved capable of supporting large urban populations and underpinned the Classic Maya civilization that flourished until its dramatic collapse in the ninth century (Demarest, 2004: 133–9).

Scholars long argued that the Maya were responsible for denuding the forest, and that this destruction was fundamental to the collapse, but Ford and Nigh (2009: 216) contend that the "Maya milpa cycle is an ancient system of land use that sequences from a closed canopy forest to an open field dominated by annual crops (the milpa), to a managed orchard garden, and then back to a closed canopy forest." The last stage does not mean abandonment of the fields. Rather, the trees and bushes designed to make up the woodland are selected and planted while the annual crops – peppers, taro, beans, squashes, maize – are in the ground. Long-lived perennials include pineapple, pawpaw, cassava, guava, avocado, and other fruit trees.

Although by the beginning of the twenty-first century relatively few people lived within forest ecosystems and derived their food directly from the plants and animals indigenous to their habitat, modern evolved versions of the food forest were common. In these adaptations, the structure of the vegetation might be closely managed and, indeed, planted and cultivated by farmers. In most cases, it included introduced and domesticated plants together with indigenous species, the former naturalized and regarded as part of the landscape. It was a farming method attractive to small-scale producers but not confined to this class. In Kalimantan, Indonesia, for example, *simpukng* or "forest gardens" were a traditional farming system of the Dayak people, constructed from managed secondary forests planted with economic fruit trees, such as mango, rambutan, and durian, as well as vegetables and medicinal plants, bamboo, rattan, and timber (Mulyoutami, Rismawan and Joshi, 2009). In addition, the Dayak hunted, and gathered from the forest nuts and honey, the latter from honeycombs found in a variety of tall "honey trees." The use and inheritance of these forest gardens was regulated by communal rules founded in indigenous knowledge to prevent excessive exploitation of the resources, but by the end of the twentieth century the system was threatened by logging and mining enterprises.

A similar mode was found in many regions of New Guinea, particularly in central mountain zones, where outside influences remained minimal until the middle of the twentieth century. For example, in the 1980s, the Seltaman people of the Western Province of Papua New Guinea effectively combined gardening with hunting and gathering, accepting into their system new plants and technologies but retaining the essentials of forest-mountain food ecologies (Whitehead, 2000: 42–6). Their gardens were cut from the forest and designed to slope down steep hillsides, to ensure the necessary drainage to cope with frequent heavy rain. Cultivated plants grew alongside wild grasses and tree ferns, while the larger trees of the forest started their regrowth. Ancient domestications such as the banana and sugar cane, and native varieties of taro and sweet potato, flourished along with imports such as Chinese taro, cassava, maize, pumpkin, tomato, and cabbage. Each Seltaman family cultivated several gardens simultaneously, at different stages of ripeness and with a different emphasis on the primary tubers. Some of the native taro was cooked and fed to domesticated pigs. Lesser quantities of meat came from the hunting of game (including wild pig), but this was an unreliable source of protein, and overall the consumption of meat was meager except for the excesses of feast days. Oils and starches were extracted from the nuts of semicultivated trees and palms. Further food came from shoots foraged from the surrounding forest, wild yams and mushrooms, worms and large wood grubs, frogs, snakes, and lizards, and the very large eggs of the brush turkey and cassowary. In the 1980s, traded foods remained a relatively distant prospect for the Seltaman, difficult to acquire though seductive: canned meat and fish, rice, and sugar.

In West Africa in the nineteenth and twentieth centuries, farmers combined taro with cocoa and coconut, allowing vines to grow on the trunks and branches of the taller trees and planting short-term crops in the spaces between. In Ghana, the fruits of these complex agroforests were a mix, some of them destined for consumption by the farmer's household, some for local sale, and some for export. Cocoa was, however, the most valuable crop and increasingly funneled into the export market, feeding demand from the rising metropolitan chocolate makers such as Cadbury's and Fry's (Ruf and Schroth, 2004). Traditional "cocoa forest gardens" or "chocolate forests" were also found in the humid forests of Cameroon, the Ivory Coast, and Brazil, where they are now valued for their capacity to protect forest species from logging, to sustain smallholders, and, through their biodiversity, aid the regulation of pests and diseases (Bisseleua and Vidal, 2008).

Something similar occurred in parts of the Americas, within the plantation system based on slavery, beginning in the seventeenth century. Rather than providing food for enslaved people, sugar planters chose to allocate land on which the people were required to produce their own. These plots were often in distant hilly zones, fertile but not suited to the cultivation of the major export crops, and in these niches the people created food forest farms. Tubers such as yams, cassava, taro, and sweet potato grew down into the soil, while peas, corn, and melons served as ground cover. Above these, plantain, banana, and coffee trees rose to 16 ft (5 m), lightly shaded by pawpaw (22 ft [7 m]) and cocoa (26 ft [8 m]), with large shading timber trees forming the canopy. Avocado (65 ft [20 m]) and other indigenous fruits were collected from the wild. Nearer to their houses, enslaved people grew fruits and vegetables, and over time new plants were added as they were introduced: ackee (40 ft [12 m]) from western Africa, jackfruit (50 ft [15 m]) from India, breadfruit (65 ft [20 m]) from Tahiti, and mango (115 ft [35 m]) from India.

The great attraction of the constructed food forest was that it replicated the natural ecosystem, providing shade for plants below the canopy, support for vines and creepers, and mulch from leaf drop. It also maximized the use of vertical space and produced a variety of foods that could contribute to avoiding seasonal shortages and nutritional stress. In addition, the food forest was sometimes favored because it was more likely to be an organic mode of farming and more protective of the soil. This was not always true, however, as farmers came to appreciate the advantages of sprays and fertilizers. Further, although some indigenous plants might be retained in this model of the food forest, it was more common for the farmer to select productive species for cultivation and for the food forest to be combined in a single farm with crops such as maize or sugar cane or cassava planted in cleared openings. Both these crops and the food forest depended on the destruction of original forest. The food forest replaced the ancient forest with a new variety, making a milder assault on the landscape, but was often reduced to minor niches and pushed to the fringes of broadacre crop farming systems. In these ways, the food forest and the forest garden stood at the margins of agriculture.

Crop farming landscapes

Throughout the world, the first requirement of crop farming was the destruction of forest. The thick forest that clothed the world at 5000 BP was itself a relatively recent feature of the landscape, a product of the changed climate that came with the Holocene. It represented a challenge to hunters and gatherers, and a barrier to agriculture. People set about creating openings and treeless ecological niches, on a small scale at first but eventually, and largely in response to the demands of agriculture, removing most of the trees.

The clearing of the forest was easily the most important factor in the creation of new landscapes around the world (Williams, 2003: 37–8). It opened up vistas and created an environment in which humans might feel safe and secure, able to look out over their fertile fields. Even in the early Holocene, before agriculture, forest had been burned for similar reasons by hunters and gatherers, to encourage the development of park-like clearings. In the tropics, these open clearings generally remained small, but in some regions, for example temperate North America, extensive grasslands were formed. Thus, although not all forest removal was designed for crops or grazing, the plants and animals cultivated and raised for human food systems dominated the process for most of history. Agriculture also provided fibers such as flax, cotton, and wool, and industrial raw materials, while managed forests or plantations produced a variety of commodities, from timber to rubber and coconuts. In the late twentieth century, vast swathes of tropical forest containing endangered wildlife were cut down and burnt in order to cultivate the oil palm, a vital element in the production of a wide range of industrialized foods. Popular opinion came to link the deforestation of the Amazon with North American consumption of hamburgers, but the depletion of rainforest was driven increasingly by demands other than food production (Bonti-Ankomah and Fox, 1998).

These destructive events came at the end of a long drawn out process and are merely dramatic modern examples. In the nineteenth century huge areas of Australia and Argentina were cleared of forest by settler colonists encouraged by their imperial governments to plant wheat and raise cattle and sheep. In the eighteenth century, Caribbean islands were set on fire to remove the forest in a single operation, in order to prepare the land for sugar cane cultivation, smoke from the fires filling the sky for months. In ancient times, the spread of agriculture across Eurasia had similar effects.

Only occasionally was deforestation reversed. Japan is perhaps the best example. In the early medieval period, the thirteenth century, the spread of intensive cultivation encouraged the growth of smallholders and larger, more densely settled, villages. To maintain the fertility of poor soils on newly terraced hillsides, farmers collected increasing quantities of mulch from the surrounding forests, using it as green fertilizer. In important regions of Japan, this development set villagers against local large landholders, who wished to preserve high forest for themselves, whereas smallholders valued landscapes dominated by grass, scrub, and coppice, the latter exploited for chestnuts and charcoal-making. By the sixteenth century, however, it was commoners who led the move to close the forests from predation, in order to protect the resources essential to agriculture, followed by the ruling elite, the daimyo, whose interests were different. In saving its forest, Japan had the great advantage that its food system did not demand the milk and meat of large mammals, whose herds would have damaged the roots of trees and trampled the undergrowth that held the hillside soils in place (Totman, 1998: 37–49).

In general, the agricultural societies of the world came to fear the forest as a place of wildness and hazard, and indeed the forest did and does still provide sanctuary for wild animals. Thus, the destruction of forest was typically seen not only as necessary to the expansion of cultivation but also as vital to making the world a more secure place for human beings and providing the environment needed for the development of complex civilized societies.

The first agricultural societies depended on individual small producers. They worked with limited technologies and limited knowledge, which in turn inhibited their potential output and the area they could efficiently manage. It was these limits that made people increasingly sedentary, while the security of their crops and their lives was similarly increased by living close to other people working the land in the same way, in small settlements. This pattern persisted into modern times, with small nucleated groups of homesteads around a square huddling the people together, with their fields stretching out toward the more dangerous frontier of forest or foe. As these settlements grew and as ancient farmers became more productive, they came to support larger urban centers in which some people found it viable to abandon agriculture and take up alternative specialized occupations. People began to purchase food rather than producing enough to feed themselves and their immediate household or group. Farmers in turn produced to meet this new demand. Gradually, they became separated from communal settlement sites, and the conduits of food chains began to develop locally and over greater distances. Emerging states took a close interest in these developments, anxious to ensure the supply of food and to encourage and control the agricultural population, the mass of the people.

For the ancient farmer, it became necessary to make choices about what to produce and in what quantities, in order to meet the demands of a market, though often required to do so according to directives and controls applied by governments of one sort or another. Where essential resources were limited, central management emerged early along with hegemonic state systems. The best example of this type of development is the so-called "hydraulic society," a problematic concept, in which the management of water was vital to food production and might be controlled centrally (Manning, 2010: 36–41). In ancient Egypt, the annual flooding of the Nile brought water and fertile soil to the lower stretches of the river, and this provided the foundations for dynastic rule, in which the pharaohs were regarded as part of a pantheon of gods with direct influence on the natural world, including the annual flood. In ancient China, dynastic rule was closely associated with the control of river systems through drainage and irrigation. Dependent on the cultivation of wet rice and other thirsty plant crops, farmers benefited from the great engineering schemes that could only be built by a state with control over large armies of laborers. Recognized as one of the world's first water projects is the system of stonework levees initiated in 256 BC, during the Qin Dynasty, at Dujiangyan on the Mingjiang River in Sichuan province, designed both to control the flow, by releasing sediment and preventing the annual flooding of farmland, and to irrigate the dry Chengdu plain now a major food producer (Li and Xu, 2006).

Other forms of hydraulic control important in increasing food production included the terracing of hill slopes and draining of wetlands. Terracing became common in Mesoamerica and the Andes by 3000 BP, used particularly to prevent erosion and to retain water. The drainage of wetlands was common on a small scale from early times but making large areas dry enough for agriculture required central control of labor and landscape. Modern examples include the empoldering of lands below sea level, as in the Netherlands and the Guyana coast of South America, where it was necessary both to construct a wall against the sea and to pump out saltwater. The construction and maintenance of such large-scale works was always expensive and profitable only when the crops were of high value, such as the cheese and tulips of the Netherlands and the sugar of Guyana. All of these projects of land-forming had the effect of creating level, geometric landscapes, most often planted in monocultures that contributed further to the openness and flatness of the scene. The development of modern cultivation technologies had a similar impact, flattening plowed fields. Most recently, lasers have been used to ensure lands are level in order to maximize the efficiency of irrigation water reaching all parts of the field equally. These were artificial agricultural lands, a long way from the food forest.

Other agricultural trends that had a significant impact on economies and landscapes include the tendency toward monoculture, the increasing scale of farming enterprises, and the increasing size of individual fields. In nature, plants and animals typically exist together in diversity, forming complex ecosystems and occupying hierarchical positions within the food chain. The idea of monoculture was born with domestication, particularly the domestication of grain crops. Rather than gathering grain from the favored plants that happened to be found in an area, incipient agriculturists recognized that it was efficient to weed out those which did not contribute, and then to collect seed and plant it in a dedicated field, reducing the need to separate the wheat from the tares.

Once a field was planted exclusively with the seed of a particular favored cereal crop, it became possible to harvest, thresh, and winnow the whole of it, with hopes of obtaining a relatively pure product which could safely and efficiently be made into flour and bread. Much the same process applied to all the grain-bearing grasses, as well as sugar cane, and to legumes and fruit. In recent times, chemical sprays were used not only to kill the pests that attacked crop plants but also to weed out unwanted species, further encouraging the monocultural status of a field. Fertilizers have similarly been targeted at specific growth characteristics. In very recent times, GM seeds have been used to cope with some of these natural hazards and to increase the quantity and quality of yields. These principles were important but could be operated on a small scale, within a strongly diversified farming unit made up of a number of distinct monocultures that produced primarily for household subsistence.

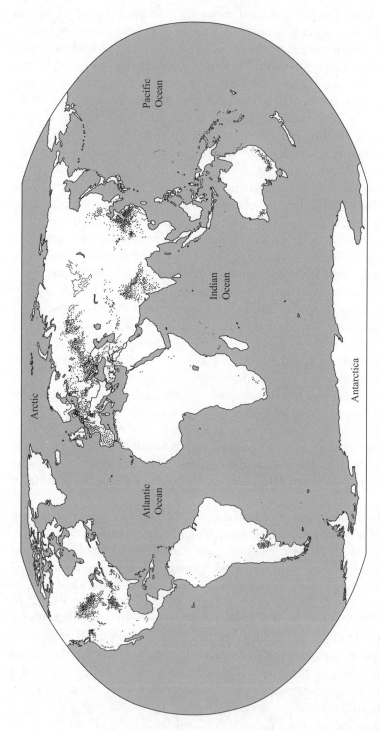

Figure 3.2 Wheat-growing regions, circa 1914. Each dot represents 50 000 hectares planted in wheat. Based on Erich W. Zimmermann, *World Resources and Industries: A Functional Appraisal of the Availability of Agricultural and Industrial Resources* (New York: Harper and Brothers, 1933), 246.

Monoculture moved to a new level when applied on a large scale within highly commercialized farming systems. Grain crops were at the forefront once again, though for reasons somewhat different from those that connected specialization with domestication. Particularly from the eighteenth century, commercial farmers in Europe and parts of the European imperial world began to see advantages in producing a single main crop, not just in some of their fields but in most of them. The process was worked out over centuries but it emerged essentially from recognition of the ecological suitability of particular conditions of soil and climate for particular plants, and from the advantages of specialist knowledge and investment in specialized tools and machinery. Generally, these advantages applied over large regions, resulting in the creation of monocultural zones, for example the wheat belts of Argentina and Australia, and the US corn belt which developed in the nineteenth century and persisted (Figure 3.2). Increasingly, these monocultural farms became dedicated commercial producers, with little interest in production for consumption by the farm household, further exaggerating the uniformity of their regional landscapes.

Raw colonial capitalism produced similar outcomes in the sugar and coffee plantations of the eighteenth century, in which there was little place for any crop other than the most profitable one. Once again, investment in technologies was an important driver of this development. Sugar plantations, for example, located the primary processing of their crops, the making of raw sugar, in factories located on their lands, requiring substantial capital investment. As with the cereals, this enabled the marketing of relatively pure products, demanded by the modern world, which could be consumed without fear of foreign bodies. It was the great growth in demand for these prime foods – wheat, rice, corn, sugar – coming particularly from urban populations disconnected from agriculture that created these highly specialized monocultures and clothed much of the agricultural landscape in a uniform vegetation that contrasted strongly both with the forest and the open-landscape diversified systems it had supplanted.

Loosely connected with the long-term development of monoculture was growth in the scale of farming units. In the ancient world, plantations of olives and vines emerged as early examples of large specialized units, though more often they were elements in varieties of mixed farming practices (Foxhall, 2007: 77–83). On the other hand, the great estates and domains that dominated Europe in the Middle Ages, some of them ruled by warlords, others by church foundations, tended to be internally diversified. After 1492, some of the largest farming units were the sugar and coffee plantations of the Americas, and these were indeed highly monocultural. Landholdings on this scale had something in common with the great estates of the Middle Ages, with nucleated settlements and integrated internal food economies, but outside these relatively rare examples of early large-scale agriculture, small farmers often operated independently, able to make their own choices about what crops to grow and how to distribute the product.

From the eighteenth century, powerful forces worked to increase the scale of farms. New technologies, particularly those driven by steam and oil, encouraged the spread of grain growing into new regions and enabled the expansion of the frontiers of individual enterprises. The railroad made accessible lands previously thought too distant from markets and ports to be profitable. The internal combustion engine powered the farm machines of the twentieth century, notably the tractor and the combine harvester, which were most profitable when employed on large fields and large properties. By the end of the century, many of these machines were so big and expensive they could never be used on small units. For many functions, particularly the harvesting of cereals, it became more efficient for the farmer to employ seasonal contractors than to purchase such machines.

Something similar occurred in tropical plantation agriculture. Steam power greatly increased the scale of sugar factory capacity, thus increasing the demand for cane. At the same time, the steam railroad enabled the collection of cut cane from distant fields, and plantations grew rapidly in acreage as a result. In 1750 a sugar plantation of 2000 acres was a large one, but by 1900 it needed to be 10 000 acres to qualify. These tropical plantations provided models for the development of large-scale horticulture, as in the vast orchards of southern California.

A more recent example of the shift from small-scale diversified production to large-scale monoculture is provided by the dramatic history of the banana (Wiley, 2008). Domesticated in the forests of southeastern Asia before 5000 BP, bananas came to be cultivated widely throughout the tropical and subtropical world. For millennia they formed part of the food forest subsistence system, and then grew among the diversified plantings of peasant farmers in the Americas. From the late nineteenth century, however, bananas came to form the basis of great plantation industries linked into international supply chains. This transformation occurred when steamships first made it profitable to carry ripening fruit to metropolitan markets in North America and then Europe, to feed rapidly growing populations of enthusiastic consumers. Banana plantations quickly became monocultural and massive, the fruit delivered to processing plants and ports by small internal railroads similar to those used on sugar plantations. These giant plantations were owned by multinational corporations, such as the United Fruit Company, which placed their stamp on Central America, creating "banana republics" where the voice of the company was louder than that of any local government.

Bananas and plantains are now the fourth-most-important crop in the developing world, serving as a starch staple in many of the poorest nations. In 2009 world output was 95 million tons of bananas and 34 million tons of plantains. Plantains are eaten unripe, boiled, or roasted, or ripe when fried or baked as a tart, but never raw. Unripe green bananas are boiled or deep fried (to make chips) or juiced to ferment beer. Bananas exported from the tropics to the developed world are almost all eaten ripe and raw. The leaves of the banana plant are not edible but are used as serving plates for food and for wrapping food parcels for steaming.

Roots and tubers, together with the bananas and plantains, are far outweighed by cereals. In 2009 the world produced 2 489 million tons of cereals but just 750 million tons of roots and tubers. The most important of the latter was the potato (330 million tons), followed by cassava (240), sweet potato (108), yam (54), and taro or cocoyam (12), and a range of other types which when heaped together amounted to eight million tons. Locally, several of the roots and tubers were important in diets, particularly in Africa and Southeast Asia. Africa accounts for more than half of world cassava production (51 percent), and Asia 29 percent and Latin America 19 percent. The two biggest countries in cassava are Nigeria and Brazil, accounting together for about one-third of world production. Everywhere, however, the roots and tubers faced a heavy onslaught from the cereals.

The three major cereal grains – maize, wheat, and rice – supply 50 percent of the world's calories. In 2009, the most important was maize (817 million tons), more than 40 percent of it grown in the United States, but an increasing proportion of this was used for the production of ethanol and the feeding of animals. Next came wheat (682), closely followed by rice (678), with all the rest much less significant: barley (150), sorghum (62), millet (32), oats (23), rye (18), and triticale (15). The dominance attained by the cereals depended partly on the increased area of cropland devoted to their growth but also on improvements in yield which had occurred only slowly and in tiny increments down to the eighteenth century but then speeded by the second Agricultural Revolution.

Breeding, hybridization, and seed improvement made greater gains possible in the twentieth century, particularly after 1950. The global spread of these and associated agricultural technologies followed fears for food security and world peace in the Cold War. The most dramatic response to such threats was the Green Revolution of the 1950s, deployed by the West as the vanguard of modernization and development in the struggle to curtail the spread of Communism, particularly in the ricefields/battlefields of Southeast Asia. When the Cold War thawed, many features of the agricultural achievements of the Green Revolution were replicated in China, resulting in massive increases in output and the establishment of new trade flows in food as well as industrial products.

The core elements of the Green Revolution, directed at increasing yields without increasing cropland, were widely adopted around the world regardless of political ideology. The significant exceptions were Africa, where the cultivation of wheat and rice was less important and little scientific attention was given to the genetic improvement of crops like cassava, sorghum, millet, and yams; and the Soviet Union, where commitment to an archaic model of plant-breeding held back yields until the 1960s and efforts to increase wheat production by plowing up drought-prone grasslands ultimately proved unsuccessful. From the 1960s, genetic manipulation and the chemicalization of cultivation reigned supreme. Unwillingness to adopt these technologies typically meant soil erosion, rationing, and the importation of grain, and living in fear of food shortages. The Soviet push into the steppe had failed and left behind an environmental disaster. On the geopolitical stage, the technologies of the West, symbolized by American farming systems, won the day, with the capacity to create abundance at home and still have substantial surpluses for export and aid (Olmstead and Rhode, 2008).

Ironically, the Green Revolution handed opportunities to large landowners that small farmers could not profit by, leading to increasing corporate concentration of land tenure and to massive fields, empty of people and planted in a single crop. In Australia, for example, agricultural output more than doubled in the second half of the twentieth century, in spite of protracted droughts, a contracting workforce, and a declining farm population. Around the world, farm numbers fell while productivity soared. Even in India, where more than one-half of the workforce continues to be directly engaged in agriculture, market forces and logistical challenges shifted the balance from fresh fruit, vegetables, and pulses to the production of grain, especially wheat.

In these ways, the Green Revolution contributed significantly to the reduction in the number of food sources on which the world depends, making the system vulnerable to devastating disease in a single crop. The use of pesticides increased in proportion, with the effect of further reducing the biodiversity of the world's agricultural landscapes, and by seeping out into streams, ponds, and reefs – along with large doses of chemical fertilizers – destroyed marine life as well. For example, the Great Barrier Reef, off the sugar-growing coast of Australia, suffered coral bleaching and loss of species. In the Gulf of Mexico, the Black Sea, and the Yellow Sea, the results were much worse, characterized by "dead zones." The rapid spread of irrigation systems took water from natural lakes and marshes, and depleted soils. The building of thousands of large dams around the world to supply these irrigation systems similarly changed the ecology of streams and, in China and India, required the massive resettlement of communities.

Industrialized agriculture

In the recent trend toward large-scale, industrialized farming, the leader was the United States, where the objective was to "make farming modern" and "every farm a factory" (Fitzgerald, 2003: 12). Agriculture accounted for three-quarters of all American workers at the beginning of the nineteenth century but by the beginning of the twentieth, and in spite of the powerful myth of the family farm as the foundation of the nation's society, the proportion had fallen to less than one-half. By the beginning of the twenty first-century, farmers made up less than 2 percent of the US population.

Whereas the nineteenth-century decline in the American farming population had much to do with the rise of alternative forms of employment, the dramatic twentieth-century collapse was driven by the transformation of farming. The labor power of humans and animals was replaced by coal- and oil-dependent machines, engineered to be capable of cultivating and harvesting vast acres of a limited range of crops for increasingly distant and urbanized markets. Between 1950 and 2000, the number of farms in the United States was halved, but the total area devoted to crops remained unchanged. Agribusiness took control, dominated by a small number of vertically integrated multinational corporations. Industrialization and economies of scale made farmers immensely productive, capable of feeding many more people and delivering food at cheaper prices, but at the same time emptied the rural landscape of people as well as animals (Centner, 2004: 14). Where human hands remained indispensable, notably in the harvesting of fragile fruits and vegetables, workers were brought in on a short-term seasonal basis, many of them from developing countries.

The industrialization of agriculture had significant implications for the nature of the food produced. The use of machines demanded varieties of plants which were amenable to such handling in the field and, equally important, amenable to transportation technologies that could deliver commodities to distant markets in good condition. It was the demand for out-of-season fresh foods (rather than their canned versions) that drove these developments, in which the largest markets were located in the urbanizing eastern seaboard of the United States. A good example of the outcome of these demands was the modern tomato, regularly reviled as tasteless but tough enough to withstand the rigors of cultivation, harvesting, and shipping, while still having a good shelf-life. The salad tomato was smoother and rounder, qualities appreciated by consumers, than its heritage varieties. Much later, in 1994, the FlavrSavr tomato became the first genetically engineered whole food.

Another example is the lettuce, a fragile leafy green plant which was never canned or frozen. Down to World War I most of the lettuces consumed in the United States were leaf or butter varieties, the most successful being the "Big Boston," but after the war the growing market dominance of California was followed by a shift to crisp head varieties, notably the iceberg or "New York" lettuce, with characteristic compact heads and resistance to damage in the near-freezing temperatures that made possible their journey across the continent, packed in crates and resting on layers of chipped ice. By the 1920s the iceberg lettuce had emerged as the first truly seasonless fresh vegetable. It was this status that enabled cultivation on mass production principles, the geometric regularity of monocultural fields and large-scale farming units. It also limited the number of producers who could enter the field to those who had the resources to capitalize on mechanical systems of cultivation and distribution (Petrick, 2006).

From the beginning, there was also a fundamental conflict between cultivation and livestock. Animals, both domesticated and wild, saw carefully planted fields and orchards as ideal places to graze. It was this threat to agricultural productivity that led to the construction of fences or walls, designed to keep animals out of cropped fields and corralled in pens and pastures where they could be controlled and prevented from wandering off and rejoining their wild relatives. Fences, walls, and ditches were also used, less successfully, to keep out human predators. In the long run, the adoption of the fence as a barrier between animals and plants had a dramatic impact on the rural landscape, with the fencing of land units of all sizes from plot to landholding. The concept also spilled over into the idea of the fence as a boundary marker and symbol of property in land, in town as well as country, connecting with the palisades thrown up around Neolithic villages. All of these applications had their origins in the role of the fence in food production systems, directed at improving quantity, quality, and yield, as well as improving the characteristics of selected plants and animals by separating them from the wild and from one another.

Fences and walls took many forms, but generally used materials at hand, mostly bushy hedges, wood or stone, and in some places were combined with earth mounds and ditches. Hedges might be grown and shaped using plants with many thorns, such as briars, or with simple density. More important to the food system was the use of "living" or economic fences in which the plants included in a hedge bore fruit which could be eaten or harvested for sale. With their prickly branches, orange and lemon trees were ideal for the purpose, and might be draped in vines such as the passion fruit and granadilla. Only in the industrial age did steel wire and mesh replace natural materials, and even then they typically replicated the briars of nature in the form of barbed and razor wire, or delivered electric shocks to deviant animals. Broadly, the contested integration of plants and animals within crop farming systems was responsible for the creation of a rural landscape distinguished from nature by the geometry of hedges, walls, and fences that increasingly came to contain a single crop, with its particular color, texture, and pattern. It was another way in which cleared and cultivated landscapes were separated from food forest and woodland.

Although the domestication and farming of plants and animals typically went hand in hand, the role of animals in food production systems was changing and variable. As observed earlier, some of the first animals to be domesticated were not regarded primarily as sources of food but rather commensal companions or working livestock. Cattle, buffalo, and horses were valued more for their capacity to pull plows and carry loads than for their meat. Animals used to perform work on farms did, however, often end up in cooking pots. Exceptions occurred where particular animals were associated with taboos, as in Hindu India where the sacred cow was not eaten by the higher castes, though used for work and milked. Other work animals, such as horses, donkeys, and llamas, were not excluded by prohibition but simply not preferred. They might enter the human food system in times of stress and shortage, but normally were not regarded as good to eat.

Shortage and rationing helped horsemeat enter the diet of Americans during the Civil War and of the British during World War I. Generally, however, throughout the long period in which horse-drawn transport dominated the cities of Britain and the United States the eating of horsemeat was rare, whereas in France and Germany it was common. Elsewhere, much the same was true of camels, which were regularly used to perform work, but were eaten as well in some cultures. Even preferred animals were often not particularly attractive as human food because they had been selected for different characteristics. Their long years of heavy work made their flesh tough and sinewy, and even when they were sent to fattening pastures in their last days their flesh did not come close to the standards expected by modern consumers.

For most of history, only the rich and powerful in society could afford to kill the young of their domesticated cattle for meat. Even specialist herders could not sacrifice young animals, which, alive, could provide a reliable supply of milk and blood. In the modern world, only the relatively affluent industrial societies have made fresh meat a common part of diet. The reasons for this pattern are not so much that animals are now rarely used for work on the farms of the industrialized world but rather that urban consumers have become relatively wealthy and animals are raised for meat or milk in new ways. At the center of this recent development is the selection of cattle for their qualities of flesh and lactation rather than their strength to pull tools and wagons.

Specialization and industrialization came early to dairy farming. Although milk is avoided by the people of large regions, it is a central commodity in world food history and increasingly significant in modern times. Specialization meant the selection of cows for their ability to yield large volumes of milk. This process was an extreme example of herd manipulation typical of domestication, in which males are reduced to a minimum in order to emphasize the desired characteristics of behavior as well as products. In dairying, cows were central and bulls marginal, and lactation was maintained significantly longer than in wild herds. In addition, dairy cows came to be grazed on specialized pastures and, particularly in the colder latitudes, handfed in barns. Industrialized approaches to milking gave machines a large role in the dairy, beginning in the late nineteenth century, and from the middle of the twentieth century large-scale rotolactors were used to milk cows stepping onto a rotating platform. Later, microchips allowed the monitoring of independent cattle movements, spreading milking through the day, and robots were used to perform various tasks in the process. In most parts of the world, however, hand-milking of small numbers of cows remained the norm.

A more dramatic impact on the rural landscape occurred in the industrialized farming of cattle for the production of meat. Selected animals had long been hand-fed in pens and barns with this intention but the high cost restricted such practices to the wealthy. Only in the nineteenth century did the commercial production of beef for the rapidly expanding and relatively well-off urban populations of Europe and North America become viable. As with grain-growing, the initial effect of the railroad was to expand dramatically the geographical extent of open-range livestock-raising, which enabled the shipping of large numbers of live animals to central city abattoirs. In the twentieth century, particularly in the United States, wherever cattle farming was located, it tended toward the confinement of animals in feedlot sheds. The outcome was a rural landscape in which cattle became rare, whether grazing or performing agricultural work (Centner, 2004). Horses, raised for the task of pulling carts and carriages on rural roads and city streets, disappeared with the coming of the motor truck and car, and the many acres devoted to the production of fodder were freed for alternative crops. The working livestock on farms were replaced by machines. Beef cattle were hidden in sheds.

The confinement of domesticated pigs was a feature of the early farming societies of southwestern and eastern Asia. Important reasons for keeping pigs in yards and pens was that they were typically destructive of planted crops, including underground tubers, and they were great converters of household waste, making it useful to locate pens close to habitations. They were also fed special fattening foods (Grigson, 2007). Much the same applied to domesticated dogs in those places where they were used as human food, and indeed in the Pacific dogs were sometimes herded along with pigs, and penned and fed breadfruit poi.

Pigs were not domesticated as working animals or exploited for their milk but always regarded as specialized meat producers. The milk of pigs was avoided partly because of the pig's reputation as an unclean omnivore but more importantly because sows can have as many as fourteen teats and let down their milk for just 30 seconds or less compared to as long as five minutes in cows. Thus, even in the earliest farming economies, pigs stood out from the other domesticated animals used for meat: sheep, goats, and cattle. Pigs were highly specialized, delivering fat-rich protein but not much else, and they had the advantage of rapid breeding so that even the very young, including suckling piglets, could be slaughtered for human food without jeopardizing the viability of the herd. Similarly, it was possible to slaughter large numbers for feasting purposes without endangering the stock, something continued in New Guinea until recent times. In addition, pigs did not need to be driven to pasture and their commensal habits in fact encouraged sedentarism, as opposed to the nomadic behavior that seemed to flow naturally from the keeping of cattle, sheep, and goats. Pigs have low tolerance for heat and need to drink regularly. They prefer shaded habitats, analogous to natural woodland. In spite of these advantages for small-scale, household production in the environment of southwestern Asia, it was there that the pig came to be prohibited as human food.

Confinement came later in northwestern Europe, where until medieval times pigs were herded in woodland, before making the transition to farmyard animals by 1400. One reason for this transition was the deforestation of the more densely populated regions of Europe by the twelfth century, which destroyed the natural habitats most suited to herding (Ervynck *et al.*, 2007). In spite of the contrast with cattle, under industrial conditions, pigs were increasingly confined in close pens, in large sheds, the pregnant females constrained by close metal stalls designed to prevent them attacking one another. Industrial practices also led to the feeding of varieties of animal waste which had implications for the health of human consumers as well as the livestock.

Less often intensively farmed, and rarely confined except for seasonal sheltering in cold places, were sheep and goats. Both of these were sometimes used for their milk and more frequently for their wool and hides. Goats were relatively omnivorous and capable of the destruction of gardens and orchards, but like sheep typically allowed to graze on poor pasture at low densities. Sheep and goats, together with cattle and pigs (before the taboo), were the main sources of meat for the early farmers of southwestern Asia.

The industrial confinement of animals reached its most extreme version in poultry after 1945. For millennia, widely spread across Eurasia, domesticated fowls had scratched and pecked their way through loosely fenced gardens and dunghills, laying their eggs in unsuspected nests as well as henhouses, being killed for their meat only on special occasions and when they were old and tough. In some places, however, poultry were long regarded as more important as fighting cocks and as sacrificial birds used for divination or spiritual purposes, rather than for their food uses. This was true of Japan until the nineteenth century. In China, on the other hand, eggs (including eggs with well-developed fetuses) and chicken meat were popular from ancient times, and in the nineteenth century the opening of trade in eastern Asia led to the export of superior poultry breeds to Europe. Chicken meat and eggs gained a global significance only in this late period but continued to be produced largely by small farmers as part of a diversified agriculture and horticulture.

Specialized commercial poultry-raising emerged first in the United States in the 1930s, when large sheds filled with cages began to replace the barnyard style of husbandry. Poultry farmers entered contracts with suppliers of feed, baby chicks, and veterinary services, and ultimately marketers, resulting in considerable vertical integration within the industry. By the 1950s, automated systems were in place, from hatchery to feeding and egg collection. In this way, the environment within the shed was controlled, disease monitored, and high-protein factory-made feed standardized. Specialized egg-box containers were developed. The slaughter of broilers, six- to twelve-week-old chickens selected for their meat qualities, also became highly automated, as did their plucking, dressing, dissection, and packaging. Chicken farmers in the United States typically had flocks of 50 to 100 in the 1930s, but by the end of the century a broiler house with a capacity of 25 000 had become the norm and farmers often had five or more of these. Bright white lights were on all day and night, to make the birds eat to their fill. Flocks of laying chickens increased from a maximum of about 300 in the 1930s to three million by 2000 (Hart, 2003: 118, 146).

World production of poultry meat increased from nine million tons in 1961 to 91 million tons in 2009. Chicken meat made up 80 million tons of this total, and chickens produced 1182 million eggs. Although other birds, such as ducks, were also exploited for their eggs and meat, it was the chicken that proved most amenable to industrial production. Ducks are less willing to accept a uniform diet and are unhappy in cages. In 2009 ducks supplied four million tons of meat; geese and guinea fowl two million; and turkeys five million. By the end of the twentieth century, industrial-scale production of chicken meat and eggs was massive, but surrounded by criticism of the health conditions and the lack of physical and social life allowed the caged bird. The poultry industry of the United States provided a model of industrialized animal farming followed both by other industries, pigs and turkeys, for example, and other countries. The model was accepted in many places, however developed or underdeveloped their economies, with dramatic consequences for farm populations, cutting out the small farmer, and increasing dependence on imported feeds, medicines, and even breeding stock.

By 2010 the world cattle population reached 1 368 million and sheep 1 028 million. The goat population was then 764 million but growing much more rapidly than cattle and sheep. More than 90 percent of the goats were found in Asia and Africa, whereas populations were shrinking elsewhere. Goats have many advantages for poorer farmers and households in the developing world: they are small and therefore cheap, flourish in relatively harsh conditions, and are adaptable to a range of climatic conditions not tolerated by sheep. Cattle produced 62 million tons of meat in 2009 and goats five million, but were easily outranked by the pig (106 million tons), which was exploited only for its meat. As a source of meat, the pig's closest rival in 2009 was the chicken (90 million tons, as noted earlier), followed by sheep (8).

In China cattle numbers grew dramatically after the mid-1990s, with a dairy herd of more than ten million by 2004, responding to demand from the increasingly well-off urban population and encouraged by government promotion of the health benefits of milk-drinking (Fuller *et al.*, 2006). The Middle East has 7 percent of the world's goat population and 11 percent of the sheep, producing 1.3 million tons of goat milk (11 percent of world production), and 2.7 million tons of sheep milk (34 percent of world production). In Europe, the goat population declined from a high of 20 million in 1920 to 12 million in 2000. By 2009 cows produced a total of 580 million tons of milk, much more than their rivals: buffalo (90 million tons), goat (15), sheep (9), and camel (2). Surprisingly, fresh cow's milk had become the world's most valuable food product, leaving rice in second place.

Five claims

First, it is claimed that the biological, physical, and mechanical characteristics of particular domesticated plants (and to a lesser extent animals) have a determining role in how they are produced and processed. Some plants are amenable to large-scale monocultural plantation-style production, employing large numbers of (sometimes unfree) workers, whereas other crop plants suit small-scale peasant farming systems. Some require substantial capital investment in processing facilities, at the site of cultivation. Taken together, this set of claims represents a mode of historical interpretation that can be labeled "crop determinism." Once a society makes the choice to depend on a small range of specific crops, the structure of its agrarian system is created directly by the technological demands of the crop itself.

Second, a related form of determinism is associated with the claim that the particular types of resources employed in the production of food have consequences not only for agrarian systems but also for government and social domination. In "hydraulic societies," the necessity of managing water resources distributed through irrigation and drainage systems demands central authority and strong (often despotic) government.

The third claim is that in some periods of history the ambition of states to control and capture territory through warfare and imperialism is driven by a desire to increase their available cropland, either to support settlers in such new territories or to feed the population of the metropolitan center or imperial homeland. An associated sub-claim is that invasive colonization is commonly followed by the imposition of agrarian systems that match the food cultures of the imperial society, typically contributing to the long-term replacement of tubers by grains as dominant food sources.

Fourth, technological elaboration is said to have contributed substantially to the growth of agricultural production and productivity. Industrial technologies, together with species modification, transformed the agricultural landscape and made food cheap for most of the world.

The final claim is that the demand for food and the spread of agricultural and pastoral systems was the major cause of deforestation and a major source of much other environmental change and degradation. Agrarian systems transformed the face of the earth.

REFERENCES

Bisseleua, D.H.B. and Vidal, S. (2008) Plant biodiversity and vegetation structure in traditional cocoa forest gardens in southern Cameroon under different management. *Biodiversity and Conservation* 17: 1821–35.

Bonti-Ankomah, S. and Fox, G. (1998) Hamburgers and the rainforest: A review of issues and evidence. *Journal of Agricultural and Environmental Ethics* 10: 153–82.

Centner, T.J. (2004) *Empty Pastures: Confined Animals and the Transformation of the Rural Landscape.* Urbana, IL: University of Illinois Press.

Demarest, A. (2004) *Ancient Maya: The Rise and Fall of a Rainforest Civilization.* Cambridge: Cambridge University Press.

Ervynck, A., Lentacker, A., Müldner, G. *et al.* (2007) An investigation into the transition from forest dwelling pigs to farm animals in medieval Flanders, Belgium. In U. Albarella, K. Dobney, A. Ervynck and P. Rowley-Conwy (eds) *Pigs and Humans: 10,000 Years of Interaction*, pp. 171–93. Oxford: Oxford University Press.

Fitzgerald, D. (2003) *Every Farm a Factory: The Industrial Ideal in American Agriculture.* New Haven, CT: Yale University Press.

Ford, A. and Nigh, R. (2009) Origins of the Maya forest garden: Maya resource management. *Journal of Ethnobiology* 29: 213–36.

Foxhall, L. (2007) *Olive Cultivation in Ancient Greece: Seeking the Ancient Economy.* Oxford: Oxford University Press.

Fuller, F., Huang, J., Ma, H. and Rozelle, S. (2006) Got milk? The rapid rise of China's dairy sector and its future prospects. *Food Policy* 31: 201–215.

Grigson, C. (2007) Culture, ecology, and pigs from the 5th to the 3rd millennium BC around the Fertile Crescent. In U. Albarella, K. Dobney, A. Ervynck and P. Rowley-Conwy (eds) *Pigs and Humans: 10,000 Years of Interaction*, pp. 83–108. Oxford: Oxford University Press.

Hart, J.F. (2003) *The Changing Scale of American Agriculture.* Charlottesville, VA: University of Virginia Press.

Headland, T.N. (1987) The wild yam question: How well could independent hunter-gatherers live in a tropical rain forest ecosystem? *Human Ecology* 15: 463–91.

Hladik, C.M., Hladik, A., Linares, O.F. *et al.* (eds) (1993) *Tropical Forests, People and Food: Biocultural Interactions and Applications to Development.* Paris: UNESCO.

Li, K. and Xu, Z. (2006) Overview of Dujiangyan irrigation scheme of ancient China with current theory. *Irrigation and Drainage* 55: 291–98.

Manning, J.G. (2010) *The Last Pharaohs: Egypt under the Ptolemies, 305–30 BC.* Princeton: Princeton University Press.

McKey, D., Rostain, S., Iriarte, J. *et al.* (2010) Pre-Columbian agricultural landscapes, ecosystem engineers, and self-organized patchiness in Amazonia. *Proceedings of the National Academy of Sciences of the United States of America* 107 (27 April): 7823–8.

Mulyoutami, E., Rismawan, R. and Joshi, L. (2009) Local knowledge and management of *Simpukng* (forest gardens) among the Dayak people in East Kalimantan, Indonesia. *Forest Ecology and Management* 257: 2054–61.

Olmstead, A.L. and Rhode, P.W. (2008) *Creating Abundance: Biological Innovation and American Agricultural Development.* Cambridge: Cambridge University Press.

Petrick, G.M. (2006) "Like ribbons of green and gold": Industrializing lettuce and the quest for quality in the Salinas Valley, 1920–1965. *Agricultural History* 80: 269–95.

Ruf, F. and Schroth, G. (2004) Chocolate forests and monocultures: A historical review of cocoa growing and its conflicting role in tropical deforestation and forest conservation. In G. Schroth and G.A.B. da Fonseca (eds) *Agroforestry and Biodiversity Conservation in Tropical Landscapes*, pp. 107–134. Washington: Island Press.

Totman, C. (1998) *The Green Archipelago: Forestry in Preindustrial Japan.* Athens, OH: Ohio University Press.

Whitehead, H. (2000) *Food Rules: Hunting, Sharing, and Tabooing Game in Papua New Guinea.* Ann Arbor: University of Michigan Press.

Wiley, J. (2008) *The Banana: Empires, Trade Wars, and Globalization.* Lincoln, NB: University of Nebraska Press.

Williams, M. (2003) *Deforesting the Earth: From Prehistory to Global Crisis.* Chicago: University of Chicago Press.

CHAPTER FOUR

Hunting, Herding, Fishing

Hunting and fishing are like activities, involving the pursuit and capture of wild animals. Although "fishing" identifies its prey and "hunting" does not, the difference between the two is generally taken to be rooted in a contrast between water and land. In essence, however, both terms refer to technologies of capture, and fishing may therefore be understood as simply one branch of hunting. Thus, these activities, in so far as they are directed at the acquisition of food, fall outside domestication and agriculture. They may seem therefore to be the province of hunter-gatherer peoples. In the modern world, however, the principal hunters and fishers are not hunter-gatherers but rather representatives of agrarian cultures, anxious to feed growing urban populations hungry for fish and, where they can get it, the meat of wild land-animals. Quite often, the outcome of this transition has been severe depletion of stocks and ultimately the extinction of species. The more extreme examples of this process mimic the narrowing of species that marked the impact of industrialized agricultural technologies, resulting in large part from the application of killing and capturing technologies derived from modern mechanized warfare.

A striking difference between agriculture and hunting and fishing is that the severe depletions and extinctions seen in wild stocks commonly occurred in species favored as human food, whereas in the agricultural economies of the world domestication created a new balance which enabled the breeding and raising of vast herds and vast acreages of select crops. Agriculture depended on a limited, narrowed range of species but it did ensure the"husbandry" or conservation of the plants and animals at the core of the world's food systems. Hunting and fishing lacked most of these conservative attributes and letting loose capture technologies derived from agrarian economies (including their

How Food Made History, First Edition. B. W. Higman.
© 2012 B. W. Higman. Published 2012 by Blackwell Publishing Ltd.

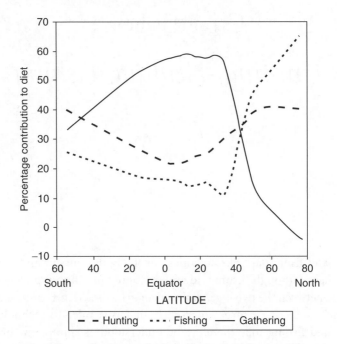

Figure 4.1   Diet of hunter-gatherers, by latitude. Derived from Frank W. Marlowe, "Hunter-Gatherers and Human Evolution", *Evolutionary Anthropology* 14 (2005) 59.

capacity for industrialized warfare) proved devastating. This imbalance is largely a recent phenomenon but examples can also be found in ancient times and among hunter-gatherer peoples.

What really pulls hunting and fishing together is their focus on the wild, which subsumes a failure to domesticate successfully these particular kinds of animals. Herding constitutes a compromise, in which humans claim ownership over herds even though the animals are not fully domesticated and are pursued rather than enclosed and subdued. Patterns of variation and change in hunting, herding, and fishing have been driven in part by regional climatic variation and by climate change but they are also products of differences in technology.

Using a sample of almost 400 past and present "forager" peoples, Frank W. Marlowe (2005) has shown that the components of diet vary directly with latitude (Figure 4.1). In the tropics, gathering accounts for near to 60 percent of the diet consumed by such peoples, hunting around 25 percent and fishing about 15 percent. The contribution of gathering declines towards the poles, becoming less than both hunting and fishing at about 45° North latitude (a line running through Mongolia, France, and Minnesota) and disappearing in the Arctic Circle, where fishing dominates. In these latitudes the low density of available food sources requires foragers to cover large home ranges and to abandon hope of finding plant materials to eat. In the southern hemisphere, hunting increases in importance toward the pole, never overtaken by fishing.

Several significant findings, and questions as well, arise from Marlowe's analysis. One important finding is that (excluding the arctic regions) hunter-gatherers do not typically occupy ecological niches which are marginal habitats in terms of their capacity to produce food. Land types that are good for arable farming are not necessarily the same as those preferred by hunter-gatherers, and incipient farmers did not necessarily emerge where hunter-gatherers were most successful. Indeed, the opposite was often the case, as we have seen, with agriculture frequently a creation of challenging environments. Hence the common lack of enthusiasm for shifting to agriculture demonstrated by the most long-lasting and successful of hunter-gatherer groups. It may be, however, that the habitats favored by hunter-gatherers were creations of the climate change associated with the coming of the Holocene, with its particular combinations of plants and animals. Arctic hunter-gatherers are the most obvious example, unable to survive in this habitat until about 20 000 BP.

Hunting

The hunter's essential toolkit is ancient, almost all of it in place before the beginnings of agriculture. All of these tools needed to be portable, to enable regular movement across a habitat or to exploit varied niches, sometimes in seasonal pursuit of particular prey. Spears of various sorts have been used for more than 400 000 years, predating the emergence of early modern humans. These weapons enabled fresh kills rather than scavenging the meat of large animals at unpredictable locations and times (Marlowe, 2010: 277). The related harpoon, used for fishing, is known from the Congo from about 80 000 years ago. Spears and harpoons were joined by blunter instruments, such as throwing sticks and clubs, and the more sophisticated and distance-capable boomerang. Spear throwers (woomeras or atlatls), strips of rigid wood on which the spear was carefully balanced and directed, greatly increased the capacity to throw hard and accurately against large animals. The earliest of these accessories is dated to 17 000 BP, though much earlier dates appear plausible.

A more important innovation was the bow and arrow, which enabled effective killing at a distance, increased the male contribution to food acquisition, and helped to increase consumption of meat and expanded population densities. Arrow points, microliths, chipped from stone to create sharp blades, are known from eastern and southern Africa about 70 000 years ago. These suggest the coexistence of bows to make them effective, and yet the earliest certain bows are from Germany, dating to about 11 000 BP. Nets, important in

Figure 4.2   Hunting traps, gazelle and reindeer. Based on Tim Ingold, *Hunters, Pastoralists and Ranchers: Reindeer Economies and Their Transformations* (Cambridge: Cambridge University Press, 1980), 59–63.

fishing, are known from about 20 000 BP, and hooked lines from about 12 000 BP. The use of poison, generally applied to arrow points in order to kill large animals, occurred first in Zambia around 11 000 BP, but came to be used also for taking fish. Finally, among the ancient inventions, the use of iron to tip spears and arrows and make axes is dated to about 3500 BP. Thus hunters early learned to trade with iron-producing peoples in Eurasia and Africa.

More ancient than any of these tools was the use of fire to create clearings in which animals might graze while hunters hid in the surrounding bush, and the use of fire to direct animals herded toward their fate, as in a pitfall or snare. More labor and planning were needed to construct landscapes which could funnel wild animals to a point where they could easily be killed in numbers. At sites in Syria dating from about 11 000 BP, for example, specialized gazelle hunters probably used local stone to build large circular enclosures, with extensive flanking walls that converged on a single opening (Figure 4.2). These walls fanned out in the path of migrating herds of gazelles, allowing hunters to drive the animals into the enclosure where they could be slaughtered with bow and arrow. The result was a large seasonal resource of meat, which when dried and salted or smoked could supply a settlement for many months (Crowe, 2000: 179–80). Here the hunting technology was designed to counter the gazelle's swiftness and agility by gradually narrowing the opportunities for escape. The strong bond between members of a massed herd, moving forward as a group, was exploited in other animals, notably reindeer for which even simpler guiding markers were sufficient (Ingold, 1980: 56–8). Not all hunting technologies constituted weapons designed to instill fear, however. In Australia, for example, lures made of feathers were used to entice emus closer to the hunter's hiding place (Anell, 1960). Alternatively, a person standing in a billabong or pond could cover their head with an attractive cover and when waterbirds landed close by simply grab their legs underwater.

The diversification of technologies made it possible for hunting peoples to prosper in a wide variety of environments, well beyond the range favored by agriculturalists and pastoralists. However, as shown earlier, hunting was hardly ever more important in diet than gathering or fishing. It was always high risk, compared to the digging of roots and tubers and the taking of fish and mollusks from shallow waters. In most situations, it made no sense to depend entirely on what hunters could bring back to their community. On the other hand, a successful kill resulted in an above-average quantity of food. A hunter who failed to kill an animal, as was often the case on any particular day, might bring back to his group some other rich and rare food, such as honey, or at worst more of the roots and fruits which were typically regarded as the work of women and children.

Honey found its way into this scheme because it was something to be hunted for, taken from wild animals (even if some bee species are stingless), rather than dug from the earth. Honey represents a prime source of concentrated sugar and protein, hunted for not only by humans but also by other vertebrates, including bears of course. Thus honey hunting and harvesting is very ancient. Collection from owned nests began in the Neolithic and the first horizontal hives with fixed-honeycombs were established in Egypt by 5000 BP, followed sometime after by vertical hives. Moveable combs were known by the seventeenth century. The use of artificial nest sites probably occurred first in southeastern Asia, at a date unknown (Crane 1999: 2). However, although honeybees were widespread throughout Eurasia and Africa, they were not known in the Americas, Australia, or New Guinea until introduced at various dates down to 1800. A vast range of hive technologies developed, imitating nature or applying pottery, wooden and woven models derived from other activities (Figure 4.3), yet bee colonies still needed to be hunted and attracted to hives and remained dependent on the surrounding habitat for their nectar.

At the end of the twentieth century, roughly 30 percent of the world's land remained in forest, much of it in patches too small and too degraded to provide the needs of large non-domesticated mammals such as elephants, rhinoceroses, and giant hogs. The depletion of these wild animals was very much a part of the story of food. Much of this reduction resulted from the clearing of forest in order to cultivate crop plants and graze (domesticated) animals, with most

Figure 4.3   Traditional log and box bee hives, China. Based on Eva Crane, *The World History of Beekeeping and Honey Hunting* (New York: Routledge, 1999), 271–72.

of the product intended for human food. The other side of the depletion was a direct function of the killing of hunted animals, including apes, for food, to meet a growing global demand for protein (Peterson, 2003). In large regions of the developing world, notably Africa and southeastern Asia, bush meat remained cheaper and more readily available than meat from domesticated animals, in urban as well as rural areas. Some of these populations, the people of the Congo Basin, for example, eat as much meat as citizens of developed countries do (about 155 lb [70 kg] per capita per annum) but up to 80 percent of the meat consumed by rural groups in these societies comes from hunted wild animals (Wilkie and Lee, 2004: 360).

Hunters generally preferred to kill large animals because they yielded high volumes of meat, as well as valuable byproducts such as horns, hides, and bones, elements of which were important in medicine. Thus, these large mammals were likely to be killed whenever encountered. Overhunting led to increasing proportions of smaller animals, notably rodents such as the cane rat or "cutting-grass" of West Africa, weighing about 11 lb (5 kg), which was hunted with dogs. Much the same pattern occurred elsewhere, as, for example, the extinction of the 550 lb (250 kg) sloth in the Caribbean as early as 4000 BP (as discussed in Chapter 1), followed by the modern hunting of small rodents such as the coney or hutia, using dogs. Indeed, it seems to be a principle with very few exceptions that the commercial hunting of wild animals is rarely sustainable and that, at least since the time of Columbus, extinctions follow quickly on the heels of technologies designed to supply a market larger than the local group of hunter-gatherer people. A similar transition from the hunting of large mammals of the open forest to smaller rodents occurred in the highlands of Papua New Guinea about one thousand years ago, long after these societies had become essentially agrarian (Feil, 1987: 22).

In complex agrarian societies, the hunting of large wild animals was rarely an important source of food for the common people but continued to contribute to elite diets. This was true of classical Greece and Rome, though it can be argued that the physical environments of the Mediterranean, with their poor supplies of grass and other fodder, offered hunters slim pickings, compared to the abundance of the tropics and the African savannas or even the grasslands of central and northern Europe. Hunting was more often understood as sport, designed to produce trophies, and directed at animals (including lions, bears, and wild goats) that were dangerous or caused damage to flocks and fields but not necessarily regarded as good food (Anderson, 1985). When the common people of Athens received distributions of red meat it was frequently the product of sacrifice, and sacrificial victims were taken exclusively from the domesticated mammals, which "exist with a view to the good of man," said Aristotle, never the untamed, whose hunting and slaughter is an act of pure violence (Detienne and Vernant, 1989: 8–9).

In ancient China, a wide range of wild animals, from deer, rabbit and dog to antelope, panther, and tiger, was hunted, though generally in small numbers and frequently for medicine more than meat. The pattern persisted but deforestation and population growth meant that by the time of the Tang (618–907) venison was most common in the north and some species of deer were already extinct (Schafer, 1977: 99–101). The elite organized hunts and employed trappers, while the poor depended on bow and arrow and snares, the emphasis shifting to smaller targets such as bamboo rats. In the south of China, elephants remained abundant and their meat highly regarded.

In the medieval Low Countries (the region of the modern states of Belgium and the Netherlands), red deer and other game account for 20 percent of animal bones excavated at high-status archeological sites. Seals were hunted on the beaches, wild boar, beavers, otters, and hares on the coastal dunes, and brown bears, badgers, and aurochs (primitive oxen) in the forests. The right to hunt was gradually reduced from an entitlement of all free men to a privilege of nobles and domain lords. European monarchs began to claim exclusive rights to hunt game in their royal forests. As game became less plentiful as a consequence of the reclamation of forest and wasteland habitats, the poor were turned into poachers (Bavel, 2010: 124–5).

Feudal rules extended beyond the hunting of wild animals, such as red deer, brown bear, and wild boar, to the herding and hunting of pigs in woodland. This made the consumption of pork a symbol of power and prestige. An important element of this prestige derived from the fact that pigs were exploited exclusively for their meat and therefore not only enjoyed for their tender flesh but also understood as indicators of plenty. To achieve this end, pigs were slaughtered young, typically less than 24 months old, whereas multipurpose cattle and sheep lived longer, to be slaughtered only when their flesh had grown tough. The conspicuous consumption exhibited in noble banquets took the roasted pig, cooked on a spit, as its central icon. Wild boar remained among the most dangerous of the game hunted in medieval forests, and therefore served to make the link with male bravery and bravado. So long as the domesticated pig remained an animal of the woodland, feeding on acorns and beech mast, as it did until the end of the medieval period, it continued to serve such symbolic roles. Once pigs were reared in close confinement, they lost these associations and their meat became pink rather than purple, with a less muscular texture.

Where natural forest suited for hunting was lacking, it might be manufactured. In medieval Britain, for instance, aristocratic estates typically included an extensive park designed specifically as a hunting ground, where the lords could enjoy the atavistic pleasures of chasing and killing animals, particularly deer, using crossbows. The meat of these game animals was eaten and played an important part in defining social status, the close-guarded parks themselves an affront to popular culture and the notion that wild animals were fair game to all comers. The system persisted into the modern period but lost its importance as a source of meat, being confined increasingly to birds such as pheasants, and it came under fire for the cruelty of the hunt. Even in the medieval period, the amount of venison returned was small compared to the labor of managing parks and most of the meat consumed by aristocrats came from domesticated animals raised in fenced fields and pens.

Hunting from the back of a strong, large mammal, particularly a horse, gave the human hunter many advantages. Equestrian hunters were able to cover much wider habitat zones, and therefore able to support larger populations. In the Americas, the introduction of the horse was enough to shift the balance for hunters in many habitats. For example, the Native Americans of the Great Plains quickly took to riding when horses brought by the Spanish to the Americas reached them in the eighteenth century, thus substantially increasing their ability to hunt bison with bow and arrow, following these high-yielding animals over long distances. The use of firearms took the hunt to yet another level of unequal combat, leading by the early twentieth century to the virtual extinction of the bison. Something similar occurred in Eurasia in the late twentieth century where several species, including the long-favored gazelle of Syria, were reduced to remnants by hunters using high-powered semiautomatic firearms, riding in the backs of four-wheel-drive vehicles capable of crossing rough, desiccated, sandy, and icy terrain. In Africa, the great apes faced the same fate at the hands of hunters loaded with military-style weaponry (Peterson, 2003: 255).

On the Tibetan Plateau, where traditional pastoralism coexisted with abundant wildlife for centuries, wild animals came by the late twentieth century to be seen as competitors with the growing (domesticated) yak, sheep, and goat populations for the scarce plant food of the region. Fences inhibited movement, and men with rifles riding motorbikes were able to run down groups of animals. In 2003 the Chinese government started a program of "ecological migration" intended to restore the degraded rangeland by relocating at least half of the more than two million nomadic herders on the Tibetan Plateau, selling off the livestock to prevent overgrazing.

On the other hand, in some places, introduced large mammals became feral, placing pressure on indigenous species of animals as well as plants. In northern Australia, for example, camels introduced as pack animals in the nineteenth century ran wild after 1945 when they no longer performed work. The population blew out to one million by 2000. To control numbers, camels were shot from helicopters in remote locations, the carcasses left to rot because it was too costly to bring the meat to market. The global market for camel meat was substantial but Australians generally were reluctant to eat it, even though it is low in fat and cholesterol and tastes much like beef.

Slaughter did not always depend on overwhelming technologies. Where animals had evolved in the absence of effective natural predators, they proved immediately vulnerable and often suffered from demand for their exotic food products. The most notorious among these is the dodo, a flightless bird of Mauritius weighing about 45 lb (20 kg) and so trusting that it stood still in the presence of human predators, oblivious to the fact that it was about to be clubbed, and indeed clubbed to extinction by the end of the seventeenth century, though its meat was rarely praised by those who ate it. Some species of seal behaved in a similar manner, the monk seal of the Caribbean, for example, effectively wiped out by 1800 though not formally declared extinct until 1996. Weighing over 440 lb (200 kg), the monk seal came to be killed more for its fat (used to make oil) than its meat, coming ashore to rest and sun, lulled into vulnerability.

Another example from tropical America is the manatee, which grew to 1 100 lb (500 kg) and was highly regarded for its meat. Although they did not come on shore and possessed acute hearing which alerted them to the presence of predators, manatee were lethargic and grazed on seagrasses in shallow bays and brackish estuaries, so that they were easily killed with harpoons or taken in nets. The manatee was already rare by the early nineteenth century and by the beginning of the twenty-first century faced extinction. Its relative, the dugong, survived better, though increasingly confined to the waters of northern Australia, having been an easily hunted mammal for millennia. An even larger mammal, growing to 4 400 lb (2 000 kg) and supplying vast quantities of flesh, the walrus recovered its population after heavy depredations in the nineteenth and twentieth centuries. In the Arctic, the walrus spent much of the year in shallow shelf environments and on sea ice, hunted with harpoons from kayaks.

More important in their contribution to diet were turtles, once abundant in the Caribbean and a sustainable resource for the Amerindian peoples for whom the turtle was the major source of animal protein. When they came ashore to lay their eggs, female turtles could be easily turned on their backs, because they were "indifferent to disturbances" for the two or more hours it took (Higman, 2008: 295). Millions of turtles lived in the "rookeries" of the Caribbean when Columbus reached the islands but by the end of the eighteenth century they had been reduced to a remnant, many of them consumed by European settlers and some shipped live to Europe where the meat was regarded as a great delicacy. Turtle meat was subjected to culinary elaboration and recipe-making, creating soup as well as a variety of other specialized dishes.

None of these easily killed water-loving animals were fish. The turtle is a reptile, and the seals, walrus, dugong, and manatee mammals. They were hunted with specialized weapons, rarely used in fishing, and generally taken either on land or at the water's edge. Fish typically behaved quite differently, darting away as soon as they sensed danger, much like the gazelle and most birds.

Another mammal, the whale, did live almost entirely in the water, beaching only in extremis. In the region of the Arctic Circle, coastal peoples long enjoyed eating the meat, blubber, and skin of whales and looked forward to the annual migrations that brought pods close to shore. By the sixteenth century, and probably much earlier, fishermen herded pilot whales ashore by surrounding them in boats, shouting, and throwing stones (Shoemaker, 2005: 273). Slaughtered and butchered, stranded whales presented a vast resource of blubber, bone, and flesh. Some of the blubber was valued as lamp oil but much of it was eaten as lard, and the flesh which could not be consumed fresh was salted and dried.

The killing of whales at sea did not begin until the seventeenth century because their size and strength made them more than a match for most men in a boat. The largest whales could grow to as much as 150 tons. Only with modern industrialized fishing methods, using explosive harpoons and powerful winches, did their catch become viable but it was then their oil rather than their meat that was in demand. Depletion of the population led to the establishment of the International Whaling Commission (IWC) in 1946, which by 1982 declared a moratorium on the commercial hunting of large whales, though exceptions were made for a small number of traditional Arctic consumers of whale meat. At first the indigenous hunters were limited to canoes and kayaks, with paddles or sails, but this condition was retracted because motorboats and guns were more efficient and left fewer whales wounded or uncaptured. A more controversial act of the IWC permitted the taking of whales for research purposes, using industrial fishing technologies, which resulted in protests at Japanese whaling in the southern ocean and protests that the IWC practiced a variety of "culinary imperialism."

Herding

By the beginning of the twenty-first century nomadic herders were few and far between, pushed to the extreme margins of the world's agricultural ecosystems. Looked at from a different perspective, however, about one-quarter of the earth's land surface remained occupied by pastoralists, roughly 200 million of them, who continued to raise livestock on extensive rangelands, most of which could not be used for alternative agricultural purposes. About one-half of the world's pastoralists now live in Africa, occupying large proportions of the land space of Kenya, Uganda, and Tanzania. These peoples depend on milk for two-thirds of their dietary energy, also consuming blood, cereals, and occasionally meat. Sheep and goats increasingly dominate the pastoralists' herds but are often combined with camels, yaks, and cattle, exploited for their milk and meat, as well as their wool, hair, and leather, and used as pack animals (Degen, 2007).

For thousands of years, mobile pastoralism had enabled herders to take advantage of superior forage resources and cope with fluctuations in rainfall and to survive drought. Relationships between herders, hunters, and farmers were often complex, and in many cases there was difficulty in allocating individual groups to such specialized categories. The beginnings of agricultural settlement in western Asia and elsewhere seem generally to have been associated with a continuing dependency on the hunting of wild animals as the major source of meat. But it did not make sense to encourage wild animals to persist close to crops or sedentary people, and the cost of following herds became high for non-nomadic groups. For these reasons, traditional prey such as gazelles became scarce in the perimeter zones of settled farming and incipient farming sites, encouraging people to domesticate selected species in the same manner they had applied to plants (Crowe, 2000: 185–6). As noted earlier, attempts to domesticate preferred meat animals such as the gazelle did not always succeed, and semi-domestication was the best that could be achieved. Thus, for example, deer raised to be hunted in large enclosures or parks remain essentially wild.

Reindeer, widespread in the Arctic taiga and tundra zones, typically exist as wild animals but have sometimes been semi-domesticated or tamed. Whatever their state, they continue to support large human populations, supplying meat as a staple and milk in meager amounts, though sometimes enough to make cheese. Reindeer also serve as transport, and contribute to clothing, tools, and medicine (Beach, 1990; Ingold, 1980). They have been both hunted and herded, with somewhat equivalent levels of productivity. When tamed, reindeer have been used as decoys in the killing of members of the wild herd. Thus, the reindeer is representative of animals which were never fully domesticated, and not merely in a transitional stage between the semi-wild and the fully domesticated.

Even the largest herds might, however, be corralled occasionally, as proof of "ownership" as well as to select animals for slaughter. Industrializing tendencies became strong in the late twentieth century, using fencing and motorized herding vehicles, thus more clearly demarcating property rights while at the same time distancing the herder from the herd, heading toward a variety of ranching.

Specialized herders or pastoralists made a choice to follow their food supply rather than settle to the sedentary life of domestication and cultivation. Attempting to live on preserved flesh was not attractive or viable for these peoples and keeping close to a herd had other advantages in the potential for milk and blood, as well as wool, fur, and skin. In some regions, for example alpine Europe, farmers planted grain crops where they could but depended for their survival on the grazing of (ruminant) animals, used for milk and meat, following a system of rotation that paralleled the semi-nomadic seasonal movement of people and livestock, known as transhumance. This system persisted until the twentieth century, when grain and protein feeds came to displace straw, particularly in the winter regime (Krausmann, 2004).

Sedentary stockbreeding was common across the steppes and forest-steppes of eastern Europe by 5000 BP, with an emphasis on sheep and cattle. Both goats and pigs were relatively rare toward the east, suggesting a diffusion of stockbreeding from the Caucasus. The lack of pigs can be attributed to their unsuitability to being driven across the steppes and perhaps also to negative attitudes to pork developed by the early migrant peoples. The latter interpretation is supported by a lack of enthusiasm for the hunting of wild boar which were common in the forest fringes (Shnirelman, 1992). In the long term, such migrant peoples adopted agriculture where the ecological conditions were appropriate, but persisted in their reliance on animals wherever the habitat was hostile, extremely dry or cold, often depending on them to provide the elements of clothing and shelter as well as food.

Nomadic rather than sedentary pastoralism typically had its origins in a need to find fodder. In some cases, herders simply followed in the tracks of herds as they sought out fresh grazing lands. In other cases, the herders made the decision to move, driving their animals to greener pastures or following a seasonal rotation. One consequence of such nomadism was a lack of enthusiasm for bulky technologies, but at the same time it served to stimulate trade both between different groups of nomads and between pastoralists and sedentary farmers, and an exchange of knowledge as well as goods. Nomadism also gave a strong impetus to long-term migration and to the expansion of hegemony. Decisions about which animals to herd, how and where, often were made by the rich and powerful and became matters of interest for states. Wealthy herders always had an advantage, possessing the capacity to move their herds over long distances in search of greener pastures and engaging more freely in trade than the poor were ever able to do.

Although the decline of herding as a mode of food production resulted in part from the spread of broadacre agriculture and the dominance of intensive systems of animal-raising, it also became increasingly constrained by social and political pressures. The European colonization of Africa in the nineteenth century, for example, severely restricted the mobility of pastoralists, by changing systems of land tenure and granting extensive tracts to farmer colonists in freehold tenure. In more recent times, customary rights to African rangelands have been constrained by subdivision and increased cultivation, leading to a loss of mobility. Elsewhere, the decline of socialist states after 1990 affected the viability of mobile pastoralists, for example in the central Asian states of Kazakhstan and Mongolia.

A thousand years before, the Mongols were emerging as one of the most powerful pastoral societies in world history, creating the world's largest contiguous empire and establishing what Soviet historians designated "Mongolian nomadic feudalism," a formation that was to last from the thirteenth to the nineteenth century (Bold, 2001: 24). These nomadic "predatory pastoralists" engaged in regular contact with the agrarian societies of Eurasia and with forest peoples of the steppe, dependent on farmers for grain. Pastoralism dominated the economies of these nomads and all year their herds grazed freely and without stabling. Production was directed toward subsistence and rarely included any form of cultivation.

The mobility of the people and their herds was seasonal, within a specified territorial zone. When they moved, everything moved. This, together with the carrying-capacity of the grazing lands, limited the total size of the population, the ratio of livestock to people generally falling below 20. But long distances were often covered, up to 400 miles (640 km) in the Gobi Desert and more than 600 miles (1 000 km) for some Kazak groups. The lengthier these seasonal movements, the likelier were permanent migrations (Bell-Fialkoff, 2000: 181–2). The origins and survival of such nomadic pastoralism are typically to be found in the relatively poor returns that could be won from infertile regions in periods of climatic stress. Thus, the choice to become pastoralist represented a parting of the ways that was accomplished about three thousand years ago. The consequences for transport technologies and the development of language were dramatic and "shaped the modern world" (Anthony, 2007).

By the end of the twentieth century the pastoralists of Mongolia depended on sheep but also herded cattle, goats, horses, camels, and yaks. Sheep milk was the most important part of the diet and meat often consumed only reluctantly. Herding was organized cooperatively. Under socialism, cooperative communities known as *negdel* negotiated a flexible dispersion of herders, even in the most remote regions, and these communities ensured the effective maintenance of necessary infrastructure (Okayasu *et al.*, 2010). When socialism was abandoned in the 1990s and replaced by a version of market economy, the *negdel* were not privatized and the support system quickly collapsed. From a situation in which flocks could be moved at low cost, mobility became expensive, particularly for poorer herders in drought years. The consequence was a rapid transition to sedentism, and increased social stratification. A decade-long drought beginning in 2000 saw herds of sheep and goats decimated. By then, many Mongolians raised their stock in permanent settlements but about one-quarter of them were still nomads. They relied on the wool and hides of their animals for cash income but also depended on them for milk and meat.

The Mongolian winter of 2010 was so cold that the tails of cattle snapped off. The people who depended on these animals for food as well as motive power were among the last remaining nomadic herders on earth. Five thousand years before, their situation had been much less unusual, with numerous pastoral and hunter societies scattered around the higher latitudes. Now, they stood out from the vastly increased world population as anomalies or anachronisms, distinguished by their lack of dependence on a globalized exchange economy of agricultural and industrialized foods based on a highly specialized system of exploitation of plants and animals.

Hunting and herding did not lend themselves to industrialization and as a result the production of meat (and milk and eggs) became a monopoly of industrial agricultural systems using pens and cages to raise domesticated animals rather than capturing their wild relatives. Fishing, on the other hand, did adopt technologies that enabled its effective industrialization, while remaining a determined branch of hunting, but only in recent times.

Fishing

For hunter-gatherer peoples, fresh and saltwater environments provided relatively reliable and plentiful resources, much to be desired. Whereas the hunting of wild animals was sometimes a hazardous, and often uncertain, means of obtaining food, the gathering of mollusks and crustaceans in shallow coastal waters, harbors, bays, inlets, streams, and billabongs was relatively easy and required only limited technology. This was typically the work of women and children, carried on while men fished in deeper waters or went to hunt land animals for meat. Generally, communities that depended on fishing were more sedentary than those that relied on gathering and, especially, hunting.

Along the coast of southeastern Australia, for example, Aboriginal people depended for part of their diet on the collection of a range of mollusks, such as mussels, oysters, and abalone. These could be found in shallow weed beds and rocky shelves, along the edges of beaches, and marooned in pools at low tide. Availability shifted over the long term together with changes in sea levels, and some of these resources were seasonal. The consumption of mollusks left highly visible middens or mounds of empty shells, as clear evidence of their role in diet, whereas other materials, lacking the survival qualities of shells, are harder to identify and date. The shellfish middens of southeastern Australia and Tasmania were started by 5000 BP at least. Collection was not confined to the immediate shoreline, however. Women and men dived for abalone and lobster, holding their breath for minutes and placing their catch in woven baskets.

The catching of fish could be done from the shore, from rocky ledges, as well as by wading or from a bark canoe. Larger boats carved from tree trunks, paddled by men or using sail, traveled to more distant fishing grounds. Fishing tools changed relatively little between 5000 BP and the eighteenth century. In rivers and streams, from the onset of the Neolithic, fish were speared or shot with bow and arrow, hooked or harpooned, or caught with nets and baskets, and concentrated into weirs or narrow corridors of netting. Crustaceans were trapped in fishpots. Although these techniques were simple, they proved sufficient in some places to reduce fish stocks enough to force shifts to new resources.

In Europe, from about 5000 BP early farmers along the southern coast of the North Sea exploited a diverse range of mammals, birds, fish, and shellfish but from the Middle Ages depended increasingly on fishing. Around a thousand years ago, the inland rivers and lakes of this wetland and intertidal region suffered habitat degradation and overfishing that reduced their populations of freshwater and migrating fish, leading to the expansion and commercialization of marine fisheries. Herring and oysters became important from the twelfth century, haddock and cod in the sixteenth, and then whales (Lotze, 2007).

Tidal fisheries channeled large shoals into attenuated traps as the water became rapidly shallow. Either from near shore or out at sea, seines or encircling nets were spread out like a curtain and then drawn and closed. This technique was practiced by the ancient Egyptians of the lower Nile marshlands. By 4500 BP the towns of Mesopotamia had fish ponds, while sea fish, including shark, flying fish, sole, turbot, and swordfish, were kept alive in tanks. Well-off ancient Romans had aquaria, much preferring the taste of sea fish. Asian fishers employed all of these techniques, adding to their arsenal screens of split bamboo placed across streams, dip or lift nets, plunge baskets and blow guns. Close to shore, conch was dived for in the Indian Ocean and in the Caribbean.

At sea, baited hooks were set up in various combinations, including long lines that either floated near the surface or dragged along the seabed. Large drift nets snared fish as they swam into the mesh, while trawling nets were shaped like great baskets or conical bags. The use of boats generally had little impact on catch-size, though it increased choice between species and varieties. Until the nineteenth century, fishers generally tried to stay in sight of the shore, and they depended on their own muscle power to haul nets on board. Nets made of natural fibers became heavy as they absorbed water, and had to be dried out

Figure 4.4   Shipboard processing of cod fish in the eighteenth century. When a fishing boat reached the banks, the fishermen donned leather aprons up to their chins and stood in barrels, to keep out the worst of the water and weather. Each fisherman had about ten lines, with one iron hook on each leaded line. When cod were caught, the fish were gutted by the fisherman and the gut used to rebait the hook. Working at a table, the header cut off the head of the fish and the splitter cut the fish to flatten it out, before sending it below where the salter laid the fish between layers of salt. Duhamel du Monceau and L.H. de la Marre, *Traité général des pesches, et histoire des poissons qu'elles fournissent tant pour subsistence des hommes, que pour plusieurs autres usages qui ont rapport aux arts et au commerce* (Paris: Saillant et Nyon, 1769), Part 2, Section 1, Plate 9.

every time they were used. It was the essential inefficiency and limited capacity of these tools that underpinned the continuing abundance of the world's fish stock into the nineteenth century and prevented its depletion. In addition, in many places the lack of means of preservation meant that fish could only be consumed fresh and therefore it was rational to take only what could be eaten more or less immediately. This was the case, for example, in Indonesia, where salt was expensive and the fresh resource abundant (Butcher, 2005: 68–9).

The first significant technological changes in the global transformation of marine fisheries were the use of salting and drying. These processes enabled long-distance enterprises and extended markets but were associated with only limited change in methods of capture. From the sixteenth century, European fishers began to venture into the North Atlantic to exploit the abundant cod stocks on the banks surrounding Nova Scotia and Newfoundland, and these sedentary fishers were soon joined by rivals from New England. The industry depended on the salting and drying of the catch. The large fish – cod weigh 20 lb (9 kg) on average – were caught using lines with a single hook, then split, flattened, and salted by a series of workers on board ship (Figure 4.4). This was a seasonal occupation, lasting through summer, but the boats involved were rarely more than 100 tons and were lucky to process more than one hundred cod per day. The fishers used hand lines with a single baited hook. Annual fleets numbered just a few hundred. In spite of the limited scale of these operations, they did contain elements of the future factory ship, and competition for the resource was strong enough to stir up naval conflict between competitors. Bigger boats were used in the drying industry. They anchored near shore and sent out daily several longboats, which they had carried with them, with three or four fishers using baited hand-lines. The catch was dried on shore, and shipped to the Mediterranean or, after the development of slavery and the sugar plantation economy in the seventeenth century, to the Caribbean. In the nineteenth century, these fishers gradually abandoned handlines and used instead long lines with multiple hooks that brought in many more fish. The boats became bigger and more efficient. But the basic techniques persisted in much the same manner for four hundred years.

The Industrial Revolution marks a transition in fishing for food as important as that observed in the cultivation of crops and raising of animals on land. Fishing remains different, however, because it has always been based primarily on the hunting, or catching, of wild fish. Thus, technological change has been directed principally at increasing the efficiency of "harvesting" the resources of sea, river, and wetland. On the other hand, all of the fisheries typically existed without access to domesticated fish stocks or fish farms. More importantly, fishers were rarely able to increase or improve wild fish stocks. Fisheries science, which emerged only in the nineteenth century as an adjunct of marine biology and oceanography, was largely a mathematical exercise, directed at estimating densities and stock, with the practical objective of regulating the mesh of nets, but regularly failing to achieve the control desired.

Whereas industrialized farming techniques dramatically increased the output of plant and animal food on land, the industrialization of fishing was more likely to lead to the long-term depletion of the fish stock and, in the worst case, its extinction. Fish farming on an industrial scale, in ponds or in confined sea pens, is a recent development, beginning with salmon in the 1980s. It had relatively little impact on total production or consumption. By the beginning of the twenty-first century as much as three-quarters of the world's oceans had been officially declared over-fished or fished to their limit. Aquaculture came to be seen as the only long-term solution but entailed continued pressure on marine resources because the farmed fish were fed other fish, in the form of fishmeal and fish oil, together with poultry byproducts and vegetable proteins. The fishmeal typically was made of trimmings from fish processors and from fish, or parts of fish humans chose not to eat. Some fish farmers regularly used growth hormones and antibiotics, and some fish were treated to make them appear closer to their wild varieties – as in the use of a dye to make salmon flesh similar to the pink that wild fish gained by eating crustaceans. Aquaculture grew rapidly in Asia, particularly China, moderately fast in Latin America, and in Europe (particularly salmon and trout in Norway and Turkey), balancing somewhat the overall decline in fishery.

Consumers came to be faced by a lack of choice or by limited or expensive supplies of fish. It was a very new situation, in strong contrast to the persistent perception of abundance that had prevailed for millennia. Because fishing was directed almost entirely at the production of food, excepting pearl fisheries and whaling, for example, the long-term ecological footprint of the human search for aquatic foods was particularly strong.

Industrialization came to marine fisheries only in the last decades of the nineteenth century, with the use of steam-powered ships and the mechanization of on-ship operations. Once the new system was adopted, it continued apace, placing pressure on fish stocks for the first time and leading rapidly to substantial depletion and an acceptance of the concept of overfishing. Fishers could no longer simply sail out a little further to find fresh sources of abundance. Competition became fierce and led ultimately to an international agreement in 1977 to respect Exclusive Economic Zones, stretching out 200 nautical miles, within which nations with coastlines could claim sovereignty.

Steamships grew in size and speed and possessed a reliability that could never be achieved with sail and its dependence on the wind. They could travel further and carry more, gaining greater flexibility when diesel displaced coal as the major fuel in the 1920s. They could generate electricity, enabling night fishing using deck lights. They also became platforms for machines that could shoot and haul very large seines and trawls. These large catches could be kept fresh on ice or canned at isolated wharves or on board. The ships could stay at sea longer, and indeed needed to do so by the 1920s, as stock densities declined steeply. The factory ship became almost a necessity. Emblematic was the whaling factory ship, perfected by the 1920s for long voyages in the Antarctic, with the capacity to pursue the faster whales that had not previously been captured, and equipped with explosive harpoons.

A "second industrialization" of fisheries is sometimes identified in the period between the 1950s and the agreement of 1977, with the treaty a direct product of this process (Roberts 2007: 297; Cushing, 1988: 234). Capture technologies were refined and employed increasingly effectively by newly expanded fleets, the Japanese and Russian being the most prominent, operating far from home, often in waters off the coasts of developing tropical and subtropical nations, leading to the United Nations Convention on the Law of the Sea, concluded in 1982 but not signed or ratified by all countries. These fisheries fed new markets for frozen fish and shrimp, and took advantage of demand for fish oil and meal from the chicken and feedlot-livestock industries. Stern trawlers, modeled on whaling ships, were used from the 1950s, designed to haul in heavy seines more easily than sidewinders could do, and equipped with machines for filleting, freezing, and conversion of offal to fish meal. From the 1960s massive mid-water trawls were employed in combination with sonar devices that enabled the tracking of schools of fish that were impossible to identify by surface methods. Planes and helicopters were used to search for fresh targets. Extraordinary increases in catches resulted. But they proved unsustainable.

Because of this concerted military attack and because of the fine mesh of the great seines which could not distinguish species or maturity, fish populations declined dramatically almost everywhere around the world. Moratoria had to be implemented to avert extinction but poachers and rogue fishers continued to reduce stocks. From the late 1980s, the total world catch of fish leveled off and then began to decline steadily. In the same period, the health benefits of eating fish were promoted by nutritionists, pushing up demand. Further, the global warming experienced over the period affected stocks of freshwater fish by making it harder for cool currents to well up, thus reducing the flow of vital nutrients. Lake Tanganyika, for example, suffered from this problem, greatly reducing the commercial catch of sardines and other fish on which neighboring populations depended.

By 2010 there were 35 million fishers globally and 20 million fishing boats, encouraged by government subsidies. In addition to the depletion of previously abundant stocks, the intense fishing of the period after 1950 induced a change in the structure or composition of the world's fish population. Larger high-value species, most of them predators, were eliminated or reduced, creating opportunities for smaller varieties to prosper and for those generally ignored or despised as human food to gain a more significant role in the marine food chain. Octopus, squid, and eels, as well as shrimps, crabs, and lobsters, even jellyfish, replaced cod, shark, and whale. These changes in the composition of the maritime stock derived in some cases directly from human selectivity: as in the intense demand for cod, together with the rejection of bycatch fish, and the continuing appalling demand for shark's fin, which entails the rejection of the body of the fish itself. Thus, although humans had little success in domesticating fish species through selective breeding, the composition and structure of the marine ecosystem was altered substantially by industrialized fishing technologies which created the possibility of closely targeted human choice.

Two claims

The first claim is that technologies played a greater role in determining productivity levels in hunting and fishing than they did in agriculture and the herding of semi-domesticated animals. Even small increments in capture-capacity derived from superior tools enabled hunters to substantially increase their catch.

Second, and building on the first claim, where the capture-capacity of hunters and fishers exceeded the ability of animals and fish to reproduce and replenish their populations, productivity declined. Frequently, the outcome was severe depletion of stocks and in many cases extinctions. Domesticated animals, on the other hand, rarely suffered species-wide extinctions. The consequence of this unequal balance was global dependence on a narrow range of domesticated animals, raised on industrial principles.

REFERENCES

Anderson, J.K. (1985) *Hunting in the Ancient World.* Berkeley, CA: University of California Press.

Anell, B. (1960) *Hunting and Trapping Methods in Australia and Oceania.* Uppsala, Sweden: Studia Ethnographica Upsaliensia, XVIII.

Anthony, D.W. (2007) *The Horse, the Wheel, and Language: How Bronze-Age Riders from the Eurasian Steppes Shaped the Modern World.* Princeton: Princeton University Press.

Bavel, B.V. (2010) *Manors and Markets: Economy and Society in the Low Countries, 500–1600.* Oxford: Oxford University Press.

Beach, H. (1990) Comparative systems of reindeer herding. In J.G. Galaty and D.L. Johnson (eds) *The World of Pastoralism: Herding Systems in Comparative Perspective*, pp. 255–98. New York: The Guilford Press.

Bell-Fialkoff, A. (ed.) (2000) *The Role of Migration in the History of the Eurasian Steppe: Sedentary Civilization vs. "Barbarian" and Nomad.* New York: St Martin's Press.

Bold, B.-O. (2001) *Mongolian Nomadic Society: A Reconstruction of the "Medieval" History of Mongolia.* Richmond, UK: Curzon.

Butcher, J.G. (2005) The marine animals of Southeast Asia: Towards a demographic history, 1850–2000. In P. Boomgaard, D. Henley and M. Osseweijer (eds) *Muddied*

Waters: Historical and Contemporary Perspectives on Management of Forests and Fisheries in Island Southeast Asia, pp. 63–96. Leiden: KITLV Press.

Crane, E. (1999) *The World History of Beekeeping and Honey Hunting*. New York: Routledge.

Crowe, I. (2000) *The Quest for Food: Its Role in Human Evolution and Migration*. Stroud, UK: Tempus.

Cushing, D.H. (1988) *The Provident Sea*. Cambridge: Cambridge University Press.

Degen, A.A. (2007) Sheep and goat milk in pastoral societies. *Small Ruminant Research* 68: 7–19.

Detienne, M. and Vernant, J.-P. (1989) *The Cuisine of Sacrifice among the Greeks*. Chicago: University of Chicago Press.

Feil, D.K. (1987) *The Evolution of Highland Papua New Guinea Societies*. Cambridge: Cambridge University Press.

Higman, B.W. (2008) *Jamaican Food: History, Biology, Culture*. Mona, Jamaica: University of the West Indies Press.

Ingold, T. (1980) *Hunters, Pastoralists and Ranchers: Reindeer Economies and Their Transformations*. Cambridge: Cambridge University Press.

Krausmann, F. (2004) Milk, manure, and muscle power: Livestock and the transformation of preindustrial agriculture in central Europe. *Human Ecology* 32: 735–72.

Lotze, H.K. (2007) Rise and fall of fishing and marine resource use in the Wadden Sea, Southern North Sea. *Fisheries Research* 87: 208–18.

Marlowe, F.W. (2005) Hunter-gatherers and human evolution. *Evolutionary Anthropology* 14: 54–67.

Marlowe, F.W. (2010) *The Hadza: Hunter-Gatherers of Tanzania*. Berkeley, CA: University of California Press.

Okayasu, T., Okuro, T., Jamsran, U. and Takeuchi, K. (2010) An intrinsic mechanism for the co-existence of different survival strategies within mobile pastoralist communities. *Agricultural Systems* 103: 180–186.

Peterson, D. (2003) *Eating Apes*. Berkeley, CA: University of California Press.

Roberts, C. (2007) *The Unnatural History of the Sea: The Past and Future of Humanity and Fishing*. London: Gaia.

Schafer, E.H. (1977) T'ang. In K.C. Chang (ed.) *Food in Chinese Culture: Anthropological and Historical Perspectives*, pp. 87–140. New Haven, CT: Yale University Press.

Shnirelman, V.A. (1992) The emergence of a food-producing economy in the steppe and forest-steppe zones of Eastern Europe. *Journal of Indo-European Studies* 20: 123–43.

Shoemaker, N. (2005) Whale meat in American history. *Environmental History* 10: 269–94.

Wilkie, D.S. and Lee, R. J. (2004) Hunting in agroforestry systems and landscapes: Conservation implications in West-Central Africa and Southeast Asia. In G. Schroth, G.A.B. da Fonseca and C.A. Harvey *et al.* (eds) *Agroforestry and Biodiversity in Tropical Landscapes*, pp. 347–70. Washington: Island Press.

CHAPTER FIVE

Preservation and Processing

Ancient societies generally recognized a practical and symbolic distinction between the raw, the preserved, and the processed. Often, strict rules governed the states in which specific food items could be consumed. In the Middle East and India, for example, vegetables might be eaten raw, whereas meat and eggs were consumed only when preserved or processed, but at the same time milk was acceptable in fresh, processed, and even decomposed states. What could be done to transform these foods and extend their markets remained limited, until the industrial transformation of technologies of preservation and processing, and of technologies of transport.

Ancient preservation

In the ancient world, preservation was largely directed at maintaining the original qualities of commodities, enabling their use out of season or in periods of short supply, or facilitating exchange. It was typically applied to raw ingredients rather than cooked items, the notion of leftovers having little validity. The most common methods used to achieve these outcomes were drying, smoking, fermenting, and salting. In these processes, the objective was the production of a transformed, superior, variety of food.

Early meat-eating communities attempted to extend the supply of food derived from killing animals by drying and smoking the flesh. These groups rarely had access to salt. Drying remained the dominant mode in ancient Egypt, carried out within tall and airy slaughterhouses. The slaughter of animals followed a typical model. Cattle were tethered to a stone block,

How Food Made History, First Edition. B. W. Higman.
© 2012 B. W. Higman. Published 2012 by Blackwell Publishing Ltd.

brought to the ground, and then had their legs tied before the butcher cut the animal's throat. The blood was caught and perhaps boiled for pudding. The animal was then flayed, the fat rendered, and the carcass cut into prescribed portions. By the time of the New Kingdom (1530–1070 BC), metal knives had largely replaced flint blades, not because metal was regarded as superior but rather because flint became scarce. Knives were used systematically to butcher smaller animals but cattle were often attacked with heavy axes and cleavers. The meat of cattle, sheep, goats, and pigs was dried as cuts, whereas birds and fish were preserved whole after plucking and gutting. Fish were split and splayed, and hung on a line to dry. Some of this dried meat may have been salted and spiced but the evidence is far from certain. Herodotus, in the fifth century BC, did record that the Egyptians preserved fish in brine and had fish-processing enterprises, but when these began operation is unknown.

Whereas large-scale complex societies might look to exchange to achieve food security, small isolated communities faced more extreme challenges to survival. The island communities of ancient Polynesia, for example, recognized that preservation of their food resources was essential. They had to prepare for droughts, during which it was unlikely they would be able to migrate to new places in the way continental peoples were able to do during subsistence crises, and they had also to prepare for hostile invasions which often left their fields of taro, yams, and breadfruit destroyed. One solution was the preparation of *masi*, a bread-like food made from fermented breadfruit or bananas, packed closely in a pit lined with heliconia or banana leaves. Made airtight by another layer of leaves, and covered with soil and rocks, the fruit fermented rather than rotted and was concealed from the eyes of invaders. After a month, states Cox (1980: 182), the pit could be uncovered, to reveal the "homogeneous dough-like paste" or *masi*, which was then mixed with grated coconut and kneaded into shapes for baking in a stone oven. The baked product "looked like bread and had a pungent, slightly fecal smell, somewhat like the smell of old limburger cheese" and "had a very strong taste, like a strong cheese with a dash of sauerkraut added." The *masi* could remain buried for up to a year but the baked product, packed in a series of baskets and placed in a hole up to 10 ft (3 m) deep, might be preserved for many years, completely invisible to invaders. In post-Columbian times, similar processes of fermentation were applied in Polynesia to the preservation of cassava.

The internationally known Japanese food sushi also has its origins in pickling and preservation. In ancient Japan, sushi was a cooked food prepared specially for travelers. One early variety was made by gutting an uncooked fish and stuffing the cavity with rice, which was allowed to ferment. When eaten, the rice was discarded and only the fish consumed. The use of fermenting rice in the preservation of fish imparted a sour taste, which eventually came to be appreciated. By the eighteenth century, sushi had come much closer to its modern incarnation, in which cooked rice was mixed with vinegar or pickled vegetable then rolled into balls or packed in a wooden box, for journeys. Further, as long as transport remained costly and distance-limited, the desire of inland-dwelling people for fish from the sea could be satisfied only by pickling of this type, resulting in the packing of fish and rice in layers, which served to preserve both ingredients for the days needed to transport the sushi from Japanese coastal fishing villages (Ashkenazi and Jacob, 2000: 200–211). From these early forms emerged hand-shaped sushi of the modern kind, particularly popular among the samurai.

In ancient China, eggs were preserved by the application of a coating of salt and ash to the shells, which by osmosis turned them into blue-colored jelly (Chaudhuri, 1990: 162–3). With enough salt applied, almost any cut of meat can last a long time, but to make a good-tasting product it is necessary to be sparing with the salt and allow the chemistry of the meat to complete the job. The Egyptians employed the same verb to describe the pickling of pigs to make hams as that used to name the process of mummification (though using saltpeter rather than salt). The Romans followed both a wet method, in which the hams were laid down in a jar between layers of salt before being dried and smoked, and a dry method in which the pig was boned and the meat pressed between boards to extract as much moisture as possible then rubbed with salt and hung to dry. The dry method is very similar to that used in northern Italy in modern times to make prosciutto and country hams. The preserved meat can be eaten raw, without any cooking. Cured raw, a ham can remain good for a long period, making it a strong candidate for ancient food trade.

The preservation of smaller quantities of meat, and of the byproducts of butchering, was often achieved by the making of sausages, in which salted minced meat and fat (itself a variety of preservative) was stuffed into natural casings, the elements coalescing to conceal their true origins. These sausages could be cooked and eaten immediately or alternatively made with cumin, fennel, and other spices as well as the fish sauce heavy with salt that the Romans applied liberally in their cooking. They were then hung to dry. Stuffed with enough salt and fat, a cooked sausage could survive for some time if the temperature was not too high. It did not take long for the sausage and the sausage-seller to become objects of ancient wit. As early as the sixth century BC the Greek poet Hipponax, known for his talent at parody, connected the image of the sausage with the penis and the act of copulation. Socrates was just one voice deriding the sausage-seller, indicating that the sausage was regarded as a cheap food, made of offal, and dog and donkey meat, easily adulterated (Frost, 1991).

Even in antiquity, salted fish may have been at least as common as fresh. Salted (and dried and smoked) fish came to Athens from distant places as early as the fifth century BC, from as far as Spain in the west and the Black Sea in the east. The development of fish preservation as a commercial enterprise in Spain was probably introduced by colonists from the east. It was a highly differentiated trade, the pieces of preserved fish brought to Greece identified by words describing their origins, shape, and saltiness.

The Romans had a relatively limited vocabulary for salted fish but a more refined appreciation of fish sauces and pastes, distinguishing between *garum*, *liquamen*, and *allex*, as well as *muria*, the salty liquid expressed in the process of salting fish. A simple way of making *garum* was to pack a container with whole fish which were too small to be worth salting, and the gills and innards of those which were, together with herbs, spices, and salt. Allowed to stand in the sun for a month and stirred occasionally, the liquid was strained, having by then lost its fishiness. The process changed little throughout antiquity and, indeed, continues much the same in making fish sauce in modern Southeast Asia and around the Black Sea. But here the task was not so much preservation as processing, with the intention of making a product not known in nature.

Ancient processing

Teeth, notably the molars, working together with saliva, provide a personal model of the advantages of crushing, grinding, and tearing in making food easier to swallow, a lesson easily learned. It is therefore not surprising that perhaps the most fundamental of all food-processing technologies is milling, in which plant materials are reduced in size and shape by pounding, crushing, chopping, and grinding to make them more functional and attractive to the consumer. Butchery involves some of the same principles. The essential actions are straightforward enough, and are practiced by those animals that use simple tools, as in the crushing of a nut with a stone. These natural technologies quickly transformed into much more elaborate and powerful modes.

Even relatively soft plant materials, such as yams and taro, benefit by pounding with a pestle in a mortar, while the process may be essential to making fibrous matter edible and to removing the toxic elements in others. Small stone mortars and pestles were common in the early Neolithic and taller wooden examples were used widely for pounding the softer roots and tubers. The grinding of seeds and nuts, to produce a relatively fine-grained powdery texture, was achieved better by using a fixed stone slab (or quern) and a spherical or ovoid hand stone to rub the material back and forth. This was a simple technology mastered before the Neolithic. These two technologies were both used in Mesopotamia and ancient Egypt to produce flour, the mortar and pestle separating the grain from the chaff, and the grinding stone making the

Figure 5.1 Mortar and pestle, and grinding stones. Showing: simple rubbing stone (top left); large wooden mortar and pestle (top right); grooved saddlestone (bottom left); and push-mill with stone box to hold grain (bottom right).

flour. The work of grinding was hard, typically performed by women and servants, kneeling at one end of the quern. By the time of the Egyptian Middle Kingdom, around 4000 BP, inclined saddle querns had largely replaced the flat or trough versions (Figure 5.1).

An important innovation in milling technology was made in Greece by the fifth century BC, with the development of the hopper mill, which constituted a machine rather than a set of hand tools. The hopper mill was so called because it replaced the hand stone with a large rectangular stone hollowed out and with a narrow slot in the base, the grain being fed into the hollow or hopper and trickling out through the slot to enable increased output and more uniform quality. The fixed base was now level and grooved. The hopper stone was worked back and forth using a handle. The motive power remained human but the miller could now stand rather than having to kneel. This superior mill spread quickly through the Mediterranean region.

Rotary mills emerged about the same time in the western Mediterranean, probably in Spain, but took a long time to replace reciprocal motion. Rotary querns were not known in Egypt until the conquest of Alexander the Great in 332 BC, which put in place the Ptolemies, the pharaohs of Greek descent who ruled Egypt until the time of the Romans. But rotary milling proved to have many advantages and was applied to other tasks, such as the crushing of olives for their oil. The technology was soon harnessed to animal rather than human power, using camels, donkeys, and oxen, though decentralized rotary hand mills persisted down to the present for small-scale use. The rotary mill was refined by the Romans and spread through their empire, in association with the much-improved granaries they built of stone and timber.

The grinding of grain was also the first industrial example of the application of waterpower, using both undershot and overshot mills, relieving many workers from hard labor. The watermill appeared in the first century BC and was probably an Italian invention. It quickly spread through the Mediterranean region but, because the cost of construction was considerable, including the building of aqueducts to feed the mill wheels, only the wealthy could afford them, creating the base for independent commercial enterprise. A series of mill-houses, arranged down a sloping site and powered by an aqueduct, created an impressive and rare ancient factory complex (Figure 5.2). In the early Islamic world, large-scale watermills were common, grinding millet as well as wheat. In Egypt, the town Mashtulu-t-Tawahin (Mashtulu of the Mills) was named for its flourmills, which supplied camel caravans and ships on their way to Jedda and Mecca. At Basra, mills were powered by the daily tides that rushed through the canals. By the sixteenth century, rotary mills powered by water and animals were spread throughout Asia (Chaudhuri, 1990: 162).

Modern milling

Technologies developed in ancient times for the milling of grain and the crushing of olives, harnessing the power of animals, water, and wind, maintained their importance unaffected by significant innovations down to the eighteenth century. They were, however, applied with little modification to

TO CULVERT

Figure 5.2   Water mills at Barbégal (near modern Arles, south of France), operated in the fourth century (idealized reconstruction). The sixteen millhouses were arranged in parallel lines down a slope, fed by an aqueduct. The overshot waterwheels were powered by twin millraces, with gearing arranged to turn the millstones that ground the grain fed through the hoppers.

Source: Hodge, A. Trevor, "A Roman Factory", *Scientific American* 263 (5) (November 1990). Image © Tom Prentiss by permission of Nelson H. Prentiss.

the processing of new crops. Thus, the great expansion of the frontier of tropical colonization in the Americas following Columbus depended on these rotary mills to crush sugar cane and process coffee berries. The example of sugar was particularly significant because, unlike the grinding of grain to make flour, the milling was merely the first operation in a series of processes required to produce a viable, tradable product.

Neither sugar cane nor raw cane juice constituted an item of long-distance trade. Further processing was essential, at the place of crushing, so plantations also operated factories in which the juice was boiled, crystallized, semi-refined, and drained, before shipping. Byproducts of the process were molasses and rum, the latter distilled in a separate operation. These plantation factory complexes were some of the largest private industrial enterprises of the seventeenth and eighteenth centuries. However, imperial policies, particularly as practiced under mercantilism, generally capped the degree of product modification allowed in the colonies, denying them the choice to make the refined near-white sugars preferred by European consumers. Differential tariffs ensured that refineries were located in metropolitan economies.

Sugar production in the early Islamic world – in Syria, Jordan, and northern Africa – harnessed both water and wind power to drive the crushing mills. These technologies, as well as the practice of refining, were transferred to the Americas via the Atlantic islands (Al-Hassan and Hill, 1986: 221–2). On the plantations of the Americas, down to the eighteenth century, sugar mills were driven by rotary action, the canes pushed through a set of vertical wooden rollers. In the nineteenth century, this method was replaced by more efficient horizontal iron rollers placed in a triangular configuration, and the motive power was increasingly supplied by steam engines (Galloway, 1989). Although these steam engines made use of the crushed canes as fuel, they often depended on coal and other non-renewable resources, in contrast to the renewables of animal, wind, and waterpower of earlier centuries.

The use of steam power not only increased the productivity of the mills but was also applied to the process of drying the sugar more completely, using centrifuges, and enabled the production of superior qualities of sugar, such as Demerara crystals. Steam remained significant well into the twentieth century, though electric and oil-fired motors gradually took its place, continuing the dependence on non-renewable resources. These modern engines were not confined to sugar milling but spread widely throughout the food-processing industries.

Whereas steam power was vital to the modernization of sugar-processing technologies, it did not enable the production or trade of any new commodity. The sugar was simply somewhat drier and the crystals better formed. Nor did the use of steam to power vehicles contribute much. Improved speeds on land did contribute to the expansion of plantation hinterlands, as noted in Chapter 3, but the speed of shipment to market mattered little in the case of sugar. For other commodities, however, improved speeds did transform markets, particularly for things previously thought too perishable to survive movement over any significant distance.

Packaging

For many foods, the ideal method of preservation was canning, a viable means of avoiding the deterioration that inevitably eventually attacked dried, smoked, and salted food products. Properly sealed cans made of tinplate kept their contents edible for many years. The principles of canning were known by the late eighteenth century and applied on a limited scale to the production of canned meat and vegetables, as well as "portable soup" for the British and French navies when sailing to the polar regions or the tropics. Thus, canned food had an important role in the early nineteenth century, enabling expeditions in harsh climates, including attempts to find a way through the North West Passage, and permitting blockading squadrons to remain at sea for long periods. The method remained imperfect, however, and commercial success did not come until after the 1860s, marked by the first packing of compressed cooked beef (bully beef or corned beef) in tapered rectangular cans in 1874 – a model that persisted in essentially the same form into the twenty-first century, though no longer a prominent item on the shelves of most supermarkets (Perren, 2006: 40–45).

From the late nineteenth century, industrial food-processing technologies and their products overlapped increasingly with the food cooked in homes and small-scale enterprises. The transition was gradual, however, and in many cases long-delayed. Simple preservation often remained within the home sphere for another hundred years. For example, the industrial production of kimchi – a favorite salt-cured Korean dish typically made from Chinese (white) cabbage, red pepper, garlic, and other seasonings – began only in the 1970s (Choi and Henneberry, 1999). The number of processing plants increased rapidly thereafter but many households continued to hand-prepare kimchi and preferred product that had fermented for months or even years in pottery vessels to refrigerated, fresh versions. By doing the preparation themselves, consumers could keep control of the flavors they most desired and eat the kimchi at different stages of fermentation.

In the industrial sphere, canning was central to the development of a market for cooked food, enabling the long-term preservation of complete meals (Irish stew, for example) rather than separate elements (meat, carrots).

Great commercial empires were built on these foundations, from the 57 varieties of Heinz to the cans of Campbell's Soup immortalized in the pop art of Andy Warhol. All of these meals were the products of factories.

Factories also turned to the production of snack foods, having the capacity to apply machines to the bulk preparation and cooking of standardized commodities. Here the potato chip stands out as a leader. In the United Kingdom, the Smith's Potato Crisps Ltd began purchasing potatoes on a large scale in the 1930s. The potatoes were washed, peeled, sliced, and roasted, then salted and packaged, on assembly line principles. In order to control the process, Smith's signed contracts only with farmers planting the Dutch variety Muizen, and accepted only tubers with preferred characteristics of quality, size, and shape. Soon, Smith's established its own major growing estate, thus enabling the company to command the complete chain from cultivation to distribution.

Supply chain control became increasingly sophisticated in the second half of the twentieth century, particularly through the use of electronic tracking and tagging systems that enabled the identification of poor-quality batches and to trace their origins. These large-scale developments in management went together with the growing automation of industrial food processing and packaging technologies, and the embedding of sensors. By the end of the twentieth century, packaging technologies had become highly specialized and varied, but papers and boards continued to dominate, followed by plastics, metals, and glasses. Food products then accounted for about one-third of the global packaging industry, so its impact on the economy and on natural resources was considerable.

Although plastics had many attractive features for the packaging of food – transparency, softness, lightness, strength, and heat-sealing capacity – their petrochemical materials and heavy use of energy in manufacture saw a shift toward biodegradable and recyclable products. New materials including nano-composites, together with electronic functions, made possible "smart" packaging, such as self-cooling beer and self-heating coffee containers (Popov, Filippov and Khurshudyan, 2010). However, although aspects of the food-packaging industry were automated and sometimes used robots, the different demands of particular commodities produced in small runs and the high degree of manual dexterity required to prepare origami-style cartons meant that much of the labor of folding remained manual. This was particularly true in areas such as the fast food industry (Mahalik and Nambiar, 2010).

Freezing and chilling

Although the preservation benefits of storage at low temperatures were recognized by early societies, the possible technologies remained limited until the eighteenth century. Perishable products such as meat could be placed in caves, which remained relatively cold all year, and ice collected from ponds might be used to create chilled storage pits, but these solutions depended on specific environmental conditions not found in many large regions of the world outside the Arctic Circle. Trade in natural ice and compressed snow also began in antiquity but the cost of carriage was high, for example the carting of mountain ice to ancient Rome, where it was a luxury used to cool drinks. For the same purpose, in India, ice was brought from distant mountains, by horse and boat, when the sixteenth-century Mughal emperor Akbar's court was in residence at Lahore.

It was not until the middle of the eighteenth century that the principles of artificial ice formation were discovered and applied to mechanical refrigeration. Commercial operations did not begin for another 100 years. Chilling and freezing quickly transformed the possibilities of preservation for a wide range of foods previously excluded from trade by their perishability and unsuitability for drying, salting, or canning. Further, these technologies enabled the consumption of foods out of season and extended their shelf-life in homes as well as stores.

The freezing of foods began as a means of preservation to enable long-distance trade rather than a means of long-term storage either commercially or domestically but depended on the development of a continuous supply chain of refrigerated delivery trucks, supermarket freezers, and household refrigerators in order to create a market. This dual revolution began in the United States and remained limited until the prosperity of the period following World War II. First to be frozen were fish and poultry, in 1865, then small fruits like berries by 1908. Vegetables took longer to be successfully preserved, because of changes in color and flavor, which were prevented only after 1930, when it was discovered that they needed to be scalded before being frozen. Vegetables also benefited from refrigerated trucks and rail cars, developed in the late 1920s.

Frozen foods gained a competitive edge following Pearl Harbor, when canning plants were requisitioned by the United States government and their use of metal closely monitored. Frozen products used paper packaging and were relatively freely available from the emerging supermarket sector. Production levels increased rapidly after 1945, when vegetables came to dominate the market, green peas taking the lead. By 1957, in the United States, the linear footage of frozen display cases packed with meat in supermarkets was greater than that for fresh product. By 1961 warehouse freezer capacity exceeded cooler capacity. Highly visible multinational corporations became major players in the market, much as happened with canned foods, from Birdseye to McCain with its 20 000 employees by 2010.

World War II also saw experiments in the dehydration of foods, which led to the development of orange juice concentrate, an intermediate product, which when reconstituted by the addition of water proved much closer to the natural taste of orange juice than any canned version could achieve. It also held more of its Vitamin C. Together with the juices of several other fruits, this proved a commercial success in the domestic market. Vacuum packing, designed to minimize deterioration caused by aerobic bacteria, also became common, particularly for prime cuts of meat, which might in addition be chilled or frozen. Meat-cutting was also one of the few food-processing technologies to make use of robots. The consequence was dispute over the meaning of "fresh," with fruit brought from year-long cold storage regularly marketed this way. Consumers learned that freezing and canning offered superior freshness qualities, compared to commodities transported over long distances before reaching supermarket shelves, whether refrigerated or not.

However, freezing proved unacceptable to consumers for some products, where true freshness was demanded. This was the case with eggs. When they bought factory-made biscuits, cakes, candy, or ice cream, consumers paid little attention to the fact that these products included dried (powdered), liquid, or frozen egg materials. These processes were applied to egg preservation beginning in the late nineteenth century and facilitated an extensive trade from China to Europe that peaked between the world wars, when eggs were among the top two or three exports (Chang, 2005). For household use, however, Western cooks rejected these products and demanded fresh whole eggs for their kitchens. As a result, a continuous non-seasonal supply of chicken eggs was developed during the twentieth century by the modification of chicken life and behavior, in which birds were confined in battery cages, and deprived of both sunshine and darkness, in order to satisfy the demand for freshness (Freidberg, 2008).

By the late twentieth century, bioactive edible coatings of polysaccharides and vegetable proteins (soy, wheat, and whey) containing antimicrobial compounds were being sprayed directly on fresh, frozen, and processed meat and poultry, in order to delay moisture loss and reduce oxidation and discoloration. With the addition of ingredients such as dietary fibers, herbs, and spices (rosemary extracts, sage, oregano, garlic, and cloves), and green tea, interacting with the ancient processes of curing and fermentation, such products became known as "functional foods" (Zhang *et al.*, 2010). Claiming health benefits, these were introduced first to the Japanese market in 1988, where the varieties quickly became numerous, and then spread to the United States. Central and North European markets also proved accepting of these functional foods, though Mediterranean consumers maintained a preference for fresh and natural produce. In many cases, the bioavailability of the compounds when incorporated in foods is too small to deliver a significant health advantage, and consumers remain unwilling to eat novel foods that look, smell, or taste dramatically unlike the natural products they are intended to replace or replicate (Weiss *et al.*, 2010).

Parallel developments led to the invention of frozen meals that could be purchased from grocery and supermarket retail outlets and needed simply to be warmed up in an oven or microwave to be consumed in the home. The iconic form was the TV dinner of the 1950s, which had its origins in military demand. Frozen pies, introduced to the market in 1951, increased demand for beef, and frozen pizzas massively increased the popularity of industrial-style cheeses, notably Mozzarella. Other new products entered the frozen-food market in the 1960s, items which had previously lacked national visibility in the United States, such as the bagel, which was transformed from an ethnic food eaten but once a week, to a common item consumed universally at any time (Bernstein, 1996). The massively increased demand for such products also transformed small artisanal bakeries into huge continuous-process factories, even if they retained their original brand names, such as the homely Sara Lee and Mrs Mac's.

The multiplication of frozen foods also led to changes in domestic technologies. In space-starved postwar Japan, for example, the popularity of frozen meals led to the development of refrigerators with standardized compartments and drawers made specifically to store packages of frozen food. The packages themselves were also standardized to these specifications, with the contents identified on the narrow end, so that they could be stored rather like video discs without scrabbling about a pan or a shelf (Ashkenazi and Jacob, 2000: 57). To achieve this result required coordination and cooperation across a range of industries.

Milk, butter, yoghurt, and cheese

In order to pull together the themes of preservation, processing, packaging, and trade (the subject of the following chapter) it is useful to focus on a single food source. The example chosen for the purpose is milk, which touches on each of these aspects in interesting ways.

Before Columbus and the redistribution of mammals, the milking of animals was far from universal and restricted even within Africa and Eurasia. The world milking map around 1400 shows a more or less solid bloc of committed milkers stretching into Eurasia from northern and eastern Africa (Figure 5.3). But the milking region stopped near the border of modern Bangladesh and Burma, and in China generally milking occurred north of the Great Wall but not to the south (Simoons, 1971). Otherwise, milking appeared again only in southern Africa and Madagascar. The remainder of the map was blank, either because those regions lacked animals that could be easily milked or because people consciously chose not to milk.

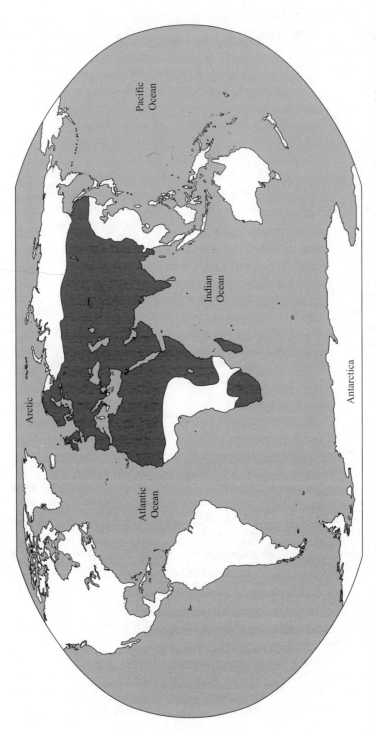

Figure 5.3 Milking regions of the world, circa 1400. Based on Frederick J. Simoons, "Dairying, Milk Use, and Lactose Malabsorption in Eurasia: A Problem in Culture History", *Anthropos* 74 (1979) 61–68, map on 63 (courtesy of *Anthropos*); and Naomichi Ishige, *The History and Culture of Japanese Food* (London: Kegan Paul, 2001), 59.

The apparent failure of otherwise omnivorous East Asians to make use of milk and its byproducts is explained by differential inheritance of the lactase gene. Lactase is a digestive enzyme that helps metabolize the sugar in milk (lactose). Whereas babies are born with a functioning lactase gene, enabling them to gain nourishment from their mother's milk, it begins to decline in the second year of life and reaches a low (adult) level by age 5. Children and adults then become incapable of benefiting from milk and drinking it is an uncomfortable experience, associated with abdominal pains, bloating, and diarrhea (Wells, 2010: 18–19; Brüssow, 2007: 6–16). However, where goats and cows were domesticated by 10 000 to 8000 BP in southwestern Asia and Egypt, human populations developed a mutation that kept the lactase gene switched on in adulthood (Simoons, 1971). It was really the milking peoples with dairy cultures who were the aberrant ones not the rest of the world, but the mutation may have provided adaptive advantages for physical growth gains.

Milk

Drinking the milk of their mothers was rarely hazardous to human babies and, indeed, it was an ideal food for them. Exclusive dependence on breast milk tended to be protracted in traditional societies down to the eighteenth century. In Africa, breast feeding typically continued to the third year, as a means of protecting the child and limiting fertility. In some societies, wet-nursing was common among those who could afford it and where maternal mortality was high, leaving infants without access to their own mother's milk. Attempts to make human milk available on a commercial basis had little success, however, because of its short shelf-life. Experiments were begun in the 1920s to extend the viable period of stored milk by evaporation and drying, then by refrigeration and freezing, and by pasteurization. In the United States, "milk banks" were established by the 1930s for the collection and distribution of mothers' milk, and these continued their work into the twenty-first century, but supplying milk only by doctor's prescription.

The first milk-producing animal to be exploited by humans was probably the goat, beginning in Mesopotamia by about 10 000 BP. The milking of cows is known first from Anatolia (modern Turkey) by 9000 BP, and the practice spread through Europe along with the first farmers. However, down to the middle of the nineteenth century, trade in milk was limited because there were no means of keeping it fresh. Most consumers milked their own cows or goats, or perhaps sheep or reindeer, or purchased from trusted neighbors. In large urban centers, dairies were established within the bounds of the cities, the cattle hand-fed with grass and hay brought from the surrounding countryside. Voyagers, from Christopher Columbus to James Cook, carried goats on board their ships in order to ensure a supply of fresh milk.

The establishment of railroad systems, particularly in Europe and North America, transformed the market for milk. From the 1870s, it became possible to move milk over relatively long distances, the product passing through several hands. By the beginning of the twentieth century almost all of the milk delivered to New York City arrived by train. Much the same applied to London, where the rapid spread of rail transport created supply regions that extended nationwide in the second half of the nineteenth century. The outcome was a decline in small-scale household milking (and butter- and cheese-making) and the emergence of specialized dairy regions. Urban dairies, which initially benefited by the railroad's ability to bring in fodder more cheaply, soon became unable to compete for space (Whetham, 1964). Throughout Europe, in particular, this new system marginalized goats and placed the cow at the center. In the United States, a specialized agricultural region along the eastern seaboard focussed on milk production for the merging megalopolis, and a second relatively distant region centered on Wisconsin, Minnesota, and Illinois specialized in butter and cheese, the products that could tolerate a longer journey to market.

A major negative consequence of the shift to rail transport of milk was large-scale adulteration. The milk was watered down, whitened with chalk, and thickened with emulsions derived from things like almonds and animal brains. Spoilage was slowed by the addition of formaldehyde. There were also problems of hygiene at the dairies themselves, with poor standards of washing down, and suspect fodder given to the animals. Milk arriving in cities by rail became carriers of tuberculosis, typhoid, scarlet fever, and other infections. Unlike many epidemics, it was the urban middle classes and their infant children who suffered most, because they were the greatest consumers of milk. Milk became regarded as a potentially poisonous food, and raw milk remained hazardous for many into the 1920s (Atkins, 1992).

Only with the passage of the Pure Food and Drug Act in the United States in 1906 did the hygiene of dairies and milk transport begin to improve. Europe followed close behind. Pasteurization, homogenization, and the cooling of milk trains and stations improved quality and gave milk a fresh image. Gradually, through the work of nutritionists and promotion by school milk programs, milk came to be viewed as a "pure" or "perfect" natural food. Delivery in sealed glass bottles rather than open cans helped, as did the replacement of copper-alloy cans with shiny stainless steel. Bottles began to be replaced by cheaper cartons made of paper, beginning in the 1930s in the United States, and plastic containers from the 1960s. Cooled tank trucks took over from rail. Milk ceased to be a generic product, but became branded and distinguished by low-fat, skim-milk, and lactose-reduced qualities or, alternatively, various forms of vitamin fortification (Tunick, 2009).

At the beginning of the twenty-first century, American consumers became concerned about the use of genetically engineered bovine growth hormone to increase milk yields and inhibit mammary cell death in cows, and it was banned from the dairy herds of the European Union and other countries. In these developed economies, consumers began to shift away from the industrial, fortified, packaged product, to favor raw milk from local, grass-fed cattle, a system rather like that which existed one hundred years before. Elsewhere, older problems persisted, for example in China where adulteration and contamination scandals appeared, in the midst of the process of globalization that brought milk-drinking culture to peoples formerly located amongst the lactose-intolerant (Wiley, 2007).

An early solution to the problems that confronted the distribution of fresh milk was to process it. Because milk consists mostly of water – with lactose accounting for only about 5 percent of its weight, and fat and protein 4 percent each – it can be substantially reduced by boiling at a low temperature in a vacuum. The thick liquid resulting from this process can be sterilized to make evaporated milk or mixed with sugar to make condensed milk. However, evaporated milk deteriorates as quickly as fresh milk once the can is opened, whereas the sugar in condensed milk enables it to last longer without refrigeration. In Europe, tinned milk consumption increased rapidly after the establishment of the Anglo-Swiss Condensed Milk Company in 1865 and an export trade emerged almost immediately. Condensed milk was promoted as a food for infants and as a nutritious substitute for fresh milk. By 1890 prices had fallen enough to make it appeal to poorer people, and local dairy industries felt threatened.

The technologies used to make condensed and evaporated milk were applied in the early twentieth century to the production of dried milk powder, which was introduced to a wide variety of processed food products, such as Milo, Horlick's and Ovaltine, then taken up after World War II by consumers as instant milk. Dried powdered milk was joined in the 1980s by ultra-high temperature or "long life" milk. These processed milk products could all be transported over long distances and sold profitably in distant markets. By the 1980s imported dried milk became a significant competitor in developing countries for people who lacked refrigeration. Trade agreements that favored large-scale producers, the heavy subsidization of European dairy farmers, and the dumping of skimmed-milk powder often led to the virtual collapse of dairy industries in the developing world.

These developments were moderated in some regions by the rapid growth of goat and sheep herds, particularly in Africa and Asia, and most importantly India and China, as noted in Chapter 3. Goats are favored by the world's shrinking pastoral communities, because they yield more milk than sheep and have a longer lactation period (Haenlein, 2007). Milk yields from sheep and goats had been increased substantially from the middle of the nineteenth century, by means of genetic selection and improved feeding, but the relatively small scale of the processing industries limited the commercial production of pasteurized beverages, evaporated milk, milk powder, butter, ghee, paneer (a soft variety of uncured cheese), and ice cream (Pandya and Ghodke, 2007).

Butter

Long before milk became popular as a drink, the attractions of cultured products, notably butter, yoghurt, and cheese, were discovered by herders and farmers of cattle, goats, sheep, and a few other mammals. This enabled them to turn the bacterial hazards of whole milk into an advantage, allowing contaminating organisms to transform the liquid into simple varieties of cheese, yoghurt, and butter. Cultured cream butter was made from raw cream, generally collected from several milkings and therefore partially fermented. Ghee, a form of moisture-reduced butter produced by heating buffalo milk, was popular only in subcontinental Asia.

Butter was an important item of transatlantic trade from the seventeenth century, shipped from Europe to colonial consumers. In cool climates the product arrived in an acceptable state but shipped to the tropics in summer it was regularly condemned as rancid and liquefied. In the nineteenth century, colonial producers such as Australia and New Zealand entered the export trade in butter, matching the Danes and the Irish in seeking to supply the demand of industrial Britain.

Down to the end of the nineteenth century, traded butter was generally packed in small kegs or glass bottles. Attempts to can butter generally failed, as there was always the problem of what to do with it once the can had been opened. Beginning about 1908, butter began to be packaged in sticks of 10 oz (280 g) or less, wrapped in paper and shipped in wooden boxes. Cream separation on a commercial scale began a little earlier and, combined with refrigeration, enabled the industrial production of butter from pasteurized cream, using continuous churning by the 1950s. Spreadable butters were developed in New Zealand in the 1970s.

The common use of butter (and lard and olive oil) in cooking had long been under threat, from new industrial products developed in the late nineteenth century. Some of these new commodities, such as coconut, cottonseed, and palm oil, had previously been made on a small-scale household model but became drawn into the plantation system and large-volume output, with sale in standardized bottles or cans. Palm oil had been an item in world trade from the middle of the nineteenth century, favored because it melted at a relatively low temperature but was hard and brittle when solid, making it an ideal article for transport. Soya bean oil appeared on the world market only after 1950.

A more direct competitor with butter was margarine. Invented in France in 1869, margarine was a truly industrial food, the product of a complex chemical sequence of processes. Early versions blended milk with animal and vegetable fats and oils, but vegetable oils, derived from coconut, palm, cottonseed, soya bean, and sunflower, came to dominate. Originally intended as a cheap alternative, margarine was promoted (and later questioned) as a health food. It was consciously created to mimic butter and is often regarded as the first successful substitute food.

Yoghurt

Simple varieties of yoghurt were made by leaving milk, sometimes heated, to stand overnight, allowing it to curdle and become sour. Doing this required no dramatically difficult innovation. The process of natural formation could be observed easily enough when milk was stood too long. Raw butter was made by churning sour milk, and probably yoghurt- and cheese-making followed close on the heels of domestication, using whey (the watery liquid that separates from curds after coagulation) and sour buttermilk (the fluid that remains after separated cream is churned).

Yoghurt and related fermented drinks were more closely associated with pastoralist peoples and only slowly became an item of trade. In lactose-intolerant East Asia, central and southern Africa, and the Americas, none of these products had any place until recent times and the development of lactase-reduced milks (Dalby, 2009). Part of the recent growth in milk consumption in Asia came from ready-made packaged milk drinks, and yoghurt-style drinks, such as Yakult developed in Japan in the 1930s (Velten, 2010).

Cheese

Cheese was known early in Europe, from about 6000 BP. In Mesopotamia, cheeses made from the milk of goats and cows, but rarely of sheep, are known from around 5000 BP. The earliest archeological evidence for Egypt dates from about the same time, but here cows were milked for medicine as well as food; words for cheese (and butter) are not known before 2300 BP. Cheese made from camel's milk was produced in northern Africa from at least 2000 BP. Thus, although the milking of animals commenced early in the Neolithic, the intensification of milk production and the diversification of secondary products occurred later, in association with the spread of woolly sheep, as well as the introduction of the plow and wheeled vehicles (Greenfield, 2010). These innovations together provided the foundations for the emergence of early complex societies.

In the Mediterranean, the ancient Minoans and Mycenaeans enjoyed cheeses made from the milk of goat and sheep. In ancient Rome, cheese was much favored over liquid milk and probably few inhabitants of the city had the opportunity to drink it. The relatively heavy consumption of cheese provided the basis for trade, since it was a product with a high value-to-weight ratio. Another reason for the significance of cheese lay in the practice of transhumance, discussed in Chapter 4. Animals were herded to upland pastures in summer, the period of maximum milk production, thus taking them further from the urban market and giving shepherds, goatherds, and cowherds an opportunity to practice cheese-making as a cottage craft. A desire for different styles of cheese created a trade not only from other parts of the Italian peninsula but also from across the Alps and as far away as Gaul.

The Romans preferred cheese made from the milk of sheep, with literary references to ewe's milk cheese (pecorino) the most common. Mare's and ass's milk are also mentioned occasionally. (Milking a mare required a delicate balancing act, though less demanding than dealing with a camel or a reindeer.) Romans enjoyed varieties of taste created, for example, by placing green pine cones in the milk while it curdled or mixing in crushed thyme (Curtis, 2001: 399–402; Thurmond 2006: 193–207). They also hardened cheese in brine and smoked it with wood from the apple tree. Generally, however, they depended on two basic types: soft curd, or cottage cheese, and hard cheese made by salting and drying.

Simple methods of butter-, cheese-, yoghurt-, and ghee-making persisted for millennia, typically associated with the labor of women. Both hard and soft cheeses were certainly consumed by ancient Europeans, and many of the better-known modern cheese varieties, such as Roquefort, Parmesan, and Brie, were already called these names by the end of the Middle Ages. The European colonization of the Americas saw cheese at the forefront, entering the food system ahead of the drinking of fresh milk. The beginnings of protoindustrialization in Western Europe, from the late sixteenth century, together with increasing urbanization and commercial farming, gave dairy products a greater role. In London, for example, cheese emerged as a cheap, convenient food, with fairly good preservation qualities (particularly through the winter) and became popular with workers. Cows replaced sheep as the major providers of milk. Women remained dominant in all aspects of dairy work. Cheese could be produced efficiently in this environment by scattered and relatively distant small farmers with access to road and sea transport.

Although artisan and small-scale cheese production on traditional lines remained important, and achieved growing popularity in the richer nations after about 1980, most of the twentieth century saw a strong shift to large-volume industrial manufacturing technologies. World cheese production increased from five million tons in 1961 to 19 million in 2007. Women ceased to dominate the making of dairy products. In the 1920s, James L. Kraft began the production of processed cheese, made by grinding together aged and fresh Cheddar, combined with emulsifying salts, then heating and pouring the mixture into cans or forms. This enabled the longer preservation of cheese and became popular, particularly with consumers lacking refrigeration.

A softer processed cheese with added nutrients, Velveeta, was developed by Kraft in the 1920s. Prepackaged cheese slices appeared soon after World War II. In the 1960s there was a shift away from using whey and sour buttermilk, to more hygienic frozen concentrated starter cultures. The very first genetically modified food ingredient to be approved by the US Food and Drug Administration was chymosin, the enzyme responsible for coagulation, made from bacteria, fungi, and yeasts, which was legalized in 1990 (Tunick, 2009: 8096). From the 1940s chemicals began to be used as preservatives, and from the 1970s antibiotics were used to inhibit yeast and mold.

Three claims

First, an extension of the claims made for crop determinism in Chapter 3 explains choices about what foods can be preserved and how they can be preserved in terms of the inherent characteristics of the foods themselves. The outcomes of these choices determined in turn what could be traded efficiently and what stored to see out seasonal or climate-related shortfalls.

A second and related claim sees technology as the main driver. Although the mechanical and chemical qualities of particular food sources determined which of them was amenable to processing, it was the availability of appropriate technologies that determined levels of output and pricing structures.

Third, a more controversial claim is that salt-deprivation followed by the consumption of over-salted preserved and processed foods contributed to high social levels of hypertension and associated health problems. The cheapness of refined sugar made it similarly culpable.

REFERENCES

Al-Hassan, A. Y. and Hill, D.R. (1986) *Islamic Technology: An Illustrated History*. Cambridge: Cambridge University Press.

Ashkenazi, M. and Jacob, J. (2000) *The Essence of Japanese Cuisine: An Essay on Food and Culture*. Philadelphia: University of Pennsylvania Press.

Atkins, P.J. (1992) White poison? The social consequences of milk consumption, 1850–1930. *Social History of Medicine* 5: 207–27.

Bernstein, E. (1996) Rising to the occasion: Lender's bagels and the frozen food revolution, 1927–1985. *Business and Economic History* 25: 165–75.

Brüssow, H. (2007) *The Quest for Food: A Natural History of Eating*. New York: Springer.

Chang, N.J. (2005) Vertical integration, business diversification, and firm architecture: The case of the China Egg Produce Company in Shanghai, 1923–1950. *Enterprise and Society* 6: 419–51.

Chaudhuri, K.N. (1990) *Asia before Europe: Economy and Civilisation of the Indian Ocean from the Rise of Islam to 1750.* Cambridge: Cambridge University Press.

Choi, S.-C. and Henneberry, D.M. (1999) Ethnic food marketing: Korean kimchi in world markets. *Journal of Food Products Marketing* 5: 19–44.

Cox, P.A. (1980) Two Samoan technologies for breadfruit and banana preservation. *Economic Botany* 34: 181–5.

Curtis, R.I. (2001) *Ancient Food Technology.* Leiden: Brill.

Dalby, A. (2009) *Cheese: A Global History.* London: Reaktion Books.

Freidberg, S.E. (2008) The triumph of the egg. *Comparative Studies in Society and History* 50: 400–423.

Frost, F. (1991) Sausage and meat preservation in antiquity. *Greek, Roman, and Byzantine Studies* 40: 241–52.

Galloway, J.H. (1989) *The Sugar Cane Industry: An Historical Geography from Its Origins to 1914.* Cambridge: Cambridge University Press.

Greenfield, H.J. (2010) The secondary products revolution: The past, the present and the future. *World Archaeology* 42: 29–54.

Haenlein, G.F.W. (2007) About the evolution of goat and sheep milk production. *Small Ruminant Research* 68: 3–6.

Mahalik, N.P. and Nambiar, A.N. (2010) Trends in food packaging and manufacturing systems and technology. *Trends in Food Science and Technology* 21: 117–128.

Pandya, A.J. and Ghodke, K.M. (2007) Goat and sheep milk products other than cheeses and yoghurt. *Small Ruminant Research* 68: 193–206.

Perren, R. (2006) *Taste, Trade and Technology: The Development of the International Meat Industry since 1840.* Aldershot, UK: Ashgate.

Popov, K.I., Filippov, A.N. and Khurshudyan, S.A. (2010) Food nanotechnologies. *Russian Journal of General Chemistry* 80: 630–642.

Simoons, F.J. (1970) The traditional limits of milking and milk use in southern Asia. *Anthropos* 65: 547–93.

Simoons, F.J. (1971) The antiquity of dairying in Asia and Africa. *Geographical Review* 61: 431–9.

Thurmond, D.L. (2006) *A Handbook of Food Processing in Classical Rome: For Her Bounty No Winter.* Leiden: Brill.

Tunick, M.H. (2009) Dairy innovations over the past 100 years. *Journal of Agricultural and Food Chemistry* 57: 8093–97.

Velten, H. (2010) *Milk: A Global History.* London: Reaktion Books.

Weiss, J., Gibis, M., Schuh, V. and Salminen, H. (2010) Advances in ingredient and processing systems for meat and meat products. *Meat Science* 86: 196–213.

Wells, S. (2010) *Pandora's Seed: The Unforeseen Cost of Civilization.* New York: Random House.

Whetham, E.H. (1964) The London milk trade, 1860–1900. *Economic History Review* 17: 369–80.

Wiley, A.S. (2007) The globalization of cow's milk production and consumption: Biocultural perspectives. *Ecology of Food and Nutrition* 46: 281–312.

Zhang, W., Xiao, S., Samaraweera, H. *et al.* (2010) Improving functional value of meat products. *Meat Science* 86: 15–31.

CHAPTER SIX

Trade

Although there were grounds for the exchange of food items from the earliest times, rooted in ecological differences, the emergence of systematic and substantial trade occurred only with the Neolithic and Urban Revolutions. Agriculture quickly led to active exchange between specialists. The growth of urban settlements dominated by people who did not produce food at all had an even larger impact. Such dependent communities remained only a small proportion of the world's population for most of history, however, and most peoples remained largely self-sufficient until recent times.

The great urban centers of the ancient world were highly influential in terms of government, and social and cultural development, but they were few and far between. They rarely contained more than 20 000 people. The exceptions stood out prominently. In Iraq, Uruk reached 40 000 as early as 5000 BP and Ur 100 000 by 4000 BP. Rome exceeded one million by 100 BC; Chang'an in China was as big by AD 700; and Baghdad by 1100. Even in the fifteenth century, at the very end of what can be considered broadly the ancient world, few cities exceeded 100 000. Rome had declined to as few as 20 000. Tenochtitlan, the Aztec capital, probably never exceeded 200 000. Beijing reached one million by 1500, and Istanbul 400 000. But London passed the one million mark only in 1810. In Africa, Timbuktu and Djenné were the largest cities but approached 100 000 only in peak periods. Vast regions of the world had no substantial urban concentrations and most people kept to themselves, only occasionally consuming foods produced at any distance.

The world was fundamentally transformed by the Columbian exchange, which laid the foundations of extensive trade in food products. By the beginning of the nineteenth century, with the Industrial Revolution about to

How Food Made History, First Edition. B. W. Higman.
© 2012 B. W. Higman. Published 2012 by Blackwell Publishing Ltd.

radically restructure the productive foundations of many economies, trade had become essential to the feeding of important segments of the world's population, even outside cities. Changes in transportation technology underpinned the development of this interdependent world economy.

After 1950, a combination of factors led to unprecedented urban growth, so that by 2007 more people lived in cities than in rural regions. The urban revolution that had begun over five thousand years earlier had finally conquered the countryside. Only now did it become common, on a world scale, not to live on some kind of farm, producing food for immediate consumption or exchange. This intense urban concentration occurred together with remarkable growth in the world's population, from three billion in 1960 to almost seven billion by 2010. Further, the burgeoning urban populations experienced increasing prosperity, demanding many new consumer goods, including foods from near and far. At the same time, cities in the developing world attracted the rural poor, who came to fill marginal shantytowns and favelas (home to more than one billion people by 2010) thus creating a resource of cheap labor for the middle classes.

Even the substantial numbers of people who remained abjectly poor in the midst of this world of plenty found themselves drawn into the international food economy, some of them dependent on international aid. In 2010, 60 percent of the world's people lived in Asia; 40 percent in China and India. Immense urban conglomerations, including Tokyo (32 million), Mexico City (20 million), and Beijing (15 million), created vast non-agricultural communities and an insatiable market for food.

The development and survival of such large dependent populations required the articulation of extensive and elaborate food supply systems, and complex chains of distribution. Underlying the emergence of this system were changes in technology, preservation, and processing as well as transport. Throughout most of history, trade in food was severely limited by the perishability of commodities and the high cost of moving bulky cargoes across land and sea. Only with the development of efficient and reliable technologies of preservation did the long-distance movement of many commodities become viable, and only with the development of modern technologies of bulk transportation did it become profitable to move great quantities of basic foodstuffs around the world.

Ancient trades

Early long-distance trades in food commodities consisted largely of items with a high value-to-weight ratio. They needed also to be resistant to deterioration. Raw organic items were rare, because most required preservation or processing to make them viable. Liquids were especially difficult to transport. If in small amounts, the containers were likely to be relatively expensive (and heavy), for example olive oil, wine and garum shipped in pottery vessels, which could bear the cost. Bottles made from skins, particularly goatskin, also held small quantities. The large-scale Roman style of container made from the complete hide of a cow and retaining its essential form, with the liquid poured in through a headless neck and emptied through a plugged hind leg, had to be mounted on a cart and was only practical over short distances (Thurmond, 2006: 163).

The best-known articles fulfilling the requirements of ancient trade were salt and spices. Salt is an essential source of the minerals needed by the human body but can be obtained in a variety of ways. So long as communities remained largely dependent on meat-eating, they might obtain all the salt they needed from the meat, blood, and milk of animals. Thus the shift to plant foods, particularly grains, that occurred with the Neolithic contributed to a demand for salt, whether obtained locally or through trade. Salt proved addictive, an early narcotic. Spices, on the other hand, are by no means a necessity. Nor are they addictive, though they have sometimes been used as medicine. Salt was also to prove important as an early preservative but, like spice, initially its significance derived from the taste it added to foods. Salt and spices were used typically only in small quantities – a pinch of salt was enough to enhance the flavor of a dish.

Salt

Salt quickly came to have economic as well as culinary significance, often emerging as one of the first non-agricultural commodities to be produced on an industrial scale and one of the first enterprises to fall under state regulation. In the ancient Mediterranean, most salt came from local sources, particularly coastal saltpans, which generally belonged to the state. In ancient Mesoamerica, communities lacking profitable alternatives might trade sea salt inland, as did the people of Yucatan to the urbanized Maya. Away from the sea, notably in the Middle East, salt was sometimes more a problem than a blessing, being seen as a barrier to agriculture, but a natural product rather than something that required active production. In these regions, trade in salt was limited. Elsewhere, in places where salt was much more hard won, for example the high Andes, the boiling of brine from salty springs could form the foundation of trade over quite long distances.

Ancient China, by 2000 BP, employed varied advanced salt-producing technologies. The Chinese pioneered the drilling of deep wells from which brine was extracted and evaporated in iron pans, sometimes using natural gas as a fuel for the process. In this period, most of China's salt came, however, from natural evaporation in salt lakes located on the fringes of the steppe and the need to import salt from this frontier zone contributed to the extension of the Chinese state's power as well as establishing a long-distance trade. The consequence was the development by the Chinese of the first effective state salt administration. The system established a state monopoly in the distribution of salt, as a means of raising revenue, and continued to about AD 80, when it was discarded, not to be reinstated until the powerful Tang dynasty of AD 618–907 (Adshead, 1992: 43–5).

Salt was the earliest commodity in trans-Saharan trade, exchanged over long distances well before the development of trades in gold and in people. The desert produced abundant blocks, particularly around its southern oases, which were traded to the farming peoples of the Sudan and also to the urban settlements of West Africa, competing with sea salt toward the coastal zone. Beginning around 500 BC this trade depended entirely on the special qualities of the camel, which enabled it to carry heavy loads, over rough ground, with long gaps between drinks. The salt trade expanded throughout the northern half of Africa in association with the spread of Islam (Austen, 2010: 16–17). Early Islam existed in desert places well resourced with salt but encouraged innovations with the development of tastes for particular qualities of salt, which led in turn to an extensive camel-train trade. Caravan routes formed an intricate web across the Sahara and into the Middle East, connecting the Niger with the Nile and Benin with Algiers, surviving long beyond the early stages of European maritime intrusion. In northern Africa a standard mold of salt often served as a unit of exchange (in the absence of gold), being used to measure the relative values of traded goods, a kind of money. Although salt came to be displaced in value by other commodities in the trans-Saharan trade, it was not only the pioneer but also persisted after colonial rule and alternative transport technologies had eroded the market for other goods, long continuing to supply the salt demanded by the farmers and pastoralists of the savanna.

Salt also began to travel greater distances in Europe during the Middle Ages. In Russia, down to the time of Peter the Great (1672–1725), salt extraction was the major non-agricultural activity. There, salt was used to cure fish and meats and to pickle vegetables (notably cabbage) for the long winter months. It was also used in the tanning of hides and the dyeing of cloth. Rock salt was mined in the south (near the Dnestr River) and traded north as early as the twelfth century; sea and lake salt was sent north from the Crimea; and brine was crystallized from seawater or by evaporation of brine obtained from wells (as practiced much earlier by the Chinese). Salt also came from the many lakes of Siberia and, as in China, it was the salt trade that encouraged Russian colonization of its margins, contesting access to the resource, the scarcest essential nutrient, with the Mongols, in the early seventeenth century (Perdue, 2005: 106–7). Again, the early taxation of salt in Russia had by the time of

Peter the Great been transformed into a state monopoly (Smith and Christian, 1984: 27–9, 72–3). The beginnings of maritime venturing around the coasts of western Europe similarly made salt a vital inaugural commodity in this emerging trade network.

Spice

Spices were ideal commodities for ancient trade: valuable, easily transported, and exotic in aroma and flavor. They traveled well with perfumes, like frankincense and myrrh. Thus, although the Greeks and Romans had at their doorsteps mint, basil, and cumin, they quickly began to use pepper and other spices from Africa, Arabia, India, and the "Spice Islands" of southeastern Asia. Rather than a single trade route, following the so-called Silk Road, many complex flows developed and became increasingly complicated as trade by sea overtook land transport.

Down to the fourteenth century, at least, much of the trade was composed of a chain of elements, dependent on local traders and shippers, moving the goods along bit by bit without any clear notion of the final destinations or consumers. This intricate supply chain from east to west meant that the volume of the shipment to Europe was unlikely ever to be great, however significant the geopolitics of the spice trade. European imports of pepper were no more than about 1000 tons in 1400, and other spices added up to about 500 tons, with roughly half the imports finding their way to Venice. Trade within Asia accounted for the greater part of the volume. The countries which were large consumers, notably India and China, were not only major producers but also the dominant importers and exporters. As argued by Findlay and O'Rourke (2007: 140–141), the structure of the spice trade in the world before Columbus suggests "the utter dependence of Europe on Asian market conditions" and the fact that Asia "dictated the pace of intercontinental trade."

Black pepper was the foundation of the ancient spice routes, shipped from southern India to China in quantities much greater than the equivalent trade to the Roman Empire. Cloves and nutmegs (and their mace) came from the Moluccas, together with ginger, turmeric, and cardamom. Again, much of this product was not destined for the west but went north to the great markets found in China.

A parallel trade from the Indonesian archipelago to China flourished in commodities other than spices, items that were rarely if ever appreciated in the west, and sometimes not consumed by the producers themselves. For example, trepang, also known as sea cucumber, sea slug, and bêche-de-mer, was a Chinese culinary delicacy, known from the seventeenth century, sent north by specialist Makassar traders who sourced it from fishermen who voyaged as far as Papua and the coasts of northern Australia (Jun, 2007: 25).

Grain

In ancient times, imperial powers worked hard to secure basic foodstuffs for their cities and armies, stretching their chain of supply into colonized regions or places over which they had hegemony. The ability to ensure the food supply of a large urban population was essential to good government and shortfalls demanded political solutions. Notably, the Romans depended heavily on imported wheat, procured by a carefully monitored cohort of private traders and drawn from the vast fields they commanded, stretching from northern Africa to the Black Sea. Grain also sometimes flowed in reverse in order to resolve seasonal and climatic differences.

Fundamental to the development of trade routes in the ancient world, and indeed until recent centuries, was the relatively low cost of transport on water and the high cost of moving goods over land. In the time of the Roman Empire, it was cheaper to ship wheat from one end of the Mediterranean to the other than to move it much more than 60 miles (100 km) on land. This gave a competitive advantage to producers located close to coasts, so that Egypt could ship grain to Rome more cheaply than farmers in the Italian hinterland could cart their wares to the city. Islands, even small ones, could also compete in this regime because they had access to maritime trade, hence the importance of Sardinia and Sicily in the Roman grain trade.

This Roman imperial pattern was not based on a system of settler colonization undertaken to generate trade, and indeed in some cases the establishment of surplus populations in distant places was intended as a way of avoiding the need to move food over great distances. Nor was it an equal exchange. The best wheat was likely to find its way to Rome, whereas inferior grains (barley, millet, oats, and rye, for example) and poorer qualities (blended perhaps with beans and other legumes) were more likely to form the ingredients of the porridges and breads of the peoples of the frontier. The system enabled the well-off city dweller to eat white bread, while the common people had only black bread or, worse, bread made from bran rather than milled flour. In late antiquity and throughout the Middle Ages, European cities and towns often faced a more precarious existence because they lacked control of the surrounding agricultural countryside.

In Africa, ruling elites maintained rural bases to ensure supply. Only the great cities of the western Sudan, notably Timbuktu, were exposed to such risks in their food supply, depending on distant grain producers and vulnerable caravans. The result was the early emergence of an internal grain trade, controlled by a professional merchant class, with the capacity to choose not to provide what was wanted. There was also an export of grain from Mombasa and Malindi across the Arabian Sea. Most pre-colonial African political elites ensured their supplies by demanding annual requisitions of their subject peoples, often spread over quite large regions, creating a flow of grain and livestock, shea butter, kola, and oil, which was not a trade but rather a chain of tribute. Elsewhere in the ancient world, farmers sometimes sold produce not because it was surplus but because they needed money to pay rents and taxes. In these systems, demand and supply responded to political objectives rather than market mechanisms.

Modern trades

John Keay (2006: xii) has made the desire for spices responsible for modern world exploration, at least in its European Renaissance incarnation, and for "the developments in shipbuilding, navigational science and ballistics that eventually gave the maritime powers of western Europe superiority over other nations and led on to dominion and power." In these ways, the ancient spice routes with their complex, attenuated chains of supply were transformed by the desire of European shippers to monopolize the trade by taking control of the product from the hands of its producers and carrying the spice in a single sea voyage in a single ship. Further, European imperialism carried many of the major spices, nutmeg, cinnamon, pepper, for example, from their original homes in Asia to new regions of the Americas, establishing the foundations of global production and consumption as well as competition. This redistribution quite quickly made what had been exotic common, with significant consequences for the development of culinary styles and cuisines, as will be seen in Chapter 8.

The other major commodity of ancient trade, salt, developed in contrasting directions in the modern world, though regularly taking its traditional role as an object of state regulation (particularly in regard to prices) and taxation. European traders along the coast of western Africa from the sixteenth century stimulated the development of a thriving salt-making industry using boiling techniques. Some of this salt was sold upcountry in competition with Saharan salt and some of it used to preserve fish, which was also sold upcountry (Sutton, 1981). In China, formerly the technological leader, the market was by the early nineteenth century freed from close regulation but not opened to imports. Western Europe and particularly England, as principal beneficiary of the Industrial Revolution, massively increased output and began to export large quantities of salt almost everywhere around the globe, competing with local industries, but excluding China. Production and trade in salt increased dramatically in the twentieth century but a declining proportion of the product was used in food, much of it then going to industrial chemical processes dependent on its principal components, chlorine and sodium.

Salt lost its role as a prime medium of preservation during the nineteenth century, displaced by canning and freezing. By the end of the twentieth century, the canners and freezers of vegetables in turn began to face competition in the supermarkets of the prosperous West from fresh foods flown in from distant places out of season. Consumers were encouraged to believe that such products were superior in nutrition and taste to the preserved varieties, and encouraged to pay premium prices. It was argued, on the other hand, that these fresh vegetables had traveled so far that they had lost most of their vitamins and minerals, whereas produce "snap frozen" within hours of harvest retained their nutritional value much better. Thus, for example, frozen peas, cauliflower, carrots, and corn might be just as nutritious as fresh product imported to Austria out of season from Israel, Turkey, or Spain. Similarly, it was argued that long-life orange juice was just as healthy as the juice squeezed from well-traveled and possibly long-stored oranges. To this nutritional critique was added the voice of those who pointed to the high cost to the environment of this new pattern of trade and the staggering food miles involved.

Meat

The invention of continuous refrigeration was particularly important in enabling long-distance trades in highly perishable foods such as meat and dairy products. This innovation favored exporters in Australia and New Zealand, beginning in the 1870s, when frozen beef and mutton were first shipped to Britain. The development of large-scale supply also depended on the laying of extensive railroad systems within the settler/colonial grazing regions, a process hardly begun in 1870 but effectively complete by 1910 in the United States, Argentina, and Uruguay, as well as Australia and New Zealand.

The era of Free Trade and British dominance was, however, followed by the protectionism of the 1930s. Although the General Agreement on Tariffs and Trade (GATT) of 1947 was intended to reduce tariffs and remove quotas, many trades, including meat, continued to be bound by preferences and subsidies, particularly in Europe and the United States. Various kinds of legislation were used to inhibit the import of meat by states anxious to support their own farmers (and secure the votes of rural lobbies). From 1945 to 1985 the United States was in many years a net importer of meat, but after 1985 its long-established tradition of giving protection to its farmers made it once again a significant exporter of beef, and increasingly of pork and poultry meat. A more genuine global easing of trade restrictions after 1990 had a significant impact but some sectors grew more rapidly than others and some declined absolutely.

Dried and salted meats declined steeply as items of international trade, largely disappearing by the 1960s. Canned meat remained important much longer, world exports reaching four million tons by 2007. Trade in the meat of sheep doubled after 1950 to reach one million tons in 2007 but the trade in goat meat was much smaller, at just 40 000 tons. Growth was much greater in pork (eight million tons in 2007) and beef (seven million tons).

The most spectacular increase in the international meat trade was in poultry. As noted in Chapter 3, production of poultry meat increased ten-fold after 1950. Only about 10 percent of this total entered international trade, but exports leapt from just 50 000 tons in 1950, to four million tons in 1995, and ten million tons in 2007. Rarely canned, dried, smoked, or salted, almost all of this phenomenal increase in trade consisted of frozen chicken meat. It was not always a trade in whole chickens. The growing dissection of bodies, with legs packed in a single supermarket packet and thighs in another, created a surplus of parts unwanted by consumers in the more prosperous countries. Developing countries imported chicken necks and backs as well as prime cuts.

The same applied to the meat of other animals, though to a lesser extent. Thus the tails and trotters of pigs brought to fatness in US factory farms were exported while the wealthy lived high on the hog – meaning, literally, to eat the best of the beast. Similarly, in the late twentieth century the bellies (flaps) of sheep, almost 50 percent fat, began to be exported frozen from Australia and New Zealand, where these cuts were no longer much eaten, to markets in the Pacific Islands. This was a trade rooted in cheapness rather than taste (Gewertz and Errington, 2010). But different cultures favored different cuts, so that to some extent demand balanced out differences in taste as well as price. For example, East Asian consumers paid relatively high prices for the internal organs and offal of pigs and cows. These markets were exploited particularly by the United States, but in the 1990s it also exported grain-fed beef to Japan and Korea while at the same time importing grass-fed beef from Australia and New Zealand to make hamburgers (Perren, 2006: 182).

Counter to these trends dependent on new modes of preservation, a large trade in live animals developed in the late twentieth century. An international trade had long been important but typically this was confined to driving cattle across land borders or shipping across narrow waters, as from continental Europe to the United Kingdom, which was the world's largest market for meat in the nineteenth century. Long-distance shipping of animals for breeding involved only small numbers. The shipping of live animals with the intention of slaughtering them on arrival at market was limited and particularly from the late nineteenth century often feared because of the prevalence of foot-and-mouth disease (Perren, 2006: 23–39). By 1914 the United Kingdom had ended importation of live animals for meat from South America and Europe, and the United States had ceased exporting because it no longer had a surplus, leaving only the minor trade from Ireland. In 1945, the trade seemed near to an end.

Revival of the trade in live animals for meat began in the 1960s, with the emergence of demand from newly rich oil states and Islamic countries with rapid population growth. The supply now came mainly from Australia and New Zealand. Specialized ships, each capable of holding as many as 50 000 sheep, were devoted to carrying cargoes to places with particular market needs, notably Indonesia and the Middle East where Muslim consumers demanded meat from animals slaughtered in accordance with religious rules. Cattle and camels were also exported. Cases of heavy onboard mortality during long voyages through the tropics and questions over the treatment of the animals on arrival at their destinations led to increasingly strong protests from animal welfare groups. The trade was interrupted but, with large profits to be made, not permanently halted. In 2007 Australia exported four million live sheep, down from the peak of seven million reached in 1983.

Grain

Other twentieth-century changes in the pattern of international trade in food occurred independent of innovations in preservation technologies. One of the most significant of these was the transformation of grain exports and imports. Before the middle of the twentieth century, the world trade in grain was essentially a transfer to industrialized, urbanized Europe from the fields of their settler/colonial outposts, a modern variety of imperial reach that recalled the ancient Roman economy. Initially, this trade developed from urban European demand, where the large industrial workforces were completely dependent on other countries to produce their food. The establishment of modern plantation economies and the emergence of export-oriented peasant sectors in the tropics did foreshadow later patterns. For example, the growth of peanut- and oil-producing populations in western Africa before World War II made the people dependent on imports of rice (from southeastern Asia) and wheat flour. But Africa as a whole was not a net importer of grain until after 1970.

World trade in cereals grew from about 30 million tons in 1950 to more than 200 million tons in 1980 and 330 million tons in 2007. In contrast to the pattern of production, by the early twentieth century the most exported grain was wheat, followed by maize, with rice a distant third. Regionally, only Western Europe was a net importer of grain before World War II, with the United Kingdom by far the largest consumer. Outside this industrialized zone, states consumed what they produced or yielded a surplus for export. This balance was overturned dramatically in the postwar world. By the 1970s almost all countries had become importers of grain, the only significant long-term exceptions being the United States, Canada, Australia, Argentina, and France. The basis of this transformation was a great growth in demand from developing countries, which increased their imports from barely five million tons in 1950 to more than 100 million by 1980. The fastest growth in grain imports occurred in Latin America, followed by Africa and the Middle East. On the supply side there was a narrowing, giving an increased role to the North American producers who in 2007 accounted for almost 40 percent of cereals exports and a greater proportion of the maize (Morrison, 1984: 13–26; Wagstaff, 1982). Smaller exporters sometimes curtailed their trade in times of stress, for example when Russia suffered devastating drought in 2010 and was unable to meet demand in its usual Middle Eastern and North African markets.

The origins of this transformation were rapid population growth in the developing world and the increasing relative wealth and income of these economies, many of them emerging from long histories of European imperialism. Changing lifestyles went hand in hand with the promotion of grains by nutritionists and governments, and with the global regulation of trade policy. Gloomier interpretations viewed the growing dependence of developing states on imported food as evidence of failing agricultural self-sufficiency, a prelude to famine and conflict. This pessimistic view reflected the historical experience that economic development almost always depended on parallel growth in agricultural output and productivity, rather than a growing dependence on imported food supplies, with the possible exception of the Netherlands in the seventeenth century. Fears also surrounded the increasing concentration of production in a handful of states, which might use food as a weapon, and the climatic and genetic vulnerability of concentration on a severely limited number of plant species and even varieties.

In part, the great increase in grain imports to developing countries since about 1950 reflects an increased overall import of food. In many cases, however, the grain trade stands out as the leader in this process. Wheat and rice replaced local roots and tubers in some regions, notably southeastern Asia, as a result of a shift to bread and other baked products, signified by the promotion of white bread as a superior, industrial, food (Bobrow-Strain, 2008). African rice had a comparative disadvantage compared to Asian rice, and often it became cheaper to import rice and wheat than to transport cassava and corn from their local producers to the cities of western Africa. Wheat was more important than rice in international trade, however, because about 95 percent of world rice production was consumed locally and because developing countries accounted for 90 percent of that production. In 2007 a total of 148 million tons of wheat was exported, the leading suppliers being the United States (33 million tons), Canada (18), Australia (15), Russia (14), and France (14). The leading importers were Brazil (seven million tons), followed by Egypt, Italy, Japan, Algeria, the Netherlands, Morocco, and Indonesia.

By the end of the twentieth century, food aid programs played a large role in the promotion of rice imports to countries which were not producers, displacing local starchy staples, and appealing to demand from growing urbanized middle-income populations. This trend created trouble and even civil disturbance when the price of rice rose beyond what poor people could afford, for example in Liberia in 1979 and again in 2008 when riots occurred in Haiti. The other major traded grain was corn, which played a different role in food systems, with a large proportion of it being used to feed animals in feedlots, marking a major change in consumption patterns toward meat. For this reason, middle-income countries increased their imports of grain more rapidly than low-income countries.

The global supermarket

Supermarkets are now known around the world, icons of the globalization of the food system and abundance. They represent the final stage of the food chains that supply almost everything imaginable at a single site. The supermarket appeared first in the United States, founded on the self-service grocery concept that emerged around 1912, making use of new-style cafeteria restaurants. The self-service model expanded only slowly at first, particularly because there was disjunction between the capacity of existing shopping bags and baskets and the weight of the goods that could be selected from self-serve shelves. The motor car solved the problem of getting home heavy loads of shopping, but the problem of moving the goods from the shelves to the car was not solved until 1936, when the supermarket shopping cart was developed (Figure 6.1). Long-haul refrigerated trucking came into its own in the 1950s, beginning in the United States, making possible the rapid and cheap distribution of frozen and chilled items, and giving supermarkets increasing power over the geographical pattern of production (Hamilton, 2008: 122).

The supermarket and its cart started their joint global conquest in the 1950s, spreading to places where many customers did not have cars and who sometimes captured the cart as a vehicle to push their burdens homeward, stretching the global food chain to breaking point (Grandclément, 2009). The model varied with levels of prosperity but was rarely hindered by borders or politics, flourishing in its essentials even in socialist societies by the end of the 1960s. The deregulation of foreign investment in many countries led by the 1990s to the entry of hypermarkets, which often resulted in the collapse of local smaller-scale supermarkets.

Supermarkets proved highly successful in capturing the many specialized trades of small shopkeepers and equally took customers away from traditional periodic produce markets. This occurred first in the United States and other industrialized economies but also affected developing countries by the beginning of the twenty-first century. Then, the share of supermarkets in domestic food retailing was as high as 80 percent in the United States, Germany, France, and the United Kingdom. The chains held a 60 percent share in places like Brazil and Argentina, and 50 percent in Mexico, South Africa, Poland, and Thailand. In China, where there had been no supermarkets as late as 1989, their share had risen to 10 percent, but in India the proportion remained just five percent (Francesconi, Heerink and D'Haese, 2010: 61). Typically, small shops are the first to be forced out, followed by sellers of dairy products and

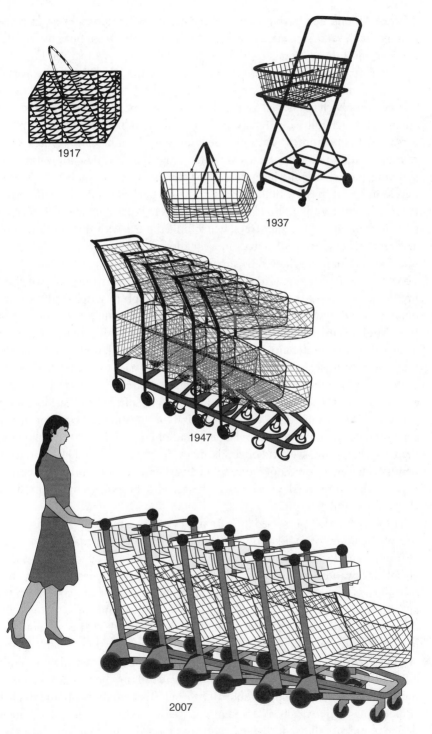

1917

1937

1947

2007

Figure 6.1   Evolution of the supermarket cart/trolley.

processed foods, and fresh produce. Niche market goods survive best. In some regions, however, a separate competition opened up between both traditional markets and modern retailers, and the growing armies of street vendors who took advantage of structural adjustment programs that made imports cheaper.

Innovations in transportation enabled supermarkets to extend their reach into the supply chain as well as distribution. Until the invention of the steam engine and the railroad, transport over land remained significantly more expensive than shipment on water. Beginning in the nineteenth century, the railroad shifted this comparative advantage significantly, but innovations in shipping, particularly the invention of the container ship in the 1950s and the development of massive bulk carriers, shifted it back again. By the end of the twentieth century the railroad had lost ground to trucks big enough to carry shipping containers on their trays, which linked ports with distribution hubs and regional agricultural sources in a far more flexible way that fed directly into the domination achieved by supermarket chains.

Before the supermarket, most goods came to the retail grocery shop or store in a large bag, box, or barrel. It was the retailer's job to weigh and measure quantities and to wrap orders in paper if necessary, serving one customer at a time. The consumer could not pick and choose but depended on the grocer for information and preference or prejudice. In the US South down to the 1960s, for example, African-American customers often had to wait while white customers were served, only to be sold inferior products which had been put aside especially. The supermarket and self-service offered partial liberation from such discrimination, through a kind of personalization. For many shoppers the supermarket offered a new kind of cultural experience, allowing them to enter a fantasy world of goods, many of which they could hold in their hands even if they could not aspire to buying them. At least on the surface, the supermarket promoted variety and choice, and bespoke a celebration of abundance (Tolbert, 2009).

The supermarket possessed a clean and hygienic – modern – atmosphere, free of the odors of moldy flour and unidentifiable putrid matter. The busy customer could move swiftly through the system, not having to wait on those ahead who wanted to gossip, even taking advantage of express lines. On the other hand, home-delivery was less commonly available from supermarkets and store credit often unknown in the era before the credit card. Selling milk cheaply in supermarkets, often at a loss, was a vital means of enticing customers into the store, and a means to the end of home delivery enterprise. Strangely, early self-serve designers hoped to introduce a scientific notion of efficient flow, laying out narrow aisles with gates along the way that ensured one-way movement. Shoppers soon subverted this concept, stopping to chat and forcing their way back to items missed or remembered. More open designs quickly followed, making the experience less mechanical and more personal and social. It was a development parallel to the social transformation of the telephone, which had been seen at first, by its designers, as a vehicle for simple and direct messages rather than expansive chatter.

In the modern hypermarket, and even in relatively small supermarkets, the shopper is bombarded by images and messages, creating the contemporary version of the omnivore's dilemma. Confronted by an abundance of variety, the consumer has to choose between maintaining a conservative list and chancing the unknown (Pollan, 2006: 15). Whereas in the forest the items to be eaten could be inspected directly, in the supermarket much of the potential food is concealed within packaging, the contents frequently bearing no simple relationship to the biodiversity of the natural world. Brand names, colors, and logos became an important part of marketing and even the shape of a bottle or package could be made distinctive and recognizable in the global market. Thus, whereas the traditional colors and lettering of potato chip packages became iconic, as used by Smith's, for example, packing them in a tube gave an innovative edge to the Pringles company. Most consumers in modern industrial societies are willing to pay more than the lowest possible price for goods they favor and it is the packaging that is most likely to lead them to do so. Very often, potential purchasers are unable to see any part of the product within a container, so they rely entirely on brand names and information printed on labels to guide them in their choice.

These images and messages track between advertising and the growth of self-service supermarket shopping where the consumer was for the first time confronted with a vast array of competing products, jostling for space on the shelves and in the frozen-food bins, all anxious to make themselves more desirable than their rivals. This gave yet another dimension to the notion of choice. Consumers were forced to make their own decisions about which brand, which mix of additives, and which price per unit offered the best buy. Products previously not regarded as unique or brandable, such as milk, came to be packed in an array of shapes, sizes, colors, and logos. Paper rather than glass containers had many advantages, not least their suitability for the printing of brands and advertising material. Supermarket chains even came to find an advantage in offering generic varieties at cut prices in order to entice those purchasers unimpressed by the hype. However, individual hygienic packaging remained the norm in these enterprises. Only cooperatives and communal consumer groups maintained bulk bins from which sugar, flour, and peas might be ladled. The notion that milk might once again be dipped from canisters was unappealing to almost everyone.

The traditional grocer's task had been much simpler and specialized because many products that are now stocked by supermarkets were formerly distributed among specialized sellers – butchers, fishmongers, delicatessens, bakers, greengrocers, pharmacists, and the like – many of whom in urban settlements provided home delivery. This was particularly true of milk and meat. Preserved and processed dairy and meat products might, however, find their way into the grocer's store, for example saltfish or pickled pork and beef. The saltfish could be stored dry and chopped into pieces to be weighed. Pickled pork and beef, on the other hand, remained in its brine, in a barrel set in the corner of the store, into which shoppers could dip their hands and arms in search of an attractive piece to purchase. These methods of storage and sale persisted to the very end of the twentieth century in the many places around the world that lacked electricity and refrigeration.

In the ancient world, specialized markets for food products had appeared early in association with the emergence of urban settlements. The larger the demographic base, the more differentiated the sellers of commodities. At the same time, the larger the market and the more complex the supply chain, the more probable the seller would not also be the producer and the more probable sellers would offer a variety of related goods. Thus, by the second century BC Rome had specialized cattle and pig markets, as did other Italian cities. Animals were brought from the countryside and sold live, then killed and quartered by butchers at their own shops. Other meat sold in these Roman markets came from animals that had been sacrificed or slaughtered in the arena, these including stags and exotic species. There was also in Rome a special area for use by sellers of fresh and preserved fish. Similar systems of food market specialization persisted strongly into the eighteenth century, throughout Europe and its colonial extensions. Typically, they were the subject of close government regulation, though often more with regard to price and availability than quality and sanitation, because food markets were reliable sources of revenue.

Two claims

The first claim is that transport technologies were the fundamental drivers of trade, determining what foods were worth exchanging and what routes viable. In the long term, the balance between the cost of land and water transport shifted significantly, several times, thus changing the viability of island and coastal producers relative to those located far from ports. As transport costs became an increasingly small proportion of the final prices of food products, as a result of technological change, patterns of land utilization were increasingly determined by global markets and patterns of consumption were made more uniform, seasonally and regionally.

Second, Freedman (2008: 128–9) argues that it was the great demand for spices in medieval European culinary styles that underpinned the most extensive early networks of world trade, and that it was a perception of the rarity and hence immense potential profit offered by spices that encouraged voyagers to brave unknown perils in venturing out across uncharted seas. A consequence was the discovery that these precious materials were less rare than imagined. The geographical redistribution that followed made some of them common, a discovery that had a large role in the development of cuisines and in the expansion of Europe.

REFERENCES

Adshead, S.A.M. (1992) *Salt and Civilization*. Christchurch, New Zealand: Canterbury University Press.

Austen, R.A. (2010) *Trans-Saharan Africa in World History*. Oxford: Oxford University Press.

Bobrow-Strain, A. (2008) White bread bio-politics: Purity, health, and the triumph of industrial baking. *Cultural Geographies* 15: 19–40.

Findlay, R. and O'Rourke, K.H. (2007) *Power and Plenty: Trade, War, and the World Economy in the Second Millennium*. Princeton: Princeton University Press.

Francesconi, G.N., Heerink, N. and D'Haese, M. (2010) Evolution and challenges of dairy supply chains: Evidence from supermarkets, industries and consumers in Ethiopia. *Food Policy* 35: 60–68.

Freedman, P. (2008) *Out of the East: Spices and the Medieval Imagination*. New Haven, CT: Yale University Press.

Gewertz, D. and Errington, F. (2010) *Cheap Meat: Flap Food Nations of the Pacific Islands*. Berkeley, CA: University of California Press.

Grandclément, C. (2009) Wheeling one's own groceries around the store: The invention of the shopping cart, 1936–1953. In W. Belasco and R. Horowitz (eds), *Food Chains: From Farmyard to Shopping Cart*, pp. 233–51. Philadelphia: University of Pennsylvania Press.

Hamilton, S. (2008) *Trucking Country: The Road to America's Wal-Mart Economy*. Princeton: Princeton University Press.

Jun, A. (2007) *Namako* and *Iriko*: Historical overview on *Holothuria* (sea cucumber) exploitation, utilization, and trade in Japan. In S.C.H. Cheung and T. Chee-Beng (eds) *Food and Foodways in Asia: Resource, Tradition and Cooking*, pp. 23–36. London: Routledge.

Keay, J. (2006) *The Spice Route: A History*. Berkeley, CA: University of California Press.

Morrison, T.K. (1984) Cereal imports by developing countries: Trends and determinants. *Food Policy* 9: 13–26.

Perdue, P.C. (2005) *China Marches West: The Qing Conquest of Central Eurasia*. Cambridge, MA: Harvard University Press.

Perren, R. (2006) *Taste, Trade and Technology: The Development of the International Meat Industry since 1840*. Aldershot, UK: Ashgate.

Pollan, M. (2006) *The Omnivore's Dilemma: A Natural History of Four Meals*. London: Penguin Books.

Smith, R.E.F. and Christian, D. (1984) *Bread and Salt: A Social and Economic History of Food and Drink in Russia*. Cambridge: Cambridge University Press.

Sutton, I.B. (1981) The Volta River salt trade: The survival of an indigenous industry. *Journal of African History* 22: 43–61.

Thurmond, D.L. (2006) *A Handbook of Food Processing in Classical Rome: For Her Bounty No Winter*. Leiden: Brill.

Tolbert, L.C. (2009) The aristocracy of the market basket: Self-service food shopping in the New South. In W. and R. Horowitz (eds), *Food Chains: From Farmyard to Shopping Cart*, pp. 179–95. Philadelphia: University of Pennsylvania Press.

Wagstaff, H. (1982) Food imports of developing countries. *Food Policy* 7: 57–68.

CHAPTER SEVEN

Cooking, Class, and Consumption

Choices about how to prepare (cook) and consume (eat) are limited by choices about what to hunt, gather, herd, and cultivate, and what to process and exchange. Before the supermarket and before the motor car made it possible, even mandatory, that consumers travel long distances to choose from seemingly endless alternatives, choices about what to cook were largely limited to what had been brought to the door by family farmers and hunters, exchanged with near neighbors, or delivered by hawkers and provisioners.

Differences across time and between cultures, in methods of cooking and manners of eating, are quite strong, driven by differences in taste and contrasting understandings of the social order, together with variant technologies. It is equally clear that decisions about how to cook and how to eat have an impact on choices about ingredients and how to obtain them, and on choices about the effort put into the development of alternative technologies. Some of these choices and decisions are made by consumers and cooks; others by commercial enterprises, institutions, and states.

Cooks

Until affordable industrial processed foods became cheap and readily available – beginning in the late nineteenth century, as discussed in the previous chapter – most of the world's peoples ate food prepared by members of their own households or by other people who belonged to their immediate communities. However, whereas everyone ate, not everyone cooked. This distinction was typically rooted in social hierarchy, notably gender, but also related to age and

How Food Made History, First Edition. B. W. Higman.
© 2012 B. W. Higman. Published 2012 by Blackwell Publishing Ltd.

physical capacity. The notion that cooking was a special skill and craft, which might be developed into a career and profession, existed from early times in unique niches, such as the royal households of the Egyptians, but for most people for most of history cooking was not much more than a task.

For most of history, cooking was merely one element in the long string of activities leading all the way through hunting and gathering or the cultivation and harvesting of crops, to their sometimes laborious processing, the collection of fuel, and the making of tools and cooking pots. Only in recent times, in industrialized societies, has household economy become limited in a way that makes the act of cooking a peculiarly active productive process in which physical materials are transformed within the household prior to consumption. Before industrialization, even in most cities, women, men, and children participated in a way of life that typically required the chopping of wood, the lighting of fires, the burning of charcoal, the fetching of water, the pounding of tubers and grains, the plucking of ducks, and the making of sausages. The idea of "housework" comprehended all of these tasks, together with a great amount of time-consuming labor on activities unconnected with food. Householders also had to build and repair their dwellings, make their own soap and candles, and make and repair their own clothes, often starting from scratch with textile and skin. Nomadic pastoralists and hunter-gatherer peoples undertook much the same range of tasks, sometimes with added complexity and difficulty.

With all these demands, the process of cooking had to be accommodated within the rhythm of daily household production, using limited sources of heat. Much the same applied to family groups across all cultures and farming systems, from hunters and gatherers to preindustrial peasants. Only the few who lived in large urban centers depended on others to perform some of the tasks associated with housework. All of the household tasks were performed without the aid of manuals, and the cooking similarly took place without reference to recipes or cookbooks. The rawness of many of the processes of food preparation meant that they were often performed in the open air, and the hazardousness and smokiness of fires pushed cooks into separate structures. The result was a relatively narrow range of meals. Among hunter-gatherers, roasting and steaming dominated. In agrarian societies based on grains, there was an emphasis on porridges and stews.

Wherever householders could afford it, their cooking was done by servants or enslaved people. In ancient Rome, the enslaved cook often had a role in literature and drama, as a symbol of luxury and decadence, but in the social life of the elite household the cook was in fact a central figure, required to take charge of the elaborate preparations essential to the staging of indulgent banquets and lesser dinners. The cook who failed, bringing dishonor to the household, might be beaten or otherwise suffer the consequences (Joshel,

2010: 17–26). The relationship was much the same in the slave societies of the Americas, even though in the long term the work of the enslaved (African) cook came to be recognized as the source of highly regarded national, regional, and ethnic cuisines.

Cooking and culture were transformed by industrialization. New technologies rapidly reduced the range of productive activities located within the household. Milled flour, readymade clothing and factory-produced candles and soap replaced homemade versions. Where this occurred (by about 1920 in the case of the United States) men and children were largely liberated from the demands of housework, making substantial gains in leisure time. The burden became focussed almost exclusively on the women of the house and the kitchen became the woman's domain (Flammang, 2009: 26–7; Cowan, 1983: 17–18). The greater the range of technologies available – from piped water to electricity and gas, toaster to microwave – the more common it became to expect the women of the house to carry the full load of food preparation. In rural China, until recent times, the cooking was typically done by the younger women of a household, most of them daughters-in-law who often took it in turns on a ten-day rotation. Whereas the preindustrial system of shared roles applied almost universally across agrarian cultures and farming systems, the emergence of the industrial model opened up a great gap between the industrialized world and all of those peoples who were slow or reluctant to follow the same path.

An even wider gap appeared after about 1960 when householders in the most advanced industrial economies, led by the United States, were able to stop cooking altogether and become almost totally reliant on commercially prepared foods, bought in ready to eat or needing simply to be warmed. The sociability (and inevitable conflict) associated with lengthy food-processing tasks was completely gone and even the communal act of eating together became a rarity.

Reaction to these trends emerged by the 1990s, with the "slow food" movement that sought to bring back elements of the more traditional pattern of task-sharing and food-sharing, often in conjunction with notions of producing food on "organic" principles and sourcing ingredients from within a narrow radius of the consumer, and often driven by a growing concern for the environment and the threat of climate change. These movements struggled to compete with the more independent, commercially driven, models. The trend was not confined to the most developed, industrialized countries. Something similar occurred in Thailand, for example, where street food, purchased from vendors, stallholders, markets, cook shops, and restaurants – displaced home-cooking after about 1970. This modern pattern was countered by advocates of the old ways, some of them setting up schools to teach traditional techniques to young Thais seeking a connection with the past.

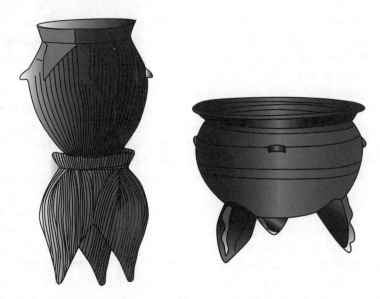

Figure 7.1   Ancient Chinese cooking vessels. Based on H.T. Huang, *Fermentations and Food Science*, Part V, Vol. 6, *Joseph Needham, Science and Civilisation in China* (Cambridge: Cambridge University Press, 2000), 77–79.

Cooking

From the earliest times, styles of cooking were most varied in China. The Chinese applied these techniques to a range of acceptable ingredients which was also broader than that eaten in most other places. Documentation begins with the Chou period (11th–3rd century BC), when the most important methods were boiling, steaming, roasting, simmering-stewing, pickling, and drying. Poaching, steeping, baking, grilling, and shallow-frying (using little oil) were also practiced but less common. Most important among the techniques missing from the list are the now-common varieties of frying, including stir-frying, that require more substantial quantities of oil.

Chou cooking vessels were made both of pottery and bronze, some of them designed specifically for steaming and others for boiling and simmering/stewing, and ranging in size from small pots to large cauldrons (Figure 7.1). Their stove, *tsao*, is known only in pottery, and pottery was also the typical material used for storage jars, whether they contained dry commodities such as grain or liquid sauces and pickles. Occasionally, cooking could be achieved without the use of a vessel. The earliest recipe for what is now called "beggar's chicken" comes from the Chou period: the bird wrapped in leaves, then coated with clay and baked in the fire. Boiling without a vessel was harder to achieve, though steaming rice in a basket over a pot of boiling water was easy enough. Boiling rice in a bamboo joint occurred in India into the seventeenth century, even longer elsewhere. In special circumstances, for example when hunters traversed forests, softer foods such as tubers could be boiled or steamed in a leaf-lined cavity dug in the ground, covered with sticks and leaves and a fire made on top.

In addition to this wide range of methods, Chou cooking was also characterized by the abiding Chinese style of careful preparation of ingredients, by slicing, chopping, and mincing, and the combining of flavors and ingredients to create distinctive dishes. In addition to flavor mixing, Chou cooking depended on the application of different amounts of heat, for differing lengths of time, together with variations in seasoning, to generate hundreds of individual dishes ranging from the simple to the complex (Chang, 1977: 31–41). These dishes, or *tshai* – particularly meat, cooked by fire, to distinguish the civilized from the barbarians who ate it raw – were from early times distinguished clearly from *shih*, the word meaning both the grain which formed the basis of every meal and the meal itself. For the rich as well as the poor, the consumption of larger proportions of grain food was regarded as a virtue.

Both millet and rice were washed and soaked before steaming to become *fan*, or cooked grain. Wheat grains are too hard to be eaten whole and were therefore ground to make *mien shih*, or flour, for breads and pastas. Pasta and noodles were made from the flour of rice and millet as well as that of wheat, and known as early as 400 BC, produced in increasing varieties of shape and thickness, leavened and unleavened, and mixed with everything from bone marrow to honey. These doughs formed the foundations for *man-thou* (steamed bun) and *hun-thun* (wonton). In the long term, beginning around AD 200, these two styles of cooking grain led to a distinct culinary contrast between the north and the south of China. In the south, cooked grains were eaten whole; in the north, products made with wheat flour dominated. Eventually, *fan* came to be used exclusively for steamed rice, and replaced *shih* as a word that might also mean a meal (Huang, 2000: 466–91). The division within China, between north and south, mirrored a wider cultural pattern, in which the Chinese alone enjoyed noodles and steamed buns made from wheat flour, but had little enthusiasm for the kinds of wheat flour breads preferred in India – the chapattis, nans, rotis, and their relatives – and the numerous variations of the early Islamic world, using skills inherited from ancient Egypt. There were, however, some larger areas of convergence in ancient cooking styles.

For the poor of ancient China, a common dish was *keng*, a thick broth made from grains and meat. This was a style of cooking well known throughout Asia and the Middle East down to the seventeenth century, in which the slow boiling together of varied grains, vegetables, and sometimes meat reflected its source in a mixed system of food production. Toward the west and the regions of dryland farming, it was matched by porridge-like dishes made from millet, barley, and rice, combined with lentils, beans, and split peas. In India this was commonly known as *khichri*, with ghee poured over it.

In the Middle East, at the interface of agriculture and pastoralism, meat and lumps of fat were more likely to be included in stewed dishes of this sort. The Prophet was said to enjoy *tharid*, a dish composed of crumbled bread, vegetables, and meat, together with a compound of butter, dates, and milk. These styles survived into the twentieth century in the form of *harisa*, a slow-cooked dish that combined meat with washed wheat, animal fat, and spices, and was the favorite of all classes, from the starving poor to the satiated elite (Chaudhuri, 1990: 165–6). This was from early Islamic times regarded as a dish best made in quantity by professional harisa cooks, being placed under regulation, particularly regarding the minimum acceptable amount of meat and the purity of the fat. In Baghdad, which had a population of more than a million by AD 1100, and other large cities, harisa sellers often provided rooms, with tables and mats, for their customers.

The origins of the cooking styles developed in ancient China seem to be located almost entirely within its own territory. Whereas China introduced numerous varieties of plants, and adapted these to their own methods of preparation, the same did not apply to cooking styles. Rather, China was a hub from which styles were diffused throughout Asia and occasionally to the West. To some extent, it was always easier to move a seed or seedling around the globe to a new location than to transfer a technology or culinary technique because the seed or seedling might successfully travel unaccompanied. For example, there is no doubt that noodles were a Chinese creation. Early, crude forms reached Japan by about AD 900, along with *hun-thun* made from a flat sheet of dough. The Japanese variety *udon*, made by slicing thinly a piece of dough rolled flat, arrived from China in the fifteenth century, a little after the introduction of *man-thou*. Tofu, a soybean product, probably reached Japan from China somewhat earlier, carried there by Buddhist monks who took the necessary presses with them. Transfer of noodles to Korea followed a similar pattern, but movement westward, to Central Asia, Mongolia, and Tibet, was quicker.

Surprisingly, *la-mien* (filamentous noodles) – produced by repeatedly stretching a loop of dough to create hundreds of thin strands – only went westward, whereas *chhieh-mien* (sliced noodles) traveled in every direction, to become the most common noodle throughout Asia (Huang, 2000: 491–7). However, the popular notion that Marco Polo brought filamentous noodles (the precursors of spaghetti) from China to Italy in the thirteenth century is not well founded. They were known in Italy much earlier, perhaps even in Roman times, and may also have traveled the Silk Road through the Islamic Middle East, centuries before Marco Polo, but failed to find favor along the way until they found a receptive home in Italy, where they blended easily with the indigenous varieties of pasta. Even in Italy, noodles attained true popularity only after the seventeenth century, with the combination of spaghetti and tomato sauce, derived from the fruit of the Americas, one of the great achievements of food-combining. The global spread of noodles was, however, a Japanese achievement, derived from the invention of instant noodles in the 1950s.

Eating places

However similar the food eaten by different groups within a single community, social distinction could always be enforced, even created, by rules governing who could eat with whom, where, and under what circumstances. Mutual refusal to eat the food of one another also serves to mark lines between religious groups, as in differences between Hindus, Muslims, and Buddhists. Denial of the right to share food was a fundamental means of inscribing class and caste. Where caste remains a central element of social organization, as in southern Asia, the social consequences of food transactions are openly political and charged with moral implications. In this hierarchical system, the most exclusive of the castes eat with nobody else, whereas the lowest in the scale accept food from almost everyone. Eating food prepared, cooked, or served by members of another caste indicates equality, or inferiority, with them; not eating demonstrates superiority, as does refusal to sit next to a person while eating. Only the lowest of the ranks, the sweeper, would eat the food left on the plates by other castes (Mayer, 1960: 34). Ethnic segregation, down to the 1960s, meant many blacks in many regions of the United States were denied access to public eating places. When they traveled, they carried prepared food with them or shared with other blacks along the way, including people unknown to one another. Civil Rights protests were frequently focussed on these sites, staging sit-ins at eateries, where demonstrators were vilified by segregationists and had food poured over them.

Even in the most exploitative situations, taste was often shared across social hierarchies, reflecting the strength of underlying local cultures. Thus, in the Americas, enslaved African people and European planters shared tastes – for things such as roast plantain, avocado, pawpaw, and saltfish – as well as cooks. The same applied more broadly to the emergence of a Southern regional style of cooking in the United States, much of it derived from the food that enslaved people consumed whether by choice or necessity (Wilson, 1964). Similarly, when white Americans went as missionaries to Hawaii in the early nineteenth century they sought to distinguish themselves culturally, by clinging to the clothing styles they had brought with them, for example, but universally adopted the food of the islands, because the alternative was likely starvation and because they quickly came to enjoy it (Kashay, 2009: 174). They refused only to eat dog, and maintained their social distance and sense of civilization by attempting to retain learned table manners.

Home

Eating together in a private place is a primary marker of kinship and belonging. The process of identification begins with the feeding of the infant child, from the breast and from the hand, in which the child becomes aware of its individuality at the same time as learning attachment and the role of sharing relationships. Households were not always classless communities, however, and commonly ordered by gender and age as well.

Servants, even where they were the cooks, typically were required to eat separately from the family household, or at least at a different time. Often they would eat in the kitchen, a location unattractive to better-off people until quite recent times. Only when the kitchen became less of a messy, workshop site, in the late twentieth century, could it begin to seem a good place to be to enjoy food. In the villages of modern China, men and women sat at separate tables to eat, the women joined by the youngest of the children and the most senior wife of the man of the household sometimes sitting with the men.

In China, sitting on a chair to eat at a table became common only in the last thousand years. In the Shang and Chou periods, the upper ranks ate kneeling on a mat, with vessels containing the food and drink that made up their meal set out before them and arranged according to strict rules. Each man was given four bowls of grain, to fill the stomach, together with a number of meat and vegetable dishes, ranging from three to eight according to their rank and age. These patterns survived for many centuries, following rules closer to those found in modern Japan.

In the sixteenth century, the Japanese typically ate from small, low portable *zen* tables, just big enough for an individual's servings. Houses rarely had spaces specifically reserved for dining, so meals were set out on these small tables, in the kitchen, and then carried to wherever the person wished to eat, kneeling on a mat. Servants generally ate closest to the kitchen. The head of the household (and perhaps his wife, who would then serve him), or a grandfather, took the most distant positions, reflecting the hierarchy of gender and age followed in the traditional family. By the eighteenth century, a common variety of *zen* table was simply a square lacquered box, with a drawer to contain utensils: chopsticks, rice bowl, soup bowl, and bowls for side dishes. When the meal had been eaten, hot water or tea was poured over the utensils and drunk, and the utensils were then wiped with a cloth. This pattern changed following modernization, and by the beginning of the twentieth century the *zen* table had been displaced by the *chabudai*, a version of the Western dining table, only about a foot (30 cm) high but big enough to accommodate several people sitting on a *tatami* floor mat. The triumph of the *chabudai* was short-lived, however, and by the 1950s it had been overtaken by "high" tables and chairs in the Western style, which accounted for 70 percent of households by the 1990s, as houses acquired reserved dining areas (Ishige, 2001: 178–87). This new pattern went together with increasing acceptance of Chinese and Western dishes, and a shift to precooked frozen meals and eating out.

During the late Chou period, around 500 BC, diners of the upper ranks, kneeling on their mats, were expected to observe a detailed list of rules governing manners that demonstrated the varying statuses of those eating together.

Among many other things, they were not to guzzle their food or swill their soup or liquor; neither to add condiments (because this would cause the host to apologize for not having the dishes prepared properly) nor to swill the sauces (which would have the host apologizing for his poverty).

The ancient Greeks and Romans placed great emphasis on the status and prestige associated with being able to recline while eating and drinking, and being served by standing waiting-people. The reclining posture was well known in Greece by the seventh century BC but had its origins in the Middle East where it was the style of powerful rulers, first depicted at Nineveh (Roller, 2006: 15–22). In Greece, it spread from the aristocracy to a wider group with wealth and leisure to enjoy, though often being an exclusive male domain. The reclining banquet followed the Greek cultural colonization of the Mediterranean, playing a particularly prominent role in Rome. As in Greece, the posture was adopted first by the upper strata of society, and then imitated by social groups lower down the ladder. Even slaves might recline when eating away from their masters. Specially designed couches were constructed, and the image of the reclining banqueter was common in art for many centuries, providing an idealized tableau of power relations, luxury, and culinary plenty (Dunbabin, 2003: 11–14, 199–202). Typically, the diner reclined with his torso upright, leaning on his left elbow, while stretching out his legs, with the right knee bent.

The image survived the end of the classical world, being taken up notably as the scheme for representations of the Last Supper of Jesus Christ, often including significant food symbolism. By medieval times, however, as artists became unfamiliar with the reclining posture, the disciples began to sit at a table, while occasionally Christ alone reclined on a separate couch in recognition of his divine status. Soon, all were depicted together at a long table, sitting or, in the case of Leonardo da Vinci's *Last Supper*, in animated posture.

Public sites

Eating out is an ancient product of urbanism. Its origins were not so much a desire for "fast food" as a means of providing cooked dishes for the poorer people who lacked the time and technologies to prepare food at the places where they slept. Ancient Rome, we have seen, had a population of more than a million by 100 BC. Most of the city's people lived in tenements and had no access to the bulky ovens and hearths needed to bake bread or make porridges and gruels. The poor had little choice but to purchase their food on the street or at the market or bazaar, whereas for the wealthy the staging of a banquet on their own premises was a vehicle for displaying their good fortune and their pretensions. Much the same applied in the cities of pre-modern Asia and the Middle East, where the better-off, especially those who could afford the large ovens and the labor of servants to bake their own bread, preferred to eat at home.

The pleasures of street food were not confined to the poor. Thus, for example, the "blood soup" enjoyed by the Chinese around AD 1200 was served in cheap restaurants as well as at imperial banquets. In ancient cities generally, where street food was the basic resource of the poor, the better-off who did not wish to jostle with unwashed laboring people at the end of the working day, and even the very wealthy, sometimes craved the same cooked foods consumed in the markets, so sent servants to purchase them. On the other hand, for the better-off there were good practical food safety reasons for choosing not to eat out. A persistent hazard of eating in the market or bazaar, or from street-sellers, was that the origins and character of the ingredients could not be monitored in the same way they could in home-cooking. There was always the fear that meat might have come from diseased animals, that the flour used to make bread had been adulterated, or that food had been boiled in tainted water. The poor could not afford to be so choosy.

The poor of fourteenth-century Cairo and Isfahan, for example, typically purchased cooked food for their evening meal, patronizing the kitchens of the bazaars where vast kettles and cauldrons were boiled on massive stoves, and kebabs were grilled over coals. In China, vendors sold cooked food items from jars and baskets throughout the night in the larger cities, serving the needs of the poor and those whose work regimes kept them up at all hours. In this situation, in which food technologies had a bulky character, economies of scale were important, and small servings could be dipped from great steaming cauldrons at relatively low cost. Bazaars and cook-shops also benefited from the scale of their markets, enabling the emergence of specialist cooks, notably pastry and confectionery makers who could devote their skills to a small range of goods produced on a large scale.

More strongly specialized were teahouses and coffeehouses. The tradition of tea-drinking was very ancient in China but the earliest-known references to "tea chambers" appeared in the Tang dynasty (AD 618–907). Some also served wine, and the teahouse became an important place to conduct business meetings or to enjoy theatrical performances and listen to poetry, sometimes with private rooms for the gentry (Wang, 2008: 6). In twentieth-century China, coffeehouses were associated with modernization, whereas the teahouse nourished traditional life and provided a stage for political argument. In the West, although coffee-drinking was little known before the sixteenth century, coffeehouses quickly emerged in European mercantile cities as vital sites, particularly for bourgeois men, for the communication of current knowledge, particularly about markets and business, and perhaps to express dangerous ideas about politics and religion (Cowan, 2005). Some of these functions spilled over into other kinds of public drinking places, such as the tavern, saloon, and café, but these were less often associated with radicalism and more often the targets of temperance movements.

By 1200, argues Chaudhuri (1990: 167), "the tradition of public and professional cuisine perhaps reached its highest forms in China and the habit of eating and dining in restaurants and tea-houses had become common." Restaurants were common in Hangchow and other major cities of China, remaining open late into the night. Their clientele was not confined to the wealthy and the poor were indeed reputedly allowed to eat in these restaurants and to use their (non-disposable) chopsticks and drink from their cups.

In Europe, public houses specifically designed for the sale of alcoholic drink emerged first in the ancient classical world and then largely disappeared until the height of the medieval period, when they once more became common in the cities and towns. Some of the latter operated as "inns," providing also meals, accommodation, and stabling, whereas "drinking houses" were at least in theory restricted to the sale of beverages and uncooked food. By 1500 the network was fairly comprehensive across most of Europe. Growth was rapid in the early modern period, directly associated with the expansion of the urban population and cross-country travel (Kümin, 2007). By the eighteenth century, the great age of coach travel in Europe, public houses came to be seen not only as disorderly and unhealthy sites of social interaction but also as potential threats to social stability through the networks they provided for the communication of political ideas and activism.

The system spread outside Europe in the wake of settler colonialism, and again came to be seen as a site of radical political discourse. The railroad and the fragmentation of the hospitality business, as well as the growth of coffeehouses and restaurants, that came with the innovations of the nineteenth and twentieth centuries undermined the central importance of public houses, as did the privatization of alcohol consumption that was enabled by new technologies of refrigeration and storage. The more sedate French version of the modern restaurant, the domicile of gastronomes and gourmands, remained rare outside Paris until the middle of the nineteenth century (Spang, 2000: 2).

Whether in public or private settings, there were vast cultural differences in attitudes to the combining of eating and drinking. In ancient Egypt, as early as 5000 BP, bakeries and breweries were typically closely associated, and it has been argued that the brewing of beer from cereals may even have predated the baking of bread. Throughout early Asia, much emphasis was placed on the supply of pure water and the making of pottery water jars that would have a cooling effect. Food might also be accompanied by weak tea and fruit juices. Only the rich could afford ice. Islamic and Hindu prohibitions on the consumption of alcoholic beverages were not always followed down to the seventeenth century. Wines were imported from European makers to India and the Middle East, and the Shiraz of Iran gained a high reputation. Elsewhere in Asia, notably China and Japan, spirits distilled from rice, wheat, sugar cane, and palm liquor were regarded from early times as vital to the enjoyment of a meal.

Institutions

Public institutions, particularly hospitals and prisons, came only gradually to take responsibility for the feeding of their inmates or patrons. Once they did embrace the concept, however, food was incorporated into the structure of the institution, used as a means of symbolizing the role of jailer, healer, carer, or teacher. Standardized menus and fixed regimes of meals and mealtimes were often imposed.

The provision of meals to schoolchildren was a European invention of the late nineteenth century, following closely on the extension of education to all classes. So long as schooling was largely confined to the better-off and associated with boarding, the nutrition of pupils was seen as a matter for the schools themselves. The idea that governments should have responsibility for the feeding of schoolchildren derived from philanthropic notions that, for the first time, saw hunger as a social problem located within the domain of the state.

Once established, the model spread quickly around the world, and survived through socialism, fascism, and varied forms of democracy. The United States established a permanently funded National School Lunch Program in 1946, but, as happened with Food Stamps and Food Aid, the initial impetus was as much a desire to find an outlet for surplus agricultural commodities as directed by nutritional objectives. The scheme was beset by problems of equity, and many poor and African-American children missed out until Civil Rights activism and the discovery of poverty in the 1960s, with the unintended consequence that school lunches came to be seen as a tool of welfare rather than democratic nutrition (Levine, 2008: 7–8). Government provision of school meals paralleled closely the promotion of free milk in schools, including the late-twentieth-century "nutritional colonization" of East Asia, most particularly Japan and China, marked by the establishment in 2000 of a World School Milk Day (Vernon, 2005). Once again, in some cases, the provision of milk to schoolchildren was initiated and driven by producers rather than consumers, and the benefits flowed to farmers rather than the children who were encouraged or forced to drink poor-quality or even contaminated milk (Atkins, 2005).

In societies with small proportions of older people, those typical of most of the pre-industrial world, age was often appreciated and acknowledged by the allocation of superior food items. Among the poor, however, older and infirm people might be treated harshly, especially in times of subsistence crisis when food was scarce. The emergence of a substantial proportion of older people (over 55 years) in the world's population occurred only toward the end of the twentieth century. The increasing concentration of these older people in institutions, particularly in Western societies, meant not only that they necessarily shared most meals with other older people but also that they tended to be fed rather than cooking for themselves. What they were fed often mirrored the standardized meals supplied in other kinds of institutions. Efforts began, however, to design meals which might delay age-related ailments such as osteoporosis, diabetes, and heart disease, while at the same time attempting to compensate for impaired taste and smell. Older people, especially those who had lived through the boom periods of the late twentieth century, came to desire meals that were enjoyable as well as nourishing: double-cheese pizza, spicy chicken, and chocolate-dipped bananas (Costa and Jongen, 2010). This attitude to mortality was a far cry from the notion that the aged should not press on the limited food supplies of a community and, with death in sight, even deny (or be denied) all food.

Eating in space

Throughout history, voyagers often faced daunting challenges in planning what to eat and how to preserve their supplies over journeys of unknown duration. Many perished in the process. A new kind of challenge confronted space travelers, who generally had a clear idea how long they needed to provide for but had to cope with life in a confined and unnatural environment. The first human to eat (and sleep) in space was Gherman Titov, a Soviet cosmonaut, in 1961, but before he did so there was doubt even whether it would be possible to swallow in conditions of weightlessness. Early space foods were restricted to pastes that could be squeezed from tubes and bite-size cubes of concentrated protein, fat, sugar, and fruit or nuts, but these lacked the qualities of aroma and mouthfeel that contribute to the enjoyment of eating on earth (Perchonok and Bourland, 2002). Much of it was left uneaten. Astronauts found it difficult to swallow, rather like eating while lying on your side on earth. Many lost their sense of taste and smell. Metabolism was upset by the lack of gravity, which moves water to the lower body (Stein, 2001).

Changes were made during the Apollo program (1968–1972), placing food in cans and retort pouches. Some food could be eaten from a bowl using a spoon but because this required two hands a special food bar was developed, made from compressed fruit packaged with an edible starch film, which could be placed in the sleeve of a suit and bitten off. Once astronauts began to spend longer periods in space, in space stations, their food became more diverse and normal, including lobster and ice cream, stored in freezers and warmed in microwaves. Tables with footholds enabled them to "sit." The objective was to make the food as earth-like as possible, in much the way voyagers had always traveled with familiar foods. For longer space voyages, it was recognized that certain crops, including the common domesticates potatoes, rice, wheat, beans, and salads, would need to be grown, generally using hydroponic principles. Again, this mirrored the carrying of sheep and goats on sailing boats, for milk and meat. For astronauts, however, the daily rhythms were disrupted. Breakfast did not accompany the rising of the sun.

Meals and mealtimes

By about 1200, the Chinese, in all regions, had three meals a day, the evening repast being the most substantial and typically consisting of several courses. For the morning meal, twice-seasoned soup, shreds of puff pastry, and small steamed buns could be bought from street-sellers. At noon, *man-thou* could be added to rice gruel, along with little steamed vegetable cakes and peppery buns. Three meals remained the norm in China into modern times, with farmers sent their midday meals in containers, while women and children ate at home.

In Western Europe, the pattern of three meals was common from the sixteenth century, but industrialization shortened the time spent at meals for the working classes whereas the bourgeoisie devoted much more time to the table and steadily delayed the times of their meals. Elites, such as the slave-owning planter classes of the Americas, demonstrated their superiority by eating large, late breakfasts, when the enslaved field workers had already spent several hours sweltering under the sun, and consuming large dinners in the afternoon, as well as midnight suppers. Only in the twentieth century, with the shortening of hours for workers in response to labor union pressures, did working people regain the time for more relaxed and regular meals.

Main meals, where such are recognized, often followed a weekly structure, repeated almost without variation throughout the year. In rural settings, these patterns were related to seasonal availability, but in industrial societies with the benefit of refrigeration the progress might be even more rigidly followed. For example, in a God-fearing Australian family of the 1950s, a leg of lamb would be roasted on Saturday night to be eaten cold with salad at lunch after church on Sunday, and the same on Monday night with the addition of hot mashed potato; Tuesday, Wednesday, and Thursday saw three boiled vegetables combined with lamb chops or cutlets, the leftovers of the roast made into a curry, or perhaps beef casserole or steak and kidney pie; Friday brought fried fish, with the usual vegetables; and Saturday sausages or lamb's fry, when the strict ritual was set in motion once again. Homemade ice cream with home-preserved stone fruit or rice pudding served for dessert.

In recent times, the last half-century or so, the growing dominance of bought meals tended to deny aspects of the specialness of particular foods for particular meals. Restaurants might offer all-day "breakfasts," echoing perhaps the view that this was in some places the best food of the day, and therefore almost qualified (in the case of the British *c*.1960) to be eaten three times a day. On the streets of Thailand, coconut pancakes, traditionally a sweet breakfast food, topped with chopped spring onions, were available, and eaten, at all hours by the end of the twentieth century.

In India, an older tradition saw midday meals delivered by lunch-wallahs to the desks and workstations of bureaucrats and business people across the major cities of India. By the end of the twentieth century, deskbound workers in the West, particularly those who spent most of their days staring at computer screens, became habituated to "grazing" or nibbling and picking at food while continuing their labors. By the beginning of the twenty-first century, the many millions in this category spent as much time grazing as they did sitting down to regular meals. The better paid the worker, the more likely they were to graze, generally with an unexpected nutritional benefit. Many grazed at home, typically while watching television, including no doubt some of the innumerable programs that made cooking a spectator sport, or playing computer games, coming to be called couch potatoes and considered gluttons, prime candidates for obesity.

At the other extreme, certain special meals attained ritual status, serving to symbolize central beliefs and doctrines of religious traditions. For example, meals had a central role in the life and teaching of Jesus Christ, from the miraculous feeding of the five thousand to the Last Supper and his breaking bread with tax collectors and sinners. These food acts were central because they confronted the Jewish understanding of the covenant between human beings and God, in which the law governing food had come to represent the whole. Thus, the Last Supper resembled in many ways the Passover, the annual feast that commemorated the sparing of the Hebrews in Egypt and, more broadly, their deliverance from captivity, also known as the Feast of Unleavened Bread. Whereas the Passover celebrated community and kinship, the sacrifice of Christ represented a covenant inclusive of all humanity.

From an essentially egalitarian "table-fellowship," in which any and every one could be equally host, servant, and guest, the early Christian Church developed a ritual holy meal, the Eucharist or thanksgiving for the crucifixion and resurrection of Christ, in which the food and drink (bread and wine) symbolized flesh and blood, as a rite served only to the faithful from the hands of an exclusive priestly class (Feeley-Harnik, 1981: 18–19). The symbolic bread-and-wine combination was not immediately accepted as the only appropriate ritual meal. Thus, one early Christian group used instead for the Eucharist bread and cheese, perhaps drawing on an ascetic tradition that recalled a meatless paradise and the cheese a soft variety or curd that could be drunk (Symons, 1999). Other early versions used salt (recognized for its purity and simplicity), olive oil, and vegetables (McGowan, 1999: 95–142). Ironically, the limitation of the Eucharist and the creation of a hierarchical priesthood went together with the grant of freedom to Christians to eat from nature without restriction.

The symbolic or actual eating of the dead, including their ashes, sometimes occurs as a means of ensuring a successful afterlife and perhaps taking on some of their powers. Placing favorite foods with the dead at the time of burial was widespread and still occurs. In parts of the Christian world, All Souls' Day is celebrated by making complete meals for the dead, reflecting their preferences in life, and laid out on a table overnight. All of these symbolic food acts or ritual meals serve to maintain and ensure good relations between family and friends, the living and the dead.

References

Atkins, P.J. (2005) Fattening children or fattening farmers? School milk in Britain, 1921–1941. *Economic History Review* 58: 57–78.

Chang, K.C. (1977) Ancient China. In K.C. Chang (ed.) *Food in Chinese Culture: Anthropological and Historical Perspectives*, pp. 25–52. New Haven, CT: Yale University Press.

Chaudhuri, K.N. (1990) *Asia before Europe: Economy and Civilisation of the Indian Ocean from the Rise of Islam to 1750.* Cambridge: Cambridge University Press.

Costa, A.I.A. and Jongen, W.M.F. (2010) Designing new meals for an ageing population. *Critical Reviews in Food Science and Nutrition* 50: 489–502.

Cowan, B.W. (2005) *The Social Life of Coffee: The Emergence of the British Coffeehouse.* New Haven, CT: Yale University Press.

Cowan, R.S. (1983) *More Work for Mother: The Ironies of Household Technology from the Open Hearth to the Microwave.* New York: Basic Books.

Dunbabin, K.M.D. (2003) *The Roman Banquet: Images of Conviviality.* Cambridge: Cambridge University Press.

Feeley-Harnik, G. (1981) *The Lord's Table: Eucharist and Passover in Early Christianity.* Philadelphia: University of Pennsylvania Press.

Flammang, J.A. (2009) *The Taste for Civilization: Food, Politics, and Civil Society.* Urbana, IL: University of Illinois Press.

Huang, H.T. (2000) *Fermentations and Food Science*, Part V, Vol. 6, *Joseph Needham, Science and Civilisation in China.* Cambridge: Cambridge University Press.

Ishige, N. (2001) *The History and Culture of Japanese Food.* London: Kegan Paul.

Joshel, S.R. (2010) *Slavery in the Roman World.* Cambridge: Cambridge University Press.

Kashay, J.F. (2009) Missionaries and foodways in early 19th-century Hawai'i. *Food and Foodways* 17: 159–80.

Kümin, B. (2007) *Drinking Matters: Public Houses and Social Exchange in Early Modern Central Europe.* Basingstoke, UK: Palgrave Macmillan.

Levine, S. (2008) *School Lunch Politics: The Surprising History of America's Favorite Welfare Program.* Princeton: Princeton University Press.

Mayer, A.C. (1960) *Caste and Kinship in Central India: A Village and Its Region.* Berkeley, CA: University of California Press.

McGowan, A. (1999) *Ascetic Eucharists: Food and Drink in Early Christian Ritual Meals.* Oxford: Clarendon Press.

Perchonok, M. and Bourland, C. (2002) NASA food systems: Past, present, and future. *Nutrition* 18: 193–20.

Roller, M.B. (2006) *Dining Posture in Ancient Rome: Bodies, Values, and Status.* Princeton: Princeton University Press.

Spang, R.L. (2000) *The Invention of the Restaurant: Paris and Modern Gastronomic Culture.* Cambridge, MA: Harvard University Press.

Stein, T.P. (2001) Nutrition in the space station era. *Nutrition Research Reviews* 14: 87–117.

Symons, M. (1999) From Agape to Eucharist: Jesus meals and the early Church. *Food and Foodways* 8: 33–54.

Vernon, J. (2005) The ethics of hunger and the assembly of society: The techno-politics of the school meal in modern Britain. *American Historical Review* 110: 693–725.

Wang, D. (2008) *The Teahouse: Small Business, Everyday Culture, and Public Politics in Chengdu, 1900–1950.* Stanford, CA: Stanford University Press.

Wilson, M.T. (1964) Peaceful integration: The owner's adoption of his slaves' food. *Journal of Negro History* 49: 116–127.

CHAPTER EIGHT

National, Regional, and Global Cuisines

A fundamental problem in history is determining why people share elements of culture over large and small regions of geographical space, and why there are relatively firm boundaries to such sharing. Even in ancient times and in places with small, diffuse populations, people typically came to depend for their food on much the same selection of natural resources. On the other hand, where people spoke different languages, there the sharing of other aspects of culture, including food, was less common, providing the basis for distinctive approaches to deciding what was good to eat and how it should be prepared and cooked. Thus, even where the variety of available natural resources was fairly uniform over large stretches of territory, people did not always eat in the same way, whereas people who shared language tended also to share food cultures across diverse landscapes.

The origins of these patterns of difference and distinctiveness, the foundation stones of identity formation, can be seen in the sharing of food and food technologies that took place within groups and clans, beyond the more limited sharing that was essential to the survival of households and family units. In the ancient food economy, whether based on hunting and gathering or on agriculture, individuals found it hard to survive without belonging to a group, and typically shared not only ingredients, cooking pots, and fires but also hoped to receive enough from the pot to ensure their survival. Thus, cooking methods and utensils came to be replicated and specialist pot-makers emerged, following traditional styles rather than introducing significant, radical, innovations. Observation and exchange worked to spread this uniformity of technologies across wider areas. Foods and food ingredients followed, though

How Food Made History, First Edition. B. W. Higman.
© 2012 B. W. Higman. Published 2012 by Blackwell Publishing Ltd.

at a slower pace and limited by the available transport technologies and geophysical situation of a community. Eventually, they might spread to the limits of a lord's domain or a state's hegemony and these bounds typically mattered more than any supposed natural boundaries created by rivers and seacoasts.

In considering the balance between nation, empire, and region, it is important to recall that nationalism is a relatively recent way of seeing the world, becoming dominant only in the late nineteenth century, and a recent form of social and cultural identification. For most of world history, the "regions" of modern states existed as autonomous or semi-autonomous domains or chiefdoms, or groupings of such entities, with their own forms of allegiance and localized identity, rooted in immediately available resources. Belonging to a tribe or clan was often the most important form of connection and closely associated with an understanding of human culture as something intimately bound up with being part of the land or country. Forms of association through language, region, and kinship also overlapped with concepts of ethnicity, based in perceptions of human diversity, both physical and cultural. Few of these smaller units of association and government produced cookbooks, whereas imperial states were more likely to do so and more likely to seek to impose their cuisines on colonized populations or to diffuse them to colonial frontiers.

Thus, although it is too much to contend that food identities always prefigured and influenced the emergence of national polities, there is good reason to give a significant role to food and food systems in the definition and demarcation of complex societies and states. This role extended also into the creation and expansion of imperial states, as noted earlier in the cases of the Roman and Inca empires, for example, through both the diffusion of foods and food technologies and through the establishment of systematic networks of exchange and storage. It is equally significant that the emergence of complex societies and empires generally served to amplify differences, of quantity and quality, in the foods consumed by different social groups within these hierarchical social structures, while at the same time contributing to the emergence of what outsiders came to see as a fundamental uniformity of techniques and dishes across the classes of such dominant political units. Thus, food was a vital tool in the exercise of hegemony, at almost every level of the social system, and a vital element in building the understanding of belonging to a larger community. However, in the long term, regional language and food cultures typically survived much more intact than did particular states and empires.

To a substantial extent, concepts of national, regional, and ethnic foods had to wait on the emergence of modern forms of nationalism. Indeed, it has been argued convincingly that many modern states came to recognize and define their national cuisines only after, or in tandem with, the birth of movements for independence and nationhood (Appadurai, 1988). Often this was a matter of giving voice to a food culture that already existed; sometimes, new and old states found themselves engaged in a much more self-conscious project, in which national cuisines were virtually invented from fragments and figments. Similarly, although regional cuisines naturally preceded national cuisines, the opposite was also possible. The temptation to conjure something from nothing became increasingly compelling in the competitive world of modern tourism. So too did ethnic cuisines often have porous boundaries, overlapping as they did the concepts of region and nation, and inevitably accepting and rejecting elements contrary to faith and tradition. At no time was this more true than in the modern "melting pot" created by global migration, imperialism, multiculturalism, and creolization (Gvion and Trostler, 2008). Food cultures and cuisines have spread around the world, causing the demise of local culinary styles and niches of uniqueness, in much the same way as a small number of plants and animals became dominant in the global pattern of food consumption, and the spread of dominant languages led to the demise of the world's linguistic richness.

Globalization has contributed powerfully to the reduction of variety and rootedness in the world's foodways, but in apparent contradiction (and matching the ambiguous relationship between nation and region) the process was also important in the emergence of national and regional cuisines. The recognition of difference always depends on comparison with something, or someone, else. Thus, the spread of people in the modern world, whether through voluntary or forced migration, created ideal conditions for the development of self-conscious notions of identity, whether derived from ethnicity, religion, history, language, or food.

Migrating people frequently try hard to maintain their language and their food cultures in the new places they find themselves. In the past, this has often been difficult or simply impossible for those moving (or moved) over long distances. In recent times, however, particularly the period since World War II, technologies and attitudes have made more possible the recreation of remembered dishes and, indeed, the integration of these styles into accommodating societies. At the same time, this recent period witnessed great growth in mass tourism, in which the tourist sometimes wished or demanded to be able to consume abroad the foods they had left at home, and sometimes complained that they could not easily find the "authentic" foods of the places to which they traveled. "Culinary tourism" emerged as a recognized special segment of the larger market (Long, 2004). Further, a more broadly self-conscious attitude emerged, in which people desired to have their particular foods and culinary styles recognized as in some way unique to their nation, region, or culture. There emerged a desire to achieve rank in a hierarchy of "cuisines."

Cuisine, high and low

The word *cuisine* is French and it is the French who have the greatest claims to achievement in this domain, elevating its superior versions to the status of *haute cuisine*, carefully distinguished from *la cuisine bourgeoise* but refreshed by occasional doses of *nouvelle cuisine*. For the French, cuisine means both the kitchen and the manner or style of the cooking undertaken there, the task of the *cuisinier*, or cook. *Cuisine* entered English only in the seventeenth century, along with its cousin *culinary*, which derives from the Latin *culina*, meaning simply kitchen.

Broadly, cuisine is now taken to include the rules of cooking (what ingredients should be selected, how they should be combined, and what processes are applied to them), the rules of eating (who should eat what, when, and with whom), and the rules of food service (how dishes should be served and in what order). These three sets of rules create the potential for many possible permutations and self-conscious respect for specific and unalterable complex norms that establish the foundation for a perception of the higher forms of culinary practice. It is from this concept that a more restricted meaning of cuisine arises, confined to identifying what Goody (1982: vii) calls "highly elaborated forms of cooking found in only a few societies such as China, the Middle East and post-Renaissance France."

Such a hierarchical understanding of cuisine does not suit a democratic approach to the study of world food history and, at the very least, several other societies would think themselves worthy of a place in this select list or wish to argue that what is high and what is low is very much a matter of taste. In this scheme, humans (who almost always cook) are distinguished from animals (which eat but do not cook); cuisine is distinguished from everyday cooking; and highly elaborated (*haute*) cuisine is in turn distinguished from its lower forms. Interestingly, the French concept of haute cuisine is matched by *haute couture* (high sewing) opposed to readymade, bulk production. Haute couture is part of the *fashion* industry but characterized by the following of rules and the use of costly materials, and distinguished by being extremely time-consuming hand-work and expensive. Much the same applies to the application of elaboration in cooking, and its audience. From these principles, it follows that cuisines are thought to be found only where surpluses are sufficient to support social hierarchies, and where those at the top of the social scale seek to differentiate themselves through the symbolism associated with being able to eat from a more exotic menu than that allowed the common folk of a culture. Generally, these requirements suggest that "cuisine" belongs among the cultural creations of complex agrarian societies, with no equivalent in hunter-gatherer societies.

An alternative understanding, advanced, for example, by Sidney Mintz (1996: 104), is to define cuisine more broadly as "the ongoing foodways of a region, within which active discourse about food sustains both common understandings and reliable production of the foods in question." With Africa in mind, McCann (2009: 5) argues for an expanded definition "by using cuisine to denote a distinct and coherent body of food preparations based upon one or more starchy staples, a set of spice combinations, complementary tastes, particular textures, iconic rituals, and a locally intelligible repertoire of meats, vegetables, and starchy textures." Similarly, Armelagos (2010: 164) calls cuisine "a cultural system that defines the items in nature that are edible; how these items can be extracted, eaten, or processed into food; the flavors used to enhance the taste of the food; and the rules about consuming it." This more comprehensive definition enables Armelagos to see cuisine as the solution to the "omnivore's dilemma."

The invention of cuisine, in Armelagos's interpretation, is not dependent on agriculture or social hierarchy but rather emerges as an element of human evolution (and the invention of cooking) and is, indeed, an essential feature of successful hunter-gatherer food culture, with continuity into the present. The Neolithic Revolution greatly reduced the variety of foods eaten, as did the industrialization of the food system, but the persistent human desire for variety was satisfied by the development of new ways of preparing and processing the increasingly narrowed range of ingredients. In this way, a deep-time understanding of the evolution of cuisine can be connected with the much shallower excavation of modern varieties of high cuisine, though stripped of their emphasis on exclusivity and hierarchy.

Developmental models of the creation of high cuisines typically focus on the role of elites, the people with power, eager to magnify their status. These classes used food to open a hierarchical space between themselves and their social rivals. In the early stages of the construction of a complex society, it might be enough to consume relatively expensive and exotic ingredients or simply to have privileged access to domestic foods in times of communal shortage. In these models, high cuisines emerged only when the upper classes elaborated their food culture by employing new prepara-tion and cooking processes, applied both to local and exotic materials, and served these dishes on exclusive special occasions, such as banquets and feasts where the rules of dining were as elaborate as those that governed the cooking itself. Specialist cooks followed detailed and complex proce-dures, which became codified and standardized, while table settings and modes of serving and waiting at table became structured in the same refined way. In this model, the example set by the rich and powerful is taken up with enthusiasm by lower-class groups who seek to emulate the dishes and some of the ceremony practiced by the elite. A third stage of development may then occur when the upper classes retaliate by inventing yet another version of their high cuisine in order to re-establish their superiority. Further iterations are possible.

High cuisines once used to establish their superiority on the fact that they possessed cookbooks. In the contemporary world such a claim may appear to have little merit, with bookshops and websites groaning with recipes from almost every corner of the globe. Before 1700, however, cookbooks were not only directed toward the higher end of style but also contained a good deal of medical knowledge, in much the same way that food and medicine were often discussed as part of a single system and guides to diet were initially the exclusive province of medical practitioners. Spiritual and philosophical matters also had a place in ancient discussions of food and culture. Thus, for example, the materialist Greek philosopher Epicurus (341–270 BC), who privileged hedonism but also advocated temperance, naturally found in food and drink a major source of pleasure. Later, Christian critics, including St Augustine, labeled epicureans gluttons.

In East Asia, Buddhist writings might combine condemnations of gluttony and pleasure with practical directions about the proper practice of butchery. When Zen came to Japan in the thirteenth century, it arrived with cookbooks stressing the relationship between food and spirituality. Again, Chinese (and Japanese) folk knowledge stressed the importance of balancing the extremes of *yin* and *yang*, in taste as in all other areas of life. Not until the eighteenth century did cookbooks emerge as a true genre, giving food and cuisine an autonomous aesthetic status independent of moralizing and medicalizing, pure pleasure.

The study of cookbooks has much to tell about the ways in which they relate to the larger history of a society and its identity. As Appadurai (1988: 3) argues, cookbooks are not merely practical manuals but also "reflect shifts in the boundaries of edibility, the proprieties of the culinary process, the logic of meals, the exigencies of the household budget, the vagaries of the market, and the structure of domestic ideologies." They depend on literacy and a desire to record and guide but also display notions of class, hierarchy, and nationhood.

The earliest cookbooks, in the Middle East, China, and Europe, were indeed designed to provide expert knowledge to the literate cooks of monarchs, emperors, and aristocrats, the people who could best afford exotic ingredients and elaborate cooking technologies and the people who most desired to impress. Thus, the objective was principally to assist cooks in the preparation of foods not known to them and to give guidance on appropriate tools and techniques. An alternative was to bring from distant places cooks familiar with these exotic materials but the uncertainty of supply meant that cookbooks quickly proved a superior solution and, in any case, cooks needed always to be ready to use substitutes.

In these ways, the cookbook often served to create haute cuisine intimately associated with central, often imperial, power and subordinated the cultures of regions and colonies. This, contends Appadurai (1988: 4), was what happened in the case of the French. In China, on the other hand, the cooking of the regions achieved separately the status of *hautes cuisines*, recognized globally as Szechwan or Cantonese, for example, and no distinct imperial or metropolitan style emerged to claim national superiority. Much the same is true of Italy. The empires of the post-Columbian world distributed elements of these dominant and regional cuisines to colonial sites, though rarely acknowledging the creative outcomes as constitutive of new cuisines.

It is striking that the very limited number of examples of high cuisines – what Goody (1982) terms "highly elaborated forms of cooking" – are confined to Eurasia. This raises interesting questions. Leaving aside for the moment the possibility that Goody's list is inadequate, and assuming the distinction between high and low cuisines really is universally valid, it can be asked why high styles did not emerge in Africa, the Americas, or the Pacific. Modern cooks in at least some of the nation-states that now occupy these lands are celebrated as highly skilled practitioners yet typically representative of styles developed elsewhere rather than achieving superior results within the context of a common national cuisine. Further, the national cuisines of the many postcolonial societies in these large regions equally appear heavily derivative rather than rooted in their natural resources.

Returning to the more fundamental question of the status of Goody's select list of high cuisines, it must be asked whether it arises directly from too narrow a definition of what might qualify and whether the definition itself reflects a particular taste or cultural style. In the case of Africa, there is the notion that the continent developed nothing worthy of the label *cuisine*, much in the way imperial historians once said Africa had no history. Indeed, it has been argued that perceptions of the continent's history have been distorted by a common emphasis on colonialism and subsistence crises, diverting attention from the complexity of African culinary styles and leading to a "failure to recognize African cookery as cuisine" (Lyons, 2007: 348).

Counter to this contention is the response that *all* nations possess national cuisines and that failure to identify haute cuisine in Africa is simply a matter of perception and cultural taste (McCann 2009: 5–7). Historians writing from a non-African (typically Western) perspective have often tended to characterize African foods as bland and undifferentiated, simply because the nuances and subtleties of the starchy staples depend on textures and flavors unfamiliar to outsiders. This lack of aesthetic appreciation and essential disparagement of African food culture fits neatly with the way in which the roots and tubers were denigrated by imperial nutritionists who sought instead to promote the virtues of grains and white bread.

Yet another reason for the lack of appreciation of African cuisine may be found in the complexity of everyday culinary practice, in contrast to the situation argued for Eurasia where there was a close association between high cuisine and social hierarchy. Perhaps Africa upsets the status of the interpretation that high cuisine begins among elites and filters down through emulation and social communication. It enables a rethinking of the relationship between abundance and cuisine, and points in the direction of what have been called cuisines of poverty and deprivation (Gvion, 2006).

Somewhat similar arguments could be advanced regarding the food cultures of the Americas and the other regions generally overlooked by food historians and anthropologists, but the example of Africa seems sufficient to make the point. In any case, the proven lack of a certified haute cuisine does not, of course, preclude strong identifications with national, regional, and ethnic foods. Indeed, prominent advocates of individuality and distinctiveness are found in many modern places, with little concern for the fact that they may not be awarded the highest status. Enthusiasm for a nation's food may be great, acting simply as an important means of expressing nationalism without belligerence, and serving as a way of claiming a distinctiveness that is increasingly hard to find in a globalized culture. In this scheme, a single food can be entirely adequate as a symbol and need not even be one desirable to outsiders, it just has to be sufficiently different. Perhaps, as Cusack (2000: 212) claims, "all nations have national cuisines."

The origins of cuisines

Two seemingly opposed sources have been proposed for the origins of cuisines. As already noticed, some scholars focus on the role of abundance, whereas others point to scarcity. The argument for abundance derives largely from the notion that only elites have the resources to access a relatively wide range of materials and to employ specialist cooks with the time and skill to refine techniques, and only elites have the leisure to create complex rules about dining. The argument from scarcity, on the other hand, contends that it was the necessity of introducing famine foods into established cooking technologies that brought about elaborated regional styles. Similarly, it has been argued that certain modern Asian and African "national cuisines" have flourished in response to poverty and deprivation, particularly within the context of closed authoritarian political regimes in a postcolonial world (Rosenberger, 2007: 342; Cusack, 2000: 211).

Although the explanation based on abundance and privilege appears contradictory to that based on scarcity and deprivation, the contrast is less striking than may appear. Thus, it could be argued that national cuisines are equally likely to develop in the midst of plenty and in the midst of shortage (though perhaps with contrasting consequences for culinary styles). Second, it could be argued that abundance and diversity can in fact coexist with scarcity and deprivation, and that this coexistence is what really matters. Thus, the notion of "abundance" is to some (quite large) extent determined by perceptions of what can be consumed, and its range might even be extended in famine conditions. It is the willingness to extend the variety of what is eaten that is crucial, not the hard fact of famine.

The survey of national cuisines that follows is intended to provide only a sample of global experience. The arrangement is neither chronological nor regional but rather follows a route that works through Eurasia, looking first at the cases of supposed high cuisine advocated most enthusiastically by food historians, then moving on to the less qualified and the more peripheral. With these assumptions in mind, it seems best to start with France, recognized as the true hearth of haute cuisine and indeed sometimes singled out as its *only* example.

France

The national cuisine of France, haute cuisine, is a seventeenth-century creation. Its emergence depended, first, on the development of distinctive cuisines within the larger region of Europe, a process which started only in the sixteenth century. Medieval culinary styles differed little from place to place, with an emphasis on spices, opulence, ostentation, and the exotic. Cooks sought to capture the attention of jaded aristocratic diners through surprise and strangeness, offering preparations like "chicken *farcie*" (stuffed chicken) in which the bird was emptied of its flesh, inflated, and the skin filled with a variety of unexpected and unrelated meats (Roux, 2009: 175). The new cuisine rejected such follies and was more firmly rooted in the local and the natural. In this way, the development of a new cuisine in seventeenth century France can be interpreted as a response to the fundamental changes in the world food map that followed the Columbian exchange. The new trade routes changed the balance between scarce and plentiful items, making some things much more cheaply available and therefore fit for introduction into the cooking of the bourgeoisie. The elite needed to find new ways of distinguishing their food culture.

A key component in the new cuisine of seventeenth-century France was the gradual abandonment of spices. One reason for this abandonment of a long-favored culinary element was that spices lost the exclusiveness derived from cost and rarity which had long made them characteristic of rich cooking. The growing availability of spices led the elite to rediscover the more subtle flavors of the land in which they lived, in a kind of local food movement, turning to chives, scallions, capers, and mushrooms. However, although this interpretation seems to work well for France, it has to be asked why the Columbian exchange did not have the same impact on Spain, Britain, or Italy, for example, where the new French model was followed only reluctantly, at a distance, and confined to a narrow elite. Attempts to explain French exceptionalism typically turn to patterns of aristocratic hierarchy and the role of courtly models, but this seems insufficient (Ferguson, 2004: 38–9; Mennell, 1985: 133).

The abandonment of spices went together with the decline of the ancient sweet-sour sauces. Instead, meats began to be accompanied by raw salads dressed with oil and vinegar. Sugar also disappeared from the many dishes in which it had previously made a regular appearance and became confined to desserts eaten toward the end of the meal. This French development reflected a polarity fundamental in modern Western cuisines, in which the opposition between sweet and savory subsumed other tastes (notably sour and bitter), and became established in the order of dishes served as a meal.

Essential to the identification of the cuisine of seventeenth-century France as distinctive in terms its connection with country, as well as finding its place in the highest ranks of culinary endeavor, was the creation of a literature and philosophy of food that emphasized its Frenchness. Doing so was an innovation, and connected cuisine with a nascent nationalism in other areas of culture. In cuisine, the beginning of the process can be found in François Pierre de La Varenne's *Le Cuisinier françois* (The French chef). Published in 1651, La Varenne's cookbook was the first to exhibit a clear break with the practices of the medieval period and a strong focus on the delicate sauces which were to become fundamental to classical French cuisine. It did, however, retain substantial medieval remnants, such as a liberal use of spices. Like almost any other cookbook, La Varenne's reflected practices already known to a wider community, but it was the pioneer and set out the pattern for the future.

More importantly, La Varenne's work and those of a number of contemporaries was laid out in a systematic manner. It also advanced codified rules for how particular recipes were to be prepared, even if they often remained somewhat vague on quantities and times. Advocacy of such a methodical approach to cooking went together with claims of French superiority, and even hinted at the beginnings of an internal ranking system that could be applied to the cuisines of individual cooks and kitchens. It also reflected the formalism that dominated French culture in the age of Louis XIV, in everything from architecture to theatre, and its philosophical foundations, above all the *Discourse on Method* (1637) of René Descartes. French distinctiveness in all these areas of culture represented not merely recognition of difference but a sense of distinction and superiority. By the end of the seventeenth century, the geographical borders of the modern nation were approaching their limits and the monarchy had established its absolute authority throughout the state's diverse and distinctive regions. Elements of the cuisine were borrowed from other places, beyond these boundaries, but always, at least in the minds of the French, so transformed that their ultimate origins were irrelevant. They had been refined, improved – made truly French dishes – by talented French hands.

Basic to the new style of La Varenne was the general rejection of separate sauces which could be poured over cooked food, to correct or smother the taste. Instead, sauces and stocks became integral elements in the process of cooking. Rather than denying the taste of the other elements, the new-style sauce was intended to bring out the subtleties and the refinement of the dish, often by the reduction of juices in the final stages of the cooking in order to concentrate the flavor. Success depended on the careful preparation of *bouillon*, or stock, as the basis of numerous soups and other dishes, flavored by a bouquet garni (to be removed at the last minute); and the precise combination of flour and fat in the making of a roux to thicken sauces. Velouté (velvet) sauce and its richer version Béchamel (named first by La Varenne) were fundamental but tricky. These and other methods placed a weight of responsibility on the shoulders of the cook (Pinkard, 2009: 123). The possibility of failure – as anyone who has been distracted while making a roux will appreciate – was never far away. Generally, it meant having to start all over again.

French haute cuisine underwent a second revolutionary transition, less than a century after La Varenne, with the emergence of *nouvelle cuisine* (alternatively, *cuisine moderne*) in the late 1730s. As in the first instance, this fresh development was marked by a series of cookbooks, but this time employing *nouveau* and *moderne* in their titles, demonstrating a heightened self-consciousness concerning the significance of food in French culture and the self-importance of the cooks. In terms of the development of national cuisines, the central feature of this second revolution was the way it extended the principles established in aristocratic kitchens to a much broader audience, by making the distinction, mentioned earlier, between *haute cuisine* and *la cuisine bourgeoise*. The latter became firmly established in 1746 with the publication of Menon's *La Cuisinière bourgeoise*, a work republished many times, under many regimes, down to the end of the nineteenth century.

Menon's title pointed to a household below the scale of an aristocratic family – identifying the cook as female (*cuisinière*), in sharp contrast to the male military operations that characterized aristocratic establishments – but not too far down the scale, with the cook and her retinue all domestic servants. It was Menon's objective to bring to such households a simplified version of this culinary style, stripped of extravagance and expensive seasonings, yet by no means equivalent to the food of rural peasants or the urban poor. Within this limited clientele, and putting aside its strong Parisian orientation, the cuisine had national relevance, but creation of a truly national cuisine had to wait on the cultural entrepreneurship of Marie-Antoine Carême (1783–1833). Down to the middle of the eighteenth century, however, food shortages and famine remained common. Thus, as Ferguson (2004: 43) concludes, rather like haute cuisine, "*cuisine bourgeoise* supposed abundance just as it supposed the wherewithal to procure that abundance."

Abundance underpinned French food styles into the twentieth century but by its end fresh fears had emerged, fears stirred up by the onslaught of globalization on national and regional cuisines. France was not alone in facing this challenge, of course, but not surprisingly it was the French who demonstrated particular distress, seeing the assault as central to the viability of a complete culture. Advocates of French gastronomy could rely on government enthusiasm as part of a broader defense of language and behavior. In this respect, France seems once again to be unique in the extent to which the state sought not only to regulate food production and distribution but also to support traditional processing technologies and to monitor authenticity and quality. This applied most obviously to the protection of wine varieties, through the concept of *terroir* – identifying the peculiarities of place or territory rooted in soil and microclimate – but included also cheese (such as Roquefort) and other products. Health and quarantine issues were often used to inhibit global trades.

Government promotion culminated in a successful bid in 2010 to have the "gastronomic meal of the French" declared worthy by UNESCO of a place on its list of world-class Intangible Cultural Heritage, in the company of celebrated art forms and traditions. Although scholarly advocates such as Jean-Robert Pitte (2002: ix) argued that the French campaign was not about claiming French food was better than that of anyone else or about attempting to preserve recipes for specific dishes, President Nicolas Sarkozy, launching the bid in 2008, stated bluntly that "We have the best gastronomy in the world – at least from our point of view." This bid was not centered on any one single dish, ingredient, or culinary style but comprehended the pairing of dishes and wines, and the setting of the table, from the precise placing of glasses to the orientation of the knife and the fork tines down (Iverson, 2010).

The French, said critics, sought this level of recognition because their cooking was in fact no longer a favorite and had slipped in world approval, supplanted by Chinese, Italian, and Spanish cuisines. Others rejected the claim that gastronomy was "France's most enduring empire," and argued to the contrary that cuisine was a "universal language," common to all peoples. From a practical point of view, the listing was seen as part of an attempt to hold back the onslaught of globalization, through the regulation of authenticity and the granting of subsidies to French farmers.

Although by the beginning of the twenty-first century France had a large immigrant population, the country resisted multiculturalism and sought to police areas of life such as language and dress (leading to the banning of the burka). The defense of French food, the national cuisine, was a central element in this reluctance to embrace such a global future. School lunches became part of national nutritional policy and firmly founded on the model of the (adult) French meal, with vending machines (both food and drink) banned from schools from 2005. But French consumers found it increasingly difficult to ignore the cheaper cheeses and meats imported from other EU countries that appeared on supermarket shelves, and Muslim children began to be offered halal alternatives with their school lunches. There was even a reluctant acceptance that fast food could be good food.

China

Claims made for French superiority and precedence are challenged by Chinese cuisine. Often, this challenge is grounded in an environment of abundance, as in the French example. Thus Michael Freeman (1977: 144) contends that the period of the Sung Dynasty (960–1279) was highly successful in feeding the people of China and that this "material abundance" led also to "the development and refinement of conscious and rational attitudes about food, in all its aspects, within that substantial portion of Sung society that could afford to eat well." Further, he makes the bold claim that in this period, "particularly in Southern Sung (1127–1279), emerged the first of the world's cuisines." Priority, as we will soon see, is always difficult to be sure about – declaring an example the first is simply to encourage challengers – and probably impossible ever to pin down with certainty in something as indeterminate as the fine line between cooking and cuisine. In making his claim for the Sung, Freeman, writing in the 1970s, had in mind only the French.

Freeman (1977: 144) connected his definition, which he called a historical one, with the precondition of abundance, seeing cuisine as "a self-conscious tradition of cooking and eating" which necessarily implied "the confluence of certain material factors, the availability and abundance of ingredients, with a set of attitudes about food and its place in the life of man." Basic to the development of a cuisine, says Freeman, is a multiplicity of ingredients and, interestingly, he immediately associates a Chinese willingness to prepare and eat unlikely substances, "inspired perhaps by necessity" and rooted in "China's tradition of famine food." But the development of the cuisine depended equally on access to exotic materials from distant sources, on cooks with the time and the tools to be able to experiment, and on the existence of a large adventurous elite audience. In addition, cookbooks were circulated and written recipes exchanged.

In the longer term, repeated severe subsistence crises might also have a direct impact on food systems by inhibiting the development of prohibitions and taboos. This has been argued particularly for south China, where taboos are virtually unknown, having been eliminated by the high frequency of famines. Beggars can't be choosers, it is said, but it is the hungry who deny themselves the potential foods that surround them, for whatever reason, who expire first in a famine. The Chinese chose early not to die wondering.

In the southern capital Hangchow, in the late Sung period, numerous highly specialized markets offered such a bewildering abundance of items that visitors like Marco Polo, who encountered the Sung at the very end of the dynasty, could not find words to describe them. A vegetable seller might offer as many as seventeen kinds of beans. Butchers used knives to broadly cut, slice, sliver, and pound with the side of the blade, to the order of the customer, the flesh of pigs, sheep, horses, donkeys, rabbits, venison, pheasants, owls, and poultry. Fresh fruit was also plentiful, from peaches and pears to plums, apricots, and pomegranates, oranges, and mandarins, though perhaps only one variety of apple. Tea-drinking spread through all classes but remained an object of connoisseurship. Cane sugar became plentiful following innovations in refining. New varieties of rice were introduced from what is now Vietnam in response to famine and drought. Once again, the roles of surplus and shortage seem inextricably bound, neither one nor the other capable on its own of creating a high cuisine.

The other ingredient necessary to the making of a cuisine, argues Freeman (1977: 145), is the presence of "attitudes which give first place to the real pleasure of consuming food rather than to its purely ritualistic significance." Thus, the masses who gulped down their crudely prepared food, with one eye over the shoulder wondering where the next meal and the next predator might be lurking, did not possess cuisine. Nor, for Freeman, did those who devoted great energy to the preparation of foods for sacrificial purposes or produced grandiose banquets. What was needed to create a cuisine was a class, appropriately resourced, with time and leisure, but most importantly possessed of a pure enthusiasm and appreciation of taste. Those who had a heightened palate or capacity to recognize the intrinsic values of food performed acts of gustation – taste – and experienced gustatory pleasure, or degustation, from the Latin *degust*. By "happy coincidence," these factors came together under the Sung to create a Chinese cuisine.

Further, claims Freeman, for both the Chinese and the French, once a cuisine was established there followed a trend "away from elaboration toward a style of cooking which, though immensely sophisticated, is simpler and truer to its ingredients." An intellectual approach to "natural" foods, wild mushrooms collected in the forest, for example, contributed to this trend, and helped keep food connected with Buddhist and Taoist philosophies. Alternatively, Anderson (1988: 71) argues that the Sung tendency toward simplicity and natural foods was not so much evidence of gustatory refinement as "a retreat into otherworldly quietism" and associated with a disconnection from culinary development.

The claim that the Sung created the world's first cuisine can be disputed even within the scope of Chinese history, with varieties of "cuisine" identified as early as the Han dynasty (206 BC–AD 220). By the time of the Han, the Chinese had come to depend heavily on grains: wheat was replacing millet in the north, while rice dominated the south; soybean increased its role, while hemp seed remained a significant minor crop (Sterckx, 2005: 35). Animal fats (the lard of cattle, sheep, and dogs) began to be replaced by vegetable oils, pressed from sesame, hemp, and turnip seeds. The range of vegetables was wide, stretching from lotus root and bamboo shoot to lettuce, garlic, and taro, and the now uncommon smartweed, mallow, and oriental celery. Fruits were equally impressive in their variety: peach, apricot, cherry, pear, orange, quince, and many more. Pigs, sheep, cattle, dogs, and chickens were the primary domesticated animals used as food by the Chinese. Wild deer, rabbit, duck, goose, and quail were hunted, as well as fish, turtles, oysters, snails, and shellfish. Almost all of these food items were indigenous and many of them, particularly the plants, endemic, making China a primary center of origin for the world at large. The Han did expand the range of potential foods through territorial expansion but relatively little came from the West, except wheat, perhaps sesame, alfalfa, garlic, pomegranate, grape, cucumber, onions, peas, and coriander. Many of the species existed in China in great botanical variety. The Chinese proved themselves willing consumers across the range of this variety, providing the basis for a rich and diverse diet, extended further by the deployment of a wide range of cooking styles (Huang, 2000: 66–7). Thus, the Han satisfied several of the criteria required to acknowledge their possession of a "cuisine."

An even more dramatic rival claim finds the world's oldest cuisine much closer to the origins of domestication and agriculture, in Mesopotamia, over two thousand years before the Sung, let alone the French.

Mesopotamia

The food culture of the modern Middle East is complex, the heritages of nations and regions formed in the midst of conflict and continuity, and in the shadow of the great monotheistic religions – Judaism, Christianity, and Islam – each with its particular prohibitions and prescriptions for living, and eating, in a godly manner. Goody (1982: 127) finds evidence of haute cuisine in several places and periods throughout the long history of the region, for example in the Sassanid Empire of Persia (third to seventh century AD) when there was "a distinct cuisine for the rich" born in luxury, along the lines of imperial Rome. The ultimate origins of Middle Eastern cuisine, however, Goody derives from

Mesopotamia. Jean Bottéro (2004: 3), a French scholar, has declared this "the oldest cuisine in the world" so, rather than attempting to untangle the larger regional story in all its complexity, it seems most useful to focus on this particular ancient episode.

Bottéro's account of the "haute cuisine" of Mesopotamia is built on the evidence provided by about forty recipes, recorded on cuneiform tablets *c.*3600 BP. Each of these recipes began with a name or title, followed by directions. Some of them were brief, almost telegraphic. For example:

> **Gazelle broth.** Other meat is not used. Prepare water; add fat; salt to taste; onion, *samidu* [white flour], leek and garlic. (Bottéro 2004: 27)

Others were much more detailed, occupying more than thirty lines. All of the dishes were cooked in water (stewed) and all demanded fat, but the use of the liquid after cooking, as soup or sauce, is uncertain, whether vegetable or meat. Sheep, cattle, and birds all featured, as well as the popular (undomesticated) gazelle. Some of the recipes called for a particular cut of meat, notably the leg of mutton. It is, however, clear that most parts of the animal were cooked, with head, legs, tail, spleen, offal, and blood mentioned specifically, and sometimes these seem to have been cooked whole.

The meat was cut into serving portions when cooked, using a carving knife, rather than reduced to smaller amounts before cooking, as practiced in Chinese cuisine, for example, perhaps because this is less a cookery born in scarcity than one reflecting abundance (of meat at least). It was undoubtedly an exclusive cuisine, enjoyed by those high in the hierarchical tree. Probably elements of culinary style were shared across classes but, apart from anything else in politics or social structure, the richness of the materials included in the recipes precluded the identification of a "national cuisine." Even the "vegetable" dishes usually had meat (as well as fat) added to them. Mint, cumin, coriander, and juniper berries were sometimes added. As remained common practice until much later, quantities are never specified, leaving the cook to make the necessary judgments, depending of course on directives from the potential consumers.

What makes these ancient Mesopotamian recipes indicative of a cuisine or, more particularly, a haute cuisine? The simple fact of their existence, recorded in writing, is vital. It points to a scribal desire to document or communicate important processes and practices based on the acquisition of closely specified ingredients, in order to achieve a particular, favored, result. Further, the combination of multiple condiments – as many as ten items in a single dish – indicates a careful blending of complementary flavors. Bottéro argues (1987: 14) that these combinations "obviously presume a demanding and refined palate" and betray "an authentic preoccupation with the gastronomic arts."

There is also evidence of a wide selection of utensils, applied to a range of named processes, such as slicing, steeping, and pounding, and the presence of ovens and varieties of cooking pots. Thus, Bottéro (1987: 17) concludes that "these people show so much refinement in matters dealing with the palate that we are forced to speak of a scientifically-based, learned cuisine, and to consider as real the possibility of gastronomic research."

Japan

The concept of a distinctive national cuisine was created much later in Japan than in China. The great difference in chronology can be accounted for partly by the fact that Japan was more a borrower than an originator in the culinary field (and in other areas too) yet closed from intruders until the late nineteenth century. Indeed, it was only in this period that the term *washoku*, or "Japanese cuisine," was invented, in response to the increasing influence of foreign cuisines, following the negotiation in 1854 of a treaty with the United States represented by Commodore Perry. However, as Cwiertka (2006: 175) argues, several of the elements of this national concept had existed for centuries, as particular features of a region, community, or class, and were merely remade or reinvented in the twentieth century.

A key element in this process was the acceptance by the Japanese of rice as the dominant staple, with soy sauce as the principal flavoring, deployed in the urban meal pattern based on the fundamental "rice-soup-side dish" model. In this model, rice was sometimes replaced by an alternative carbohydrate, but typically plain steamed rice was taken as a given. The soup is generally a broth made using fish stock. Traditionally, the side dish consisted of pickled vegetable. These three or more elements were served in their own separate small bowls, accompanied by tea. In more affluent, recent times, the rice is sometimes embellished with flakes of salted salmon (*nori*) or cooked with gingko nuts or bamboo shoots, for example, or even transformed into a kind of *sushi* (itself in origin a food of scarcity and travel). The soup is open to much greater complexity, particularly through the addition of pieces of fish, shrimp, or chicken, and by the introduction of fermented soybean paste (*miso*). Further, the side dish has been multiplied to several, and often made up of meat, fish, or poultry – seeking to balance the flavors of the sea with the flavors of the mountain – but in all this the basic model remains essentially intact. The structuring of the meal was matched by the careful arrangement of the individual dishes, and the ritual character of dining behavior. The whole package certainly qualifies as a *cuisine*, and a *Japanese* one (Ashkenazi and Jacob, 2000: 67–73).

Beyond the acceptance of this basic model, the development of a Japanese cuisine also involved the spread of regional dishes across the nation, a "gentrification of taste," and a trinity of cooking styles that depended on Chinese (with Korean as an appendix) and Western modes as much as Japanese. Items introduced from outside were not simply accepted as new additions, however, but rather, as happened in France, had to go through a process of naturalization in which taste, texture, and shape, as well as decoration and presentation, might all be accommodated more closely to a "Japanese" style (Cwiertka, 2006: 175–6; Ashkenazi and Jacob, 2000: 64–8). In these ways, the notion of a national cuisine survives strongly amidst the many introductions, even though some of these, such as the consumption of beef and milk after World War II, were touted as foods which would make Japanese smarter or even more Western.

Although it had its unique features, and long delayed as it might appear, the experience of Japan had much in common with that of several other modernizing, industrializing states, opening up to a wider world, in the late nineteenth century and coming to a kind of fulfillment in the twentieth. The common discovery of national cuisines and national foods in this period was a largely self-conscious and directed process, and, once the idea had been implanted, proved contagious.

India

Surprisingly, in view of its evident culinary tradition and its long history of colonization, India constructed a "national cuisine" even later than Japan. As in China, and Japan, the culinary styles of pre-modern India were essentially regional and ethnic, and rooted in a strong medical and moral framework. Cookbooks and prescriptive texts were uncommon and, outside the royal courts, the practice of cooking was attributed only minor cultural significance in the Hindu system of thought. According to Appadurai (1988: 5–7), it was only with the rise of the postcolonial Indian middle class, in the second half of the twentieth century, that cookbooks became common and began to recognize food and cooking as independent of medical and moral issues. Often these cookbooks were published in English, matching the national cultural tendencies of this class but reflecting also the interplay between ethnic, regional – Bengali, Punjabi, and Gujarati, for example – and "Indian" cuisines experienced by the newly mobile, largely urban, populations.

The process has not overwhelmed regional and ethnic cuisines but, instead, sharpened their articulation, and given birth to new regional categories, such as the previously unknown concept of "South Indian" cuisine, which pulls together groups possessed of a more local regional and ethnic identity. This national cuisine, incorporating Mughlai and colonial British contributions, was not confined to the tables of the middle class. It also spilled over into public eating places, from restaurants to street food, and entered the industrial food processing system.

Italy

Alberto Capatti and Massimo Montanari (2003: 115–116) argue that in Italy "a strongly elitist model shaped the development of taste over the centuries, setting a trend for the consumption of rare ingredients and creating a preference for sophisticated combinations of flavors." To this extent the experience of Italy seems to follow that of France, and the cooking of the two countries has deep roots in the indulgent consumption of the ancient Roman aristocracy based on exotic and expensive foods. The imperial cuisine had itself achieved a kind of codification, preserved loosely in the collection of about 120 recipes attributed to Apicius, who lived in the time of Augustus and Tiberius (27 BC–AD 37), but put together in *De Re Coquinaria* as late as 400. Apicius, who shared his name with several other Roman gourmets, made a science of his culinary expertise. Several characteristics of the ancient cuisine, such as the combination of sweet and sour elements, the mixing of different flavors, and the use of spices, persisted through the Middle Ages and the Renaissance and remained important into the early modern period.

French claims to priority in the invention of a high cuisine in the seventeenth century have occasionally been challenged by counterclaims that this revolution had its real origins in sixteenth-century Italy, and more specifically in the kitchens of Catherine de' Medici. Although there seems no clear proof of such transfer, it is certain that circulation between the courts of Europe of cooks, cookbooks, and culinary knowledge became increasingly common in the fifteenth century. In this context, France had the advantage of existing as a relatively coherent nation-state with an established border, whereas Italy remained a congeries of states and regional fragments until unification in 1861. Further, from the seventeenth century, the French royal court was influential throughout Europe in many areas of intellectual and social life, with food culture simply one element in this larger package. Italian cuisine benefited from this outflow of ideas.

The revolutionary changes that took place in seventeenth-century France appeared slowly in Italy, partly because cooks were not allowed initiative. Italian cooks did occasionally recommend replacing spices with thyme, parsley, garlic, and rosemary, but more often persisted with the Spanish style in which cinnamon, nutmeg, coriander, and pepper reigned supreme. Eighteenth-century Enlightenment philosophers, too, sometimes promoted the banishment of strong flavors and an emphasis on lightness and refinement.

However, as Capatti and Montanari argue, the bourgeoisie took their opportunity to make choices which had long been beyond their reach, by applying spices to their dishes for the first time and persisting with sweet and sour sauces, rather than following an elite or French model. This line of development included an acceptance of the fruits of the New World, notably the tomato, which by the eighteenth century had been naturalized and increasingly came to take on an "Italian" flavor. Cane sugar similarly was at home in this food culture, sprinkled with spice on *tortelli* (little cakes) style pasta (Serventi and Sabban, 2002: 238–9). Thus, there appeared in Italy a relationship of power contrary to the developmental model proposed earlier for the creation of new or high cuisines. Alternatively, it may be argued, it was by clinging to the old and only reluctantly introducing French ideas that Italy (and Spain) created their own unique national cuisines while maintaining significant internal regional variety.

A new version of Italian cuisine emerged during World War I as a consequence of state intervention. Cheap imported wheat enabled the poor to replace rice, corn, and chestnuts with bread and pasta. The removal of the bread price subsidy in 1921 paved the way for fascism and when Mussolini took power the following year he sought to "nationalize" Italian cuisine. On the one hand, he strived to reduce consumption and encourage self-sufficiency but on the other made every effort to be seen as the nation's provider and to be associated with images of abundance. It was a role common to many twentieth-century dictatorships. The hardships of another war brought further deprivation and a reversion to the diet of the nineteenth century. In the peace that followed, Italians proved relatively reluctant to embrace the forces of globalization. Affluence allowed them to eat more but they tended to eat more of the same things and to explore regional foods rather than succumbing to outside influences. The national cuisine of Italy remained firmly rooted in the past.

Thus, the governments of twentieth-century Italy were crucial to the shaping of popular consumption patterns and what Carol Helstosky (2004: 151) calls "a national cuisine of scarcity." It was from scarcity and necessity that Italians created highly elaborate and formal systems, in much the way that has been argued for ancient China. Further, it can be seen again that scarcity and abundance are sometimes two sides of the same thing. For example, dried pasta comes in six hundred varieties and even more shapes. The same applies to bread and pizza. The apparent simplicity of the materials is transformed by an abundance of styles and ways of cooking, thus re-making the same essential product. Tiny additions, a pinch of corn meal or a knob of lard, can be enough to create something completely distinct. Further, the rules of mixing and combination can be quite strict and formal. Expensive and rare ingredients have little to do with it.

Uzbekistan

In the postcolonial world, newly created states have sometimes approached the task of nation-building by attempting to isolate themselves from the myriad influences of globalization and cultural imperialism, with an obsession far exceeding that demonstrated by the Italians. One consequence of reclusiveness has often been an emphasis on self-sufficiency, in food as well as other things. The result is sometimes vulnerability to deprivation, including famine, as occurred in North Korea in the 1990s. Another consequence of isolationism has been the viability of authoritarian rule, making the state appear directly responsible for the scarcity and/or abundance of food and its distribution. These conditions provide fertile ground for the self-conscious creation of national cuisines, through deprivation and the necessity of turning to the local, and through the suppression of the regional (as well as ethnic or religious difference) in order to promote the primacy of nation. One such is Uzbekistan.

When Uzbekistan in arid Central Asia became independent of the Soviet Union in 1991, an ideology of ethnic, linguistic, and (Muslim) religious identity formed the basis of Uzbek nationalism, closely monitored and enforced by an authoritarian regime (Rosenberger, 2007). An Uzbek cookbook, in the Uzbek language, had been published in 1958, and the notion of a national Uzbek cuisine (in which regional variation was suppressed) became established as an element of distinctive ethnic identity. Land planted in cotton under the Soviets was reclaimed for food production, cafeterias were forgotten, and imports reduced, but food production proved inadequate and expensive. Land degradation and climate change (warming) put pressure on irrigated agriculture. Livestock production, particularly sheep, collapsed throughout the region.

A range of Uzbek dishes became prominent "national" favorites, such as *palov* (made with rice, mutton, mutton fat, onions, and yellow carrots), *sumalak* (a pudding made from sprouted, malted wheat), *samsa* (dumplings made from potatoes, onions, lamb, and lamb fat), and *shipildok* (green peas, wheat, and horsemeat boiled with onions and cumin). Enthusiasm for these dishes, even when the meat was sometimes omitted from the recipe, went together with practices, such as preserving, that reflected more directly necessity rather than positive choices. In rural areas, hunger was common, the national dishes something to drool about but beyond reach. Government policy, through tariffs, prevented entry of packaged and canned global foods for general consumption, so that the dominance of national foods was more likely challenged by internal regional, ethnic, or religious diets, all of which might also be interpreted as indicators of political rebellion.

Cuba

In Cuba, a "national folk cuisine" emerged by the middle of the nineteenth century, decades before the abolition of slavery. It was given a self-consciously "Cuban" character in the cookbooks which began to be published (by elite writers) in the 1850s, as part of the recognition of a broader picture of Cuban folk culture, with the Cuban style carefully distinguished from Spanish. These early Cuban cookbooks included many recipes using ingredients unique to the island or the Caribbean region, together with African ingredients and cooking methods (Dawdy, 2002). However, from the 1850s to the 1950s, Cuban cookbooks did not so much celebrate the blending of cultures and cuisines as denigrate and downplay the role of non-European people, notably the Afro-Cuban women who were the true creators of Cuban cuisine. In this way, as Christine Folch (2008: 221) argues, Cuban cookbooks before 1959 served as "a folklore of the elite" and were used to "mythologize the origins of the cultural production of cuisine." Thus, in contrast to the French experience, for example, the cooks of Cuba long remained a socially and politically oppressed class, unrecognized for their innovations and adaptations, written out of the cookbooks that proved sites for hegemonic struggle.

The "national cuisine" of Cuba did, however, survive the denigration of its creators, and persisted relatively intact through the Revolution of 1959, when it began to be celebrated as a creole blend of African, European, Amerindian, and Asian cuisines, taken as a metaphor representing the ethnic diversity of the Cuban people themselves. Many elements of this cuisine had their roots in the hardships of slavery, blended with technologies remembered from Africa, but they typically cut across classes, rather than being the domain of a narrow elite, so that it was neither high nor low cuisine. The Revolution merely emphasized this tendency by effectively cutting out the possibility of maintaining a high cuisine dependent on imported ingredients. Thus, Fidel Castro told his people to forget imported canned peaches and to eat mangoes. In recognition of its objective of removing inequalities in all areas, including food, the Revolution promoted the slogan "Everyone eats the same."

Megaregions and pan-ethnicity

Distinguished from both regional cuisines and from modern global foods are culinary systems identified with large regions made up of multiple national units. Often these "megaregions" are constructions of outside observers rather than units with meaning to the peoples contained within them, and they exist in order to simplify and generalize rather than to demonstrate any level of political allegiance.

One such is the concept of "Mediterranean diet," a term popularized by the American nutritionists Ancel and Margaret Keys in *How to Eat Well and Stay Well the Mediterranean Way*, first published in New York in 1975. Although the term suggests broad application to the rimlands of the Mediterranean Sea, it is a "diet" (not a "cuisine") that has most in common with the everyday national cuisine of (coastal) southern Italy, the Mezzogiorno, and that of Crete (Trichopoulou and Lagiou, 1997). It was born in scarcity and persistent hardship. Sometimes seen as equivalent to the "Asiatic diet," the Mediterranean diet was in 2010 declared by UNESCO part of the Intangible Cultural Heritage of Spain, Greece, Italy, and Morocco.

The Mediterranean diet is generally described as rich in olive oil, grains, legumes, fruit (particularly grapes), and (salad) vegetables, with some cheese, yoghurt, and fish, a little wine, and not much meat. Fundamental are notions of moderation, advocated by prophets for centuries, and simplicity (Skiadas and Lascaratos, 2001). Indeed, the Mediterranean diet is, by these means, traced back to ancient civilizations and philosophies. Locally, however, and particularly in the case of Crete, the response has been a flood of cookbooks promoting the health benefits of the insular and "national" cuisines of a much more narrowly defined region (Ball, 2003). This Cretan trend is part of a broader development in the redefinition of national identity in Greece, beginning in the late 1980s, in which small-scale "diverse" landscapes have been increasingly identified as homes to distinctive local, ethnic, and rural cuisines (Yiakoumaki, 2006). These tendencies run counter to the hegemony of both nation-state and megaregion, constituting a reaction to such lumping and an embrace of difference, but, in every case, using food as the vital ingredient.

Other examples of megaregions are easy to find. Thus "Caribbean food," "Latin American food," and "South-East Asian food" all have their cookbooks, though often subdivided by nation or island in recognition of the importance of the smaller units. Dishes that are common throughout such large regions may be found, such as beans and rice in Latin America, but they are generally few and outnumbered by the dishes that are unique to the component societies. What underlies the shared food histories and unity of these megaregions is variable. Even the apparent geographical unity of the Caribbean, for example, is less than certain, and historians regularly debate whether the cultures of the rimland (the littoral North and South American mainlands) should be included with those of the islands, with quite strongly different consequences for the food histories that might be constructed. Much the same problem arises in attempts to define South-East Asia. Latin America is a cultural region, rooted in language and colonialism, while the varied histories of imperialism cross-cut notions of national or regional cuisines or food histories throughout the Americas.

Africa provides a different kind of example. Here the question – one generally associated with the views of Africans living outside Africa – arises whether it is possible to talk usefully of a continent-wide "African cuisine." It can also be asked whether "African cuisine" should be taken to incorporate the diaspora, the places across the Atlantic where people of African descent are demographically prominent. Thus, in the period since 1960, recipe books covering

"African cooking" frequently included dishes from places like Brazil, Jamaica, Martinique, and Virginia, for example (Cusack, 2000). These collections take their place beside a growing number of publications defined by the nation-state in which "national dishes" are often identified and named for the first time. The concept of a pan-African cuisine parallels notions of pan-ethnicity and expands naturally to encompass the Atlantic diaspora.

In just the same way that ethnicity is constructed through the identification of "others," so too has ethnic food often entered the awareness of its makers and consumers only when they have become migrants or recognized themselves as belonging to a diaspora. This was what happened in the case of "Italian" food and in such cases the association between nation and ethnicity was always close. Sometimes the growth of awareness led to contests over the right to claim or own a specific food or dish. Such conflict became particularly lively in Europe following the formation of the European Union, perhaps in response to the way in which the regional association stirred up local passions.

Thus, in 2002 the EU ruled that feta cheese, made from goat's and sheep's milk, was exclusively Greek. Not all such claims were easily acknowledged, however. When hummus, a dip made from chickpeas, sesame paste, garlic, olive oil, and lemon juice, began to become known as an Israeli or Greek dip, legislation was introduced to the Lebanese Parliament in 2008 seeking EU recognition that the product's nationality was truly Lebanese, but this bid failed. In all of these cases, there was a belief that protecting ownership of foods was important to local and ethnic identity, in the midst of globalization and regionalism. Often, of course, money benefits were seen to depend on the capacity to market specific foods as authentic products.

The concept of "ethnic food" overlaps ideas of nation, region, diaspora, and universalism. Although the emphasis is apparently on the foods themselves – "ethnic food" rather than "ethnic cuisine" – understanding of the meaning of the concept clearly comprehends the many elements of cuisine. Probably it is known as food rather than cuisine because the items may be consumed by people from outside the group, though the original significance of the foods came from their being prepared and consumed by a particular group and not by others. For example, Jewish food, Creole food, Soul food, and Chinese food can all be considered types of ethnic foods but their geographical spread and acceptance has been variable, suggesting contrasting roles in pan-ethnicity and globalization (Wu and Cheung, 2002). A tension always exists between the maintenance of a remembered or living unique cultural experience and the integration of new food items and culinary styles in new places. Even in the case of Creole food, born of blending and hybridity, in the cultural process called creolization, no truly global or super-ethnic cuisine has emerged strong enough to rival national cuisines, however artificial and theoretically dubious.

Global foods

A constant theme in modern world food history is "globalization," a process and experience not confined to food but often epitomized by eating cultures. The concept covers a range of developments, from the redistribution of plants and animals (discussed in Chapter 2), to trade and distribution (Chapter 6), and culinary practice (Chapter 7). The impact was greatest in the era of European imperialism concentrated between 1492 and the end of the eighteenth century, when a global redistribution of plants and animals occurred parallel to the redistribution of peoples and cultures. Because this was largely a forced migration and invasive colonization, complaints about the loss of culinary identities are hard to find in the historical record, but a longing for home and the things of home was clearly evident. A less sweeping but equally dramatic transformation occurred in Russia as a consequence of the Westernization imposed by Peter the Great (1672–1725), which introduced new foods and culinary styles, engendering complaint that the distinctiveness of Russian cuisine was lost.

In terms of cuisine and patterns of consumption, globalization now is signified most obviously by the geographical spread of multinational products and corporate retail outlets. Prime examples of "global" food products are pasta and pizza, which, as noted earlier, are attributed origins in Italy but have been accepted by a large number of countries. Pizza had its first birth in eighteenth-century Naples, where it became one of the most popular foods of the city, providing the poor with an edible plate that could be priced according to its embellishments. It did not spread through Italy until the twentieth century and in the meantime had experienced a second birth in the United States. As Helstosky (2008: 11) argues, "pizza went from being strictly Neapolitan to being Italian-American and then becoming Italian." At much the same time it became Italian, it also became European as Neapolitan migrants set up shops throughout Western Europe.

In both Italy and the United States, pizza escaped from its status as an enclave dish only after World War II, though in the process losing some of its character as a humble food of poor city-folk. From these twin sources, pizza rapidly spread to become "the world's most popular fast food" (Helstosky 2008: 9). Even where Italian restaurants and cafés had established themselves in distant sites in the postwar world, in places like Australia, it was the rapid arrival in the 1960s of the US corporate chain Pizza Hut (established in Kansas in 1958) that made pizza known to a wider (though initially mostly middle-class) global population.

By the twenty-first century, the reach of pizza was so broad and entrenched that it could appear both cosmopolitan and local, with regional versions attached to ethnicities other than Italian, which in turn conquered the globe, for example the "Hawaiian" pizza constructed with components that included chunks of pineapple and bits of bacon. In India, where Pizza Hut opened in 1996, toppings included mutton kebabs, coriander, and paneer (a curd cheese), creating a style then offered in its outlets in places like Poland as an exotic variety. A Russian Proton rocket launched in 1999 displayed the Pizza Hut logo.

By 2000, there were about 10 000 Pizza Huts around the world, widely distributed but heavily focussed in North America and Mexico, Western Europe, and East Asia, spreading down through Australia and New Zealand. South America was blank, as was Africa, with the exception of South Africa, and most of central Eurasia. This pattern of geographical distribution was matched closely by other fast food chains of American origin, such as Kentucky Fried Chicken and Burger King. The hamburger giant McDonald's had a more comprehensive footprint, with more than twice as many outlets as Pizza Hut, though still rarely seen in most of Africa and central Asia. McDonald's had much earlier become the most visible symbol of Americanization and globalization, attributed immense powers of influence, leading to the coining of the term "McDonaldization" in 1975 intended both to applaud and denigrate the virtues of efficiency and standardization. The McDonald's hamburger also gave birth to the "Big Mac Index," which compared relative national prices with exchange rates, to test their over- or undervaluation.

McDonald's had begun life in southern California in 1948, the first drive-in restaurants specialized to produce hamburgers (which had come to America from Germany in the 1870s) on an industrial assembly line system (Smith, 2009: 219). It was true fast food, largely cooked in advance, and customers ate in their cars. Franchizing began in the United States in 1955, then Canada (1967), Japan, Australia, and Germany (1971), France (1972), and then *inter alia* Russia (1990), China (1992), and South Africa (1995). The McDonald's model was modified to meet local circumstances when it went abroad, yet retained everywhere its essential simple iconography and its values of efficiency and standardization. The ability to adjust to local circumstances and cultures was vital. Failure to do so led to closures, often on a national scale, not only for McDonald's but also for other American global hopefuls such as the coffee giant Starbucks. Competitors stole market share by making concessions, such as the French chain Quick's offering halal hamburgers to Muslim customers in 2010.

In terms of international visibility and imperial expansion the McDonald's model's only real rival was Coca-Cola. Formulated in 1886, Coca-Cola was the first caffeinated soft drink, marketed initially as a tonic or patent medicine. It rapidly became popular outside the United States and, because it was bulky (with its large element of water and heavy glass bottle), distant factories quickly sprouted. From the time of World War II, Coca-Cola had a leading symbolic role in carrying things American to the wider world, a role that expanded even further during the Cold War (Weiner, 1996).

From an American point of view, Coca-Cola was a patriotic political symbol, focussed on a democratic vision of consumer abundance. In this way it was able to encapsulate the American Way of Life – something to be protected above all and something to be aspired to by other peoples. It was egalitarian because it was inexpensive and offered a simple sweet taste, but Coca-Cola's uniformity and global grip was equally seen by critics as culturally dangerous. French protests began in the immediate postwar period and the drink was soon associated with a process labeled "coca-colanization," a term first used in 1950, fitting neatly with the political, cultural, and economic colonization of an earlier imperial era and uncomfortable in the midst of rapidly moving decolonization and independence movements.

McDonaldization was no more benign. Its defenders portrayed it as a force for democracy, a vanguard of the American lifestyle, but its detractors identified it as the Trojan horse in a process of culinary homogenization that undermined national and regional cuisines, a tool of cultural imperialism. It raised the ire of French, Italian, and Chinese political leaders anxious to defend the honor of their food and foodways. Famously, in 1999, a French farmer and cheese-maker José Bové drove his tractor into a McDonald's outlet that was under construction, in protest at the use of hormone-treated beef in hamburgers and in support of "food sovereignty."

In spite of such protests and in the face of continuing conflict between the French and US governments over trade, fast food outlets, including those of McDonald's, increased their numbers rapidly in the first decade of the twenty-first century (Willging, 2008). More significantly, McDonald's was criticized for its contribution to the spread of obesity and ill-health by promoting cheap "junk food," the provision of which in turn contributed to the destruction of rainforest and to global warming. As Watson (2006: 2) argues, "McDonald's has become a saturated symbol, so laden with contradictory associations and meanings that the company stands for something greater than the sum of its corporate parts."

One response to the global reach of fast food was the establishment of a "slow food" movement. This began in 1986 when McDonald's opened a restaurant at the Spanish Steps in Rome, thrusting functionality into the heart of civilized life. Offended Italians responded by declaring speed a threat to taste and sociability. The movement spread rapidly around the world. It sought also to promote the consumption of neglected and forgotten foods, and the revival and survival of artisan methods which had been prohibited or restricted for reasons of hygiene or safety, in order to fight against blandness and machine-made food. In spite of the wholesomeness of these ideals, fast food's empire prospered and expanded in the twenty-first century, not least in Italy. Ironically, iconic Italian foods, notably pasta and pizza, were major elements in globalization.

Three claims and counterclaims

First, there is the claim that all nations have national cuisines and the counter-claim that only some nations do. This opposition is generally taken to derive from debate over the criteria necessary to classifying cuisines as high or low. The claim that only a handful of nations have high cuisines serves to justify the claim that other nations or peoples, notably hunter-gatherers, lack cuisine. On the other hand, the claim that all cuisines are equal removes the possibility of differentiation and assessment, in much the same way it can be claimed that all drawing is art or all sound music. These claims and concerns are products of modernity, matters not much worried about by ancient peoples who knew their food was superior whenever they had more to eat than their neighbors did and could afford to eat more exotic items, however prepared.

A second and related claim, or counterclaim, is that national cuisines do not really exist but are merely constructs built up from regional cuisines. The principal advocate of this view is Mintz (1996: 95–7), who argues that cuisines "are never the foods of a country, but the foods of a *place*." However large or small this place, its ingredients are always regional. An alternative counterclaim turns the argument around to argue that the identification of national cuisines underpins and even creates recognition of the regional.

Third, whereas some claim that (high) cuisine is a product of abundance, others make the counterclaim that it is the creation of scarcity or deprivation. An alternative way of looking at this conundrum might be to argue that regular exposure to famine foods inspires creativity and elaboration of variety and culinary style that carries over into intervening moments of abundance when the lessons learned in hardship can be applied to a brilliant array of superior food resources.

REFERENCES

Anderson, E.N. (1988) *The Food of China*. New Haven, CT: Yale University Press.

Appadurai, A. (1988) How to make a national cuisine: Cookbooks in contemporary India. *Comparative Studies in Society and History* 30: 3–24.

Armelagos, G.J. (2010) The omnivore's dilemma: The evolution of the brain and the determinants of food choice. *Journal of Anthropological Research* 66: 161–86.

Ashkenazi, M. and Jacob, J. (2000) *The Essence of Japanese Cuisine: An Essay on Food and Culture*. Philadelphia: University of Pennsylvania Press.

Ball, E.L. (2003) Greek food after *Mousaka*: Cookbooks, "local" culture, and the Cretan diet. *Journal of Modern Greek Studies* 21: 1–36.

Bottéro, J. (1987) The culinary tablets at Yale. *Journal of the American Oriental Society* 107: 11–19.

Bottéro, J. (2004) *The Oldest Cuisine in the World: Cooking in Mesopotamia*, (trans. T.L. Fagan). Chicago: University of Chicago Press.

Capatti, A. and Montanari, M. (2003) *Italian Cuisine: A Cultural History*. New York: Columbia University Press.

Cusack, I. (2000) African cuisines: Recipes for nation-building? *Journal of African Cultural Studies* 13: 207–25.

Cwiertka, K.J. (2006) *Modern Japanese Cuisine: Food, Power and National Identity*. London: Reaktion Books.

Dawdy, S.L. (2002) *La comida mambisa*: Food, farming, and Cuban identity, 1839–1999. *New West Indian Guide* 76: 47–80.

Ferguson, P.P. (2004) *Accounting for Taste: The Triumph of French Cuisine*. Chicago: University of Chicago Press.

Folch, C. (2008) Fine dining: Race in prerevolution Cuban cookbooks. *Latin American Research Review* 43: 205–23.

Freeman, M. (1977) Sung. In K.C. Chang (ed.) *Food in Chinese Culture: Anthropological and Historical Perspective*, pp. 143–76. New Haven, CT: Yale University Press.

Goody, J. (1982) *Cooking, Cuisine and Class: A Study in Comparative Sociology*. Cambridge: Cambridge University Press.

Gvion, L. (2006) Cuisines of poverty as means of empowerment: Arab food in Israel. *Agriculture and Human Values* 23: 299–312.

Gvion, L. and Trostler, N. (2008) From spaghetti and meatballs through Hawaiian pizza to sushi: The changing nature of ethnicity in American restaurants. *Journal of Popular Culture* 41: 950–974.

Helstosky, C. (2004) *Garlic and Oil: Politics and Food in Italy*. Oxford: Berg.

Helstosky, C. (2008) *Pizza: A Global History*. London: Reaktion Books.

Huang, H.T. (2000) *Fermentations and Food Science*, Part V, Vol. 6, *Joseph Needham, Science and Civilisation in China*. Cambridge: Cambridge University Press.

Iverson, J.T. (2010) Can World Heritage status save the future of French food? *Time* (21 November).

Keys, A. and Keys, M. (1975) *How to Eat Well and Stay Well the Mediterranean Way*. Garden City, NY: Doubleday.

Long, L.M. (ed.) (2004) *Culinary Tourism*. Lexington, KY: University Press of Kentucky.

Lyons, D. (2007) Integrating African cuisines: Rural cuisine and identity in Tigray, Highland Ethiopia. *Journal of Social Archaeology* 7: 346–71.

McCann, J.C. (2009) *Stirring the Pot: A History of African Cuisine*. Athens, OH: Ohio University Press.

Mennell, S. (1985) *All Manners of Food: Eating and Taste in England and France from the Middle Ages to the Present*. Oxford: Basil Blackwell.

Mintz, S.W. (1996) *Tasting Food, Tasting Freedom: Excursions into Eating, Culture, and the Past*. Boston: Beacon Press.

Pinkard, S. (2009) *A Revolution in Taste: The Rise of French Cuisine, 1650–1800*. Cambridge: Cambridge University Press.

Pitte, J.-R. (2002) *French Gastronomy: The History and Geography of a Passion*. New York: Columbia University Press.

Rosenberger, N. (2007) Patriotic appetites and gnawing hungers: Food and the paradox of nation-building in Uzbekistan. *Ethnos* 72: 339–60.

Roux, S. (2009) *Paris in the Middle Ages*. Philadelphia: University of Pennsylvania Press.

Serventi, S. and Sabban, S. (2002) *Pasta: The Story of a Universal Food*. New York: Columbia University Press.

Skiadas, P.K., and J.G. Lascaratos (2001) Dietetics in Ancient Greek philosophy: Plato's concepts of healthy diet. *European Journal of Clinical Nutrition* 55: 532–37.

Smith, A.F. (2009) *Eating History: 30 Turning Points in the Making of American Cuisine*. New York: Columbia University Press.

Sterckx, R. (2005) Food and philosophy in early China. In R. Sterckx (ed.) *Of Tripod and Palate: Food, Politics, and Religion in Traditional China*, pp. 34–61. New York: Palgrave Macmillan.

Trichopoulou, A. and Lagiou, P. (1997) Healthy traditional Mediterranean diet: An expression of culture, history, and lifestyle. *Nutrition Reviews* 55: 383–89.

Watson, J.L. (ed.) (2006) *Golden Arches East: McDonald's in East Asia*. Stanford, CA: Stanford University Press.

Weiner, M. (1996) Consumer culture and participatory democracy: The story of Coca-Cola during World War II. *Food and Foodways* 6: 109–29.

Willging, J. (2008) Of GMOs, McDomination and foreign fat: Contemporary Franco-American food fights. *French Cultural Studies* 19: 199–226.

Wu, D.Y.H. and. Cheung, S.C.H (eds) (2002) *The Globalization of Chinese Food*. Honolulu: University of Hawai'i Press.

Yiakoumaki, V. (2006) "Local", "ethnic", and "rural" food: On the emergence of "cultural diversity" in post-EU-accession Greece. *Journal of Modern Greek Studies* 24: 415–45.

CHAPTER NINE

Eating Well, Eating Badly

Eating too little is hazardous, indeed life-threatening. So too is eating to excess. Most often, over the millennia since the beginnings of agriculture, the people of the world shared a fear of hunger. Only in the late twentieth century could some societies afford to express an even greater fear of over-eating. Somehow, in this globalized and interconnected world, the extremes coexisted. Starving children stared goggle-eyed from television screens, as all-you-can-eat tourist ships cruised the coasts of stricken lands. For the wealthy, the global supermarket offered bounty beyond belief, but equally a new, insidious version of the omnivore's dilemma. People ate not just because they were hungry. They responded to myriad stimuli, some of them associated directly with the foods themselves and some of them emanating from a larger contextual social and cultural bubble, from the sirens of the supermarket to the joys of sociability (Wansink, 2007; Popkin and Gordon-Larsen, 2004). Even in many developing countries, once the immediate threat of famine receded a new threat loomed, that of obesity (Galal, 2002). In developed economies, obesity became a particular problem of the poor.

Nutrition and diet

Even the hungriest people make choices about what, and what not, to eat. These choices are governed by a whole range of influences, from the economic to the ethical, but only a small proportion relate directly to ideas about what is best for the maintenance of life. Food can bring satisfaction, the pleasures of taste and a sense of fullness, without necessarily delivering the

How Food Made History, First Edition. B. W. Higman.
© 2012 B. W. Higman. Published 2012 by Blackwell Publishing Ltd.

energy needed to perform work and build the body. Energy can be found in fats, sugars, and protein, but it is the carbohydrates rich in sugars and starch that have always delivered most of the calories, and still account for more than 50 percent of total calories, even in the richest countries. Most of this energy is applied to the maintenance of basal metabolism, simply keeping the body warm enough to keep running, including the energy required to eat and digest food (Smil, 2008: 120–123). Thus, it is essential to ensure that the energy expended in obtaining food does not exceed the energy supplied, a fact well understood by hunters who might run a deer or antelope to exhaustion but equally have to know when to abandon the chase. In addition to the energy-yielding macronutrients the human body also requires the digestion of essential amino acids, nine in infants, eight in children and adults, to promote and maintain the growth of muscle, bone, and internal organs.

Custom and experience over many generations contributed to an appreciation of what was best and what most detrimental, and the advocacy of specific diets started in ancient times. Such advice was, however, typically associated with philosophical and religious ideas, and closely related to arguments for the prohibition or restriction of certain items. Only in quite recent times has a science of nutrition emerged, with the goal of providing objective guidance to consumers. Yet, as everyone knows, the directives that come from this science seem to be constantly changing, and too often contradictory and full of reversals (Gifford, 2002). One day we are told eating eggs is bad, the next good; or red wine is beneficial, then not. The variety of consumption patterns and dietary recommendations are sometimes represented in "food pyramids," first constructed in the early twentieth century. Examples prepared by the Oldways Preservation Trust, to be followed in conjunction with "daily physical activity," are illustrated in Figure 9.1.

Fundamental to the development of nutrition science is the use of numerical measures. One of the most important is the *calorie*, a number representing the energy (heat) content of food: precisely, a quantity sufficient to raise the temperature of one gram of water by one degree centigrade, but expressed by nutritionists in thousands or "kilocalories." The calorie was used first in French, from the 1830s, but became a recognized unit in the measurement of nutrition only in the 1860s when experiments using a combustion calorimeter produced the first values for specific foods. Earlier investigators had not been able to make these measurements because doing so depended on a proper understanding of the circulation of the blood, the nature of combustion, and the function of respiration, a knowledge begun in the seventeenth century but not completed until the early nineteenth. Only from the 1860s did the quantitative energy concept of foods and body tissues solve the problem of how muscles work, namely at the expense of energy derived from the oxidation of fats and *carbohydrates* (a term coined as recently as 1844).

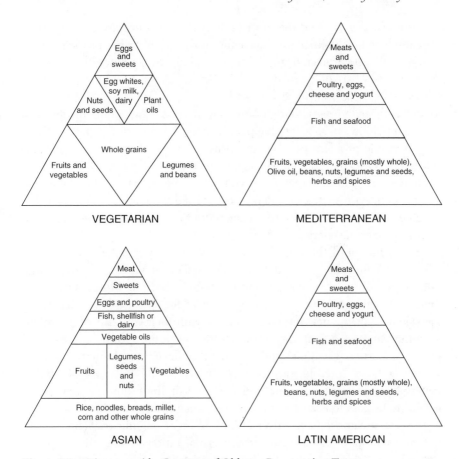

Figure 9.1 Diet pyramids. Courtesy of Oldways Preservation Trust.

Source: © 2000 Oldways Preservation & Exchange Trust www.oldwayspt.org

In addition to energy, the body needs nutrients, notably vitamins, minerals, protein, and linoleic acid. *Protein* was coined in 1838, from the Greek *protean* to indicate its power of transformation. However, the essential amino acids (discovered in the 1880s) contained in protein, which are broken down into their constituents during the process of digestion, remained little understood until the 1950s (McCollum, 1957: 115–132). These amino acids are essential to growth but needed only in small amounts and are available from both plant and animal foods. *Vitamins*, required in small quantities to prevent deficiency diseases, were identified and named by 1912. Different foods contain these elements in different proportions (Kamminga and Cunningham, 1995: 3–9). Cheese made from whole milk, for example, is rich in fat, thus delivering many calories, as well as protein, Vitamin A (good for growth and vision), and the minerals calcium and phosphorus (good for strong bones and teeth), but no carbohydrates.

It is no surprise to find that nutrition science was from its very beginning mired in ideology, politics, and academic rivalry. Such studies formed part of a larger scientific project, beginning in the middle of the nineteenth century, understood as part of a broader mission of calculability and control. In the United States, this enterprise was led by Wilbur O. Atwater, who from 1885 joined with economists, statisticians, industrialists, and philanthropists in casting nutrition as a social problem. More precisely, nutrition came to be seen as part of the problem of labor or industrial wages, in which poverty was traced largely to the poor dietary habits of the working classes. Atwater set about measuring human metabolism directly, using an airtight chamber called a respiration calorimeter, in which a subject lived for a number of days. Every aspect of the subject's activity, input and output, was monitored and measured in units of thermal energy.

Understanding of the working of the human body thus became closer to that of a machine, its fuel food rather than coal or oil. With such mechanistic notions in mind, objective measures of efficiency and productivity could replace ethical notions in the management of food, just as they did in the management of the new industrial systems with their concepts of workflow, assembly line, and standardization. On the home front, where social problems started, the model underpinned the concept of "domestic science." At its worst, it seemed like a mission to determine the least cost of labor, a measure of the minimum diet and therefore of the minimum wages that needed to be paid to keep a workforce functional (Aronson, 1982).

The calorie came to have universal application, from industrial efficiency to the provisioning of armies and the delivery of rations to starving people. It became a standard measure of the very existence of hunger, and famine, particularly when quantified on a national, regional, or global scale. In the early twentieth century, the calorie also became a tool of foreign policy, used aggressively in the advocacy of specific diets, based, for example, on models that included large proportions of grains (particularly wheat rather than rice) and animal products (particularly milk), as a means of raising the living standards and physiques of subject, colonial, peoples (Worboys, 1988). It was in this context that nutritional science was used in the 1930s by the United States, Canada, and Australia to justify the disposal of a great accumulated glut of wheat in the colonial territories, the places shown to be statistically malnourished. Doing so was seen by the developed economies as a means of correcting a global imbalance between production and consumption that was good for everyone and good for world peace (Cullather, 2007). The significance of this push was magnified after 1945 when the theories of nutritional science came to underpin patterns of world trade and food aid.

The history of nutritional science can, therefore, be written as a story of scientism and imperialism. Further, there is much evidence that ideas of nutrition continue to be used in dubious or negative ways: to encourage the eating of foods to benefit producers more than consumers and to discourage the continuing production and consumption of traditional or indigenous foods, for example. The critique is vital and important. At the same time, nutrition does have its own history, in the way people have in the long-term altered their diets with consequences for their health and wellbeing. Historians are interested to chart these transformations over time in order to correlate changes in diet with changes in other social and political indicators.

Nutritional status is best measured not in terms of the actual foods people consume but rather by physical consequences. Longevity is one such measure but complicated by the contributions of many lifestyle and environmental variables other than food. Better, though not completely independent, indicators are height and weight. Historical data relating to weight are rare until recent times but heights are available in relatively representative samples from a much wider range of samples, and stature has therefore become a preferred measure.

Stature

More than half of the variation observed in height is controlled by genetic factors. Stress, illness, and social circumstances also contribute, but the quantity and quality of food consumed by children and young people are sufficiently important to allow stature to serve as a surrogate for nutritional status and the biological standard of living. The nutritional status of the mother during pregnancy is also significant. In recent history, it is well known that modern generations show significant height gains over their parents and that the children of immigrants to developed countries show similar gains. In these societies, height correlates strongly with per capita income. It follows that height is related to class, the children of the better-off typically growing taller than those of the poor. Similarly, children conceived and brought up in times of famine and shortage are more likely to be stunted.

Achievement of appropriate weight-for-height ratios by a stunted population demonstrates a sufficient intake of energy together with chronic poor-quality nutrition. This relationship was common in sub-Saharan Africa in the late twentieth century, for example, but resolved by changes in diet and eating habits (Semproli and Gualdi-Russo, 2007). Whereas previously during times of shortage the men and boys of a group would consume most of what was offered at a meal, now women and girls partake and mothers are able to ensure the youngest of the children eat well.

Final adult heights often conceal differences in rates of growth. Children suffering protein energy malnutrition may grow comparatively slowly to adolescence but eventually catch up on the better fed of their cohorts. Thus, wherever they can be found, historians prefer to use growth data, but detailed records of measurements made at regular intervals are extremely rare for the centuries before 1900. Final heights can be found more easily, and for much longer periods. Importantly, skeletal remains found in archeological sites do not depend on the existence of a contemporary recorder or even a statistical interest in stature. Skeletal remains have an added attraction in the information they can give about nutritional status through the analysis of teeth and bones. For example, hypoplasia, evidenced by grooves in the enamel of teeth, indicates severe malnutrition (or illness) at an early age.

Something similar to the pattern of individual growth in stature can occur in the comparative heights of different countries, regions, or social groups, in which the shorter eventually catch up with the taller as they achieve parity in nutrition and health regimes. For example, in the 1920s the wheat-eating people of north China were 3–4 in. (6–7 cm) taller than the rice-eating southern Chinese, but by the 1990s this difference had been reduced to just 1 in. (2–3 cm) (Morgan, 2000: 6). Driving the closing of this gap, which had long been seen in genetic terms, was a relative standardization of diet and cultural patterns. At the same time, some socially disadvantaged small rural regions in the south showed no improvement and, indeed, sometimes suffered absolute reductions.

Generally, the effect of improvements in nutrition and wealth enable the short and poor to make bigger relative gains than their richer and taller fellow citizens. Thus, although migrant Europeans fared well in temperate North America, and from the colonial period to the middle of the twentieth century were the tallest people in the world, after 1950 they lost ground to the Europeans who had stayed put. American growth began to slow down in the Great Depression (Komlos and Lauderdale, 2007). By the beginning of the twenty-first century, the Dutch had become the world's tallest – males reaching 72 in. (184 cm) and females 67 in. (170 cm), some 2 in. (5 cm) taller than Americans – in testimony to superior and improved nutrition and health-care systems or, alternatively, relative failure of the US food system and an inferior social safety net. Black American women, but not men, actually experienced an absolute reduction in height among those born after 1975 (Komlos, 2010).

The Dutch had been the fastest-growing nation in Europe for more than a century, partly owing to superior access to high-quality milk products. Other tall populations at the beginning of the twenty-first century included Sweden (which had experienced absolute reductions in some decades of the eighteenth and nineteenth centuries), Finland, and Denmark (Hatton and Bray, 2010). Significantly, the pattern was much the same for longevity. Similarly rapid catching up in height occurred in many Asian countries in the late twentieth century, in spite of a persistent argument that there are genetic limits to growth potential (Geissler, 1993).

Long-term growth in human stature has been far from steady and consistent. Indeed, analysis of skeletal remains suggests the opposite, with reduction as likely as increase in many periods and places. Cyclical movement is also typical. These findings parallel the more pessimistic interpretations of agriculture, suggesting that its introduction and spread, together with government, urbanization, and hierarchical social structures, had negative outcomes for health status and nutrition. Similarly pessimistic views of early industrialization appear confirmed by reductions experienced in the eighteenth and nineteenth centuries.

In ancient Egypt, the intensification of agriculture improved the certainty of food supply for the previously pastoral and gathering populations, enabling them to achieve adult heights of 67 in. (170 cm) for men and 63 in. (160 cm) for women in the Early Dynastic period, around 5000 BP (Zakrzewski, 2003). This maximum was, however, followed by a reduction, probably the consequence of the development of increasingly hierarchical social systems. Inequities appeared in the distribution and consumption of food, with high-ranked men commanding the best of what was on offer, and there was a particularly striking impact on the relative heights of women. Something similar occurred in ancient Italy where skeletal data from Pompeii and Herculaneum suggest relatively short average heights of about 64–67 in. (162–170 cm) for men and 60–62 in. (152–157 cm) for women (Garnsey, 1999: 58). Under the Roman Empire, average height began to fall around AD 200, setting a downward trend that continued into the Middle Ages (Jongman, 2007: 607–9).

In the Americas, stature increased in hunter-gatherer communities down to about 5000 BP, when men achieved adult heights of close to 65 in. (165 cm) and women 60 in. (153 cm). This increase in height went together with a decline in hypoplasias and bone loss. These were tall, healthy people. The emergence of sedentary, stratified communities practicing intensive agriculture in the Americas was, however, associated with a secular reduction in heights which persisted from about 5000 BP until the 1940s (Bogin and Keep, 1999). Only at the end of the twentieth century was the hunter-gatherer maximum regained. Within this broad picture there were of course significant variations from place to place and between groups (Steckel and Rose, 2002: 564).

The Columbian impact was particularly dramatic. Enslaved Africans living in North America experienced positive growth whereas those on the most exploitative plantations suffered reductions in stature (Higman, 1979). Enslaved people did not always have the worst possible diet. In ancient Rome, for example, it has been argued there was recognition that enslaved men, as well as manual workers, athletes, and soldiers, required an energy-high diet and were therefore given above-average amounts of food. Domestic slaves had the chance to eat leftovers from the often elaborate banquets of their masters and to purloin food from kitchens. Some also had a *peculium* (property granted specifically by the master for the slave's own use) which could be turned into food, among other things (Joshel, 2010: 128–32; Wilkins and Hill, 2006: 42). It is not possible to make this argument for all of the modern slave societies of the Americas, though it has been contended that the enslaved people of the ante-bellum United States did relatively well, as evidenced by the strong natural increase of the population. Elsewhere, on the plantations of the Caribbean and Brazil, and even where the idea of the *peculium* was extended to food production, the populations survived only by replenishment through the Atlantic slave trade and slave owners showed no enthusiasm for spending their profits, even where they were exceptional, in providing food for their workforce.

One of the most troublesome questions for historians of the modern world has been the impact of the Industrial Revolution on standards of living. So-called optimists argue that industrialization brought positive benefits in material and biological wellbeing, while pessimists argue that the immediate effects were decidedly negative and took a long time to turn around (Cinnirella, 2008: 339). The optimistic interpretation of the data for Britain, the hearth of the Industrial Revolution, shows heights and hence nutritional status increasing from the middle of the eighteenth century into the 1820s but falling for children born in the following decades. The pessimistic view, which has come to be the dominant interpretation, sees the peak height (about 68 in. [172 cm] for males) achieved as early as the birth cohort of 1750, then followed by steady reduction to a minimum of about 64 in. (163 cm) for those born in the 1850s, after which heights increased steadily. The experience of females was much the same. The poor struggled to find subsistence for their growing families (Floud, Wachter and Gregory, 1990: 151–4). Thus, in spite of large aggregate gains in productivity and wealth, little of this benefit flowed to the workers. Food riots became common in the late eighteenth century. In the very long run, however, the Industrial Revolution emerges as a savior, enabling modern populations to afford nutritious food and achieve heights unknown in the preindustrial agricultural world.

The stagnant or declining trend in stature in the nineteenth-century industrializing world, observed in the United States as well as Europe, seems generally to satisfy a Malthusian model, in which the demographic transition from high birth rates and high mortality to improved length-of-life and reduced fertility, in the context of rapid urbanization and environmental degradation, placed short-term pressure on food resources and health systems (Fogel, 2004: 17–18; Haines, Craig and Weiss, 2003). The trend was repeated in white settler societies such as Australia and New Zealand (Inwood, Oxley and Roberts, 2010; A'Hearn, 2003; Komlos, 1998). In the northern hemisphere industrializing states, nutritional decline followed the growth of social inequality and the loss of diverse subsistence diets. On the other hand, there is little to suggest this deterioration was a consequence of a shift of expenditure away from food to other consumer goods or that things like sugar, coffee, and alcohol displaced healthier food choices. The populations exposed to these unintended consequences of economic development did not experience a true Malthusian crisis and the negative impact on food availability and stature was short-lived. In the twentieth century, the ultimate victory of the industrialized food system, supported by efficient technologies of preservation and transport, was undoubted throughout the developed, industrialized economies of the world. Stature ceased to be a function of income and occupation.

Whereas growth in stature naturally tends to be associated with increased body weight and body mass, and with improved health and longevity, this is something quite different from being overweight or obese. In recent times, however, some of the factors that have contributed to population-wide increases in stature have also played a part in the unhealthy global spread of obesity. In Africa and some Latin American countries, for example, successful efforts at the end of the twentieth century to prevent wasting and stunting were followed quickly by emerging problems of overweight and overnutrition, bringing new understandings of body image.

Obesity

Broadly, fatness rather than thinness has been seen to represent the perfect human body. In a sample of cultures for which data are available, Counihan (1999: 11) observes, "plumpness is preferred, especially for women, because it is associated with fertility, hardiness, power, good nurturance, and love." Fijians perceive fatness as an indication of care and generosity; Jamaicans as a symbol of kindness, ripeness, and fertility (Sobo, 1994: 136–7). Historically, fat people have been jolly, with plenty to laugh about; thin people, miserable, complaining curmudgeons. Fat people were likely to be well off, to have lived easy lives – only the rich could afford to consume enough food, and to do so little hard manual work, to achieve fatness.

The origins of these perceptions seem clear enough considered in terms of the long-term history of hunger and famine. The emaciated were no good for hard work, whereas the fat carried their own emergency reserves that might see them through the hungry times. In the Atlantic slave trade, potential slave owners paid attention to skinfold thickness, something they could pinch in the culture of the slave market, of the people they considered for purchase, and adjusted prices accordingly, while the traders attempted to fatten the enslaved to improve profits. Africans who reached the Americas as skin and bone were called "refuse slaves," wheeled away in a wheelbarrow to be fed back to health perhaps but given little hope.

Precise measures came to the fore in the late twentieth century, as obesity gained the status of a medicalized illness. By the 1980s, it was generally accepted as a definition that obesity is indicated by a body mass index (BMI) of 30 kg/ m^2 or more, derived by dividing the weight of an individual by the square of their height. In the US, however, a BMI percentile distribution was used, so that as the population fattened the bar was raised for obesity, tending to make the problem seem smaller. In spite of this sliding scale, over the twentieth century Americans went from being the tallest people in the world to being among the heaviest. In 1960 about 13 percent of adult Americans were obese, in 2000 more than 30 percent, the rate of prevalence consistently higher for women.

The range of variation in obesity rates around the world, measured in the 1990s, is striking – stretching from very high rates, exceeding 50 percent of the population in most of the Pacific Islands, to as low as two percent in Chinese populations. Ethnic heritage is important but molded by environment (Conner and Armitage, 2002: 75). For example, people of African ancestry were least likely to be obese if they lived in Africa and most likely to fall into the category if they lived in the US (even more so if they lived in cities), while the Caribbean region fell in between these extremes (Wilks *et al.*, 1996). The pattern for hypertension, which is often linked with the desire for salt and the dynamics of the Atlantic slave trade, followed much the same gradient as the rate of obesity (Curtin, 1992). Further, obesity is also linked with diabetes prevalence, which is typically high in African-heritage populations. Consequently, obese people, particularly those who are poor and exposed to malnutrition of one sort or another, suffer above-average rates of morbidity and mortality compared to other members of their societies.

Only in recent times has a substantial proportion of the world's population possessed the resources needed to eat to excess. The outcome of this new development has been a reassessment of the preferred body image, toward a thinness indicative of self-control rather than self-indulgence. In spite of these publicly proclaimed attitudes, significant differences remain embedded in developed societies, following lines of gender, class, and ethnicity. To some extent, the tables have been turned, so that it is the poor who are predisposed to consume the quantities and types of food likely to build "overweight" bodies. The better off, it is said, can more easily afford healthy food choices, memberships of gymnasiums, personal trainers, and access to knowledge about good nutrition. The poor have been tempted by low food prices, which fell by more than 10 percent across the developed world between 1980 and 2000, with a consequent increase in the intake of calories.

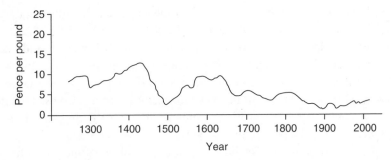

Figure 9.2   Price of sugar, in pence per pound at London, circa 1200–2010. Based on Noel Deerr, *The History of Sugar* (London: Chapman and Hall, 1949–50); J.H. Galloway, *The Sugar Cane Industry: An Historical Geography from Its Origins to 1914* (Cambridge: Cambridge University Press, 1989), 239; and FAO Statistics.

Refined cane sugar prices declined dramatically in real terms in the long term, supplying boundless sweetness (Figure 9.2). Salt followed the same downward price slide.

Physical inactivity has something to do with the global spread of obesity but far less than the increase in calories, provided by cheap industrialized food, particularly foods with extremely high caloric density typical of that delivered by fast food restaurants. The parallel growth of the obese population is related closely to the increasing proportion of people living in large urban settlements and the increasing proportion of women in the workforce, and changing notions of the relative value of time committed to household tasks and leisure (Bleich *et al.*, 2007). However, recent research has found that humans are not the only animals exhibiting obesity and that the experience of weight gain over the past thirty years is common across a wide range of species, living with or around humans in industrialized societies, from rats to chimpanzees (Klimentidis *et al.*, 2010). The explanation for this general trend seems likely to be found in the increased consumption of processed foods, by many animals as well as humans, in a broadly shared diet, through bacterial mechanisms operating in the digestive system.

Beginning in the middle of the nineteenth century, Western medical practitioners sought to label the obese as sufferers of a disease, potential patients who could be cured by dieting. By the end of the twentieth century, the problem had been recognized as "epidemic" in scale and global in extent, and increasing at a rapid rate. A "war on obesity" was declared and, in 2003, the enemy was called "the terror within." Aggressive surgical approaches, such as stomach-stapling, joined dieting in the fight against fat. Childhood obesity became a "rising epidemic," caused by eating the wrong things, particularly saturated fats, sugars, and refined foods low in fiber, and eating them too fast in the wrong situations, while living a sedentary lifestyle.

In China, the one-child policy created "little emperors," happy and fat, and given almost everything they demanded. In Britain and the United States, by 2008, obese children were sometimes removed from their parents and taken into care, even when the causes were genetic rather than due to neglect (Viner *et al.*, 2010; Gilman, 2008a: 159–63). A much broader approach was taken in Japan, a nation already low on the scale of obesity, where a law passed in 2008 required companies and local governments to measure the waistlines of employees aged between 40 and 74 years as part of annual checkups. The intention was to ward off "metabolic syndrome," a combination of health risks linked with diabetes and heart disease. Those whose waistlines exceeded the government-imposed maximums were counseled. Employers who failed to meet set targets had to pay more into health funds.

Obesity came to be seen as a product of globalization and modernization. When constructed as moral failure, gluttony and sloth, solutions to the obesity epidemic were sought in eating more naturally, avoiding the worst of the processed and modified atrocities promoted by the fast food corporate-machine, and returning to a golden age when, before the Neolithic Revolution, people lived from the land and never got fat or abused their bodies (Monaghan, 2008: 1–4). On the other hand, skeptics questioned the extent of the crisis and emphasized the continuing cultural critique that sought to create a stigmatized group, in the context of efforts to control the unruly human body (Gard and Wright, 2005: 17).

A variety of nutrition-related health issues other than obesity were recognized in the late twentieth century, but attempts to resolve them sometimes had the effect of jumping from the frying pan into the fire. For example, in the 1980s consumer advocacy encouraged United States fast food chains, including the dominant world leaders McDonald's and KFC, to shift from frying in highly saturated fats, such as beef tallow and palm oil, which elevate bad cholesterol levels. However, these were replaced by trans fats (derived from partially hydrogenated oil), which became known later to be even more harmful in their capacity to clog arteries because they both raise the bad cholesterol and actively lower the good.

The chains began to offer nutritional information on their websites but maintained that alternative oils failed to deliver the crispness and flavor demanded by consumers. Governments took steps to control or prohibit the advertising and promotion of unhealthy fast foods, particularly when directed at young children. In the United States, it became mandatory to list nutritional information on packaged foods from the 1990s, and from 2011 federal law required calorie posting in chain restaurants. Such listing proved effective in lowering consumption, though only by small amounts, and had the effect of shifting unhealthy purchases to different sites (Bollinger, Leslie and Sorensen, 2010).

Dieting

The notion that individuals should follow a prescriptive diet in order to ensure their wellbeing has ancient roots. The idea that dieting is a behavior directed specifically at the control of weight is a much more modern concept, though not a simple reaction to the spread of obesity (Gilman, 2008b). Beginning in the 1670s, eccentric European medical practitioners warned of the hazards of fatness, but these were prophets calling in the wilderness. Overeating was condemned for its gluttony and gross indulgence. The French cook Jean Anthelme Brillat-Savarin made a more direct link with diet, in his famous work *The Physiology of Taste* (1825), in which he discusses diet as one possible means of preventing or curing obesity. He suggests "moderation" but condemns particularly bread, pastry, and pasta, and all things derived from grain, including beer. In Britain, the portly image of John Bull was gradually replaced by a more svelte model, a variety of "muscular Christianity" with a nod to the Greeks.

From Europe, ideas about "dieting" spread to the United States, where the word began to appear in medical journals in the 1830s, as a cure for indigestion and the like, and associated with clean living, self-control, and chaste habits. Thus, rather than arising from a concern for the white, female, middle-class body, the origins of dieting in the United States are to be found in advice directed at middle-class men, who were told that they could increase their power and influence by reducing their waistlines (Vester, 2010). Following the views of Brillat-Savarin, men were encouraged to eat lean red meat (veal rather than fat roasts), but also told to smoke and drink, as part of a rational approach to the body – taking the initiative in achieving good career outcomes – rather than a matter of self-denial. Indeed, diets proposed for men in the 1860s sometimes recommended eating meat four times a day, making it very much a project restricted to the affluent and disconnecting the traditional association between corpulence and prosperity. Only in the 1890s did plumpness cease to be the preferred body image for American women and only in the twentieth century did they become the prime targets, encouraged to believe they could control their weight, by which time the fat woman with heavy breasts was more likely to be immigrant, low class, or black.

Issues of body image and moral behavior remained complexly interconnected into the twenty-first century. Particularly but not only in the United States, the obese came to feel pressured to slim by diet, exhorted to take back control of their bodies by exercising willpower. Secular programs were paralleled by the emergence, beginning in the 1970s, of a Christian diet movement, which called on believers to "Slim for Him" and overcome spiritual hunger (Herndon, 2008; Griffith, 2004: 172). In this model, obesity was sinful and dieting a pious act, thus bringing together modern notions of moral failure with the ancient religious forms of sacrifice and self-denial that underpinned "holy anorexia" (Hoverd and Sibley, 2007).

The fundamental difficulty for most weight-worried dieters was the sense of deprivation and the feeling of denial usually associated with programs that took away the sensual joy of eating. In 1972 the nutritionist Robert Atkins published *Diet Revolution* in which, against the consensus that slimmers should eat less fat and more carbohydrates, he argues that by eating only protein and fat the body would quickly burn off its excess, and be better equipped to stave off diabetes. His followers – his book sold 25 million copies – could eat red meat three times a day, along with butter, eggs, and cheese, so long as they avoided bread, pasta, rice, potatoes, sugar, and perhaps even fruit. His high-fiber competitors accepted that the Atkins diet had short-term benefits for losing weight but emphasized the negative effects on the heart and kidney.

Denial

The other side of gluttony is self-denial. Self-denial can take several forms, some of them highly political, others highly personal. In the modern United States, for example, thinness is cultivated as an ideal representation of self-control and individuality, but attaches more to women than men. In advertising, the image of the thin woman became dominant in the 1960s and by the 1990s was under criticism for inducing eating disorders among young women who fashioned themselves on the half-starved, cadaverous models who strutted the metropolitan catwalks. Further, it is often argued that modern women in the Western world have been driven to dissatisfaction with their body shape and weight by the promotion of such models in the media, a system controlled by men, signaling an internalized variety of gender oppression.

As discussed in Chapter 2, the denial or limitation of food consumption is an important element in several religious traditions, symbolizing a denial of the body and its earthly demands and a parallel elevation of soul and spirit. The benefits of such abstention were spiritual, quite separate from the nutritional gains expected from varieties of denial associated with dieting. In some cases, temporary fasting was limited to special periods of the religious calendar, for example Ramadan in Islam, or limited to the consumption of particular foods. More might be expected of priests and saints.

More extreme versions of denial were practiced by the Jains of southern India who, from about 2800 BP, followed a particularly austere diet in their quest to avoid harm to all things. Their philosophy of renunciation, asceticism, and non-violence meant not only fasting but also, for example, refusing to eat tubers because this required harvest before the plant's life was complete (Ulrich, 2007: 241). Among the Jains, a person who was very old or in the final stages of a terminal illness might vow not to accept further food or water, as a matter of religious discipline or acceptance rather than individual will, and with the expectation of a good rebirth (Laidlaw, 1995: 238–9). Such fasting to death contrasted with varieties of self-destruction in which Jains came to see the body as alien, and the struggle against desire and hunger no longer relevant, in the achievement of the purity of the soul and the renunciation of the body-bound self.

For early Christians, fasting was often associated with charity: by eating little, food was made available for the needy. There was also a direct link with the seasonal cycle of plenty and scarcity: fasting was allied with famine and death, so choosing denial was a way of calling on God to send an abundant harvest and renewed life. It was a means of indicating human vulnerability and dependence on the goodness of God to bring salvation. The other side of the coin was the idea that it had been the sin of gluttony that caused the Fall in the Garden of Eden.

The meaning of fasting changed for Christians in medieval times. Thus, argues Bynum (1987: 33), "Abstinence was seen less as self-control, offered to God in propitiation for Adam's sin of greed and disobedience, than as a never-sated physical hunger that mirrors and recapitulates in bodily agony both Christ's suffering on the cross and the soul's unquenchable thirst for mystical union." In this model, the fasting shared by all members of the church was balanced by the "communion" in which the bread and wine of the Eucharist, the body and blood of Christ, represented a further act of sacrifice. The practice of fasting was, however, somewhat watered down in secular medieval life. More groups were granted dispensations, and the fasting period was reduced in its duration while the range of items that could rightly be considered fasting foods was expanded. Thus, the fast might be reduced to no more than abstinence from meat. Fasting also declined in many monasteries while feast days were added to the calendar.

Some new Christian orders, on the contrary, marked themselves off by their austerity. Thus, for example, the hermitic Carthusians, founded in 1084, fasted on bread, water, and salt three times a week. More extreme varieties of fasting were practiced by individuals, particularly nuns, who sought holiness in a regime of pain and suffering. The experience of these religious people has sometimes been related to modern physiological conditions such as anorexia nervosa, which came to prominence in the 1970s. Anorexia nervosa typically affects otherwise normal young women who have an intense fear of fatness and a distortion of body image. Their aversion to food results in loss of more than one-quarter of body weight, but may be combined with periods of binge eating followed by self-induced vomiting and laxative abuse (bulimia nervosa).

Such behavior is commonly connected with emotional or personality problems.

When food-denial is practiced together with physical hyperactivity, the result can be death. In the Middle Ages, however, the denial of hunger, pain, and fatigue was felt as a victory over the senses, a means of freeing the (female) saint's soul to commune with the Almighty. To refuse almost all food was a move toward spiritual perfection and oneness with Christ. To die in such a state was a holy conclusion. Detractors claimed such extreme self-denial was impossible, that the saints in fact fed themselves in secret, or that they must be possessed by demons (Brumberg, 1988: 256; Bell, 1985: 2–13). Only after the Protestant Reformation did self-starvation cease to be understood as evidence of saintliness, gradually replaced by good works.

In the modern world, religious fasting remains common in some traditions and can cover a substantial part of the year. For example, Orthodox Christians in Ethiopia (about 40 percent of the population) fast for up to 250 days per year, made up of four long fasting periods leading up to religious festivities and regular weekly fasting on Wednesdays and Fridays. On these days Orthodox Christians do not consume any products of animal origin, including milk and dairy items. Christians in the West, surrounded by abundance, came in the twentieth century to largely abandon fasting, replacing it with "special" acts to mark dates in the religious calendar, acts which rarely involved bodily denial. In Islam, the daily cycle of fast and feast in the annual month-long festival of Ramadan, during which adults fast from sunrise to sunset, came to see people actually gaining weight over the period.

Refusing food as a weapon in modern political protest has an ambiguous history. Oppressor classes are well aware that keeping people hungry and tired is an effective way of averting revolt because their victims lack the energy required for physical resistance. Hunger was, for example, used deliberately as a weapon to control the inmates of concentration camps during World War II and Nazi commandants sometimes decreed that new internees should receive only half-rations for their first four weeks. Generally, then, hunger strikes can be effective when carried out by prominent individuals or groups but not efficient if adopted by entire communities or large populations.

In his nationalist struggle for Indian independence, Mohandas Gandhi frequently used diet as an appropriate starting point, indicating the close relationship between concepts of national identity and national food culture. Gandhi's protest was framed by the development of nutritional science as a tool of imperialism in the interwar period, as discussed earlier. Nutritional science came to underpin patterns of world trade and food aid. British advocacy of improved diet served as a means of linking public health with agricultural change and economic development, and as a justification of expanded colonial management of land tenure, irrigation, markets, and transport networks, promoted as public welfare objectives. In the process, imperial nutritionists disparaged the rice and legumes fundamental to the South Asian diet, while promoting wheat, meat, and milk as the foods of the superior races. Indian nutritional scientists came to the defense of rice and legumes, while Gandhi himself lived on fruit, milk, and uncooked vegetables which he believed delivered spiritual and physical values quite beyond the energy units of the calorie (Cullather, 2007: 359–60). More broadly, his connection of food with nationalism represented a rejection of industrial capitalism as well as colonialism.

Vegetarianism

In recent times, the past century or so, vegetarianism has often been understood as an individual decision, based on ethical and moral choices or founded on ideal models of human nutrition. In the past, such decisions were more likely to be made on a communal level, following the directives of a religion or ideology. Choices of this second type were typically constructed as taboos, justified explicitly as the will of gods though perhaps having their origin in notions of pollution that reflected nutritional realities as well as moral commandments. Thus, the varieties of denial associated with vegetarianism were sometimes imposed and in other cases the product of free choice.

In view of this variety of origins and intentions, it is not surprising that "vegetarian" has meant different things to different people. Generally, it is taken to indicate an avoidance of meat-eating, but modern adherents are typically divided into "vegans" (whose diet is strictly plant-based, the term coined in the 1940s), "lacto vegetarians" (who consume dairy products but no eggs or flesh), "ova-lacto vegetarians" (who add eggs), "pollo vegetarians" (who eat birds but not mammals), and "pesco vegetarians" (who eat seafood but not birds or mammals). In practice, individuals are often flexible, suiting their eating to convenience and social circumstance, leading to the term "flexitarian" used to describe a vegetarian who occasionally eats meat (Preece, 2008: 14–17). For example, a strict vegetarian may aspire to being a vegan but finds it too difficult to follow the rules or an animal rights advocate may be vegan in company but a meat eater at home.

The fundamental philosophical question is whether it is moral to kill animals, deserving of full lives and capable of feeling pain, in order to eat their flesh, since meat-eating is not necessary to human nutrition. This is an ancient question though its asking is hard to identify in the millennia that stretch back into the meat-eating prehistory of human societies or even the beginnings of agriculture. The question, together with vegetarian practices, surfaces first around 500 BC when it was pondered by the Indian Hindu priestly caste and their contemporaries the early Greek philosophers who flourished in the archaic period (Stuart, 2006: 40). Notoriously, Pythagoras, who flourished in the late sixth century BC, believed that a reincarnated human might return to life as another kind of animal, meaning that killing an animal was no less than murder and consuming it cannibalism.

In practical terms, these ancient arguments seem not to have been applied systematically but rather were employed to advocate particular taboos and avoidances, for example prohibitions relating to the eating of fish or perhaps only sacred fish (Garnsey, 1999: 85–91). In this connection, it has been argued that Pythagorean ideals contributed to the early Christian ascetic tradition, discussed earlier, which displaced wine (blood) from the Eucharist (McGowan, 1999: 265–7). Such practices may have been understood as principles of self-denial appropriate for philosophers and priests but not necessarily the mass of the people, and overlapped selective taboos rooted in notions of pollution.

Something similar applied in ancient China, where the vegetarian diets of Buddhist temples were influential but not followed throughout society. The Buddha, after all, was no vegetarian and he did not forbid his monks to eat meat. As Ludwig Alsdorf (2010: 6) argues, for Buddhists as well as the early Jains of India, the essential rule governing the eating of meat was "that the consumer has neither killed the animal himself, nor had it killed especially for him, so that the responsibility for the killing does neither directly nor indirectly fall upon him."

The more extreme classical Greek contention that plants also have souls was rarely extended to practical food-avoidance, though it might be thought improper to harm a plant while it was bearing fruit. More moderate ancient arguments, ignoring the issue of reincarnation, simply saw animals as things of worth, possessed of souls, and claimed that meat-eating inhibited human spiritual development. European mystics of the early modern period saw the avoidance of meat (particularly red meat with its high blood content) as a means to conquer bodily passions and aggressive behaviors. Modern vegetarian movements similarly focussed on an abhorrence of meat-eating, seeking above all to avoid unnecessary cruelty and to achieve liberation from the tyranny of physical compulsions, but they often grew out of broader spiritual and humanitarian concerns, and were closely related to wider health and medical reform. The first formal movement emerged from the ferment of improving ideas in early-nineteenth-century Britain, leading to the founding in 1847 of the British Vegetarian Society, which brought together a diverse collection of radicals and middle-class intellectuals, to challenge the excesses of the political system and dampen the desire for dominion over man and nature.

The argument that meat-eating is positively unhealthy and that human beings can live better lives without it gained strength in the late twentieth century. The development of this view occurred partly in response to the great growth of industrialized food production, discussed in Chapter 3, which was condemned for its cruelty to animals while alive, its use of chemicals and drugs, its feeding of unnatural materials, its impact on the natural environment, and its cruelty in slaughter practices. A moral responsibility was also perceived in the fact that meat-eating required a much larger ratio of natural (including non-renewable) resources in production processes and that consumers therefore contributed to the inequity of global food supplies and ecological costs. In this way, the moral and nutritional/health questions were brought together, leading some to develop preferences for "organic", free-range, and self-killed meat, eating only the flesh of animals that had been treated humanely and respectfully, whereas others argued that such practices simply ignored the fundamental ethical problems of slaughter and the question of animal rights (Rowlands, 2007). Feminists of the late twentieth century argued that, in Western societies, meat was a symbol of patriarchy and its consumption closely associated with the creation and imposition of male power. Some believed women could fight back through vegetarianism.

The model also prospered in those societies in which vegetarianism had long been not so much a choice as a requirement or expectation, at least for some groups within a community, and particularly where it was attached to hierarchical systems of social structure. Vegetarianism increased in prestige among the religious groups of South Asia over many centuries, illustrating the principle that it is easier to prohibit or deny a food than to commence the eating of something new. Among the Jains, it proved part of a larger project of ritual denial or asceticism, a process that remained active at the end of the twentieth century when more than half of the Jains (and Brahmins) in India were practicing lacto-vegetarians.

Traditionally, the Jains had understood fasting and the avoidance of certain foods (all animals, fruits with many seeds, tubers, honey, and alcohol) as a means toward self-realization and detachment from the material world. However, within this system, they considered milk an essentially spiritual food which could contribute to meditation (toward renunciation) by calming the mind and the emotions. Voices were raised in the 1990s, highlighting the violence of modern industrialized milking methods which made milk no more than "liquid meat" (Vallely, 2009: 329–31). This development reflected the spread of Jain peoples outside of India and a desire to universalize their teachings. In this way, Jains moved toward a more perfect diet, one truly vegan, which connected cosmological notions of non-violence and renunciation with the down-to-earth facts of the modern food system.

Something similar occurred in Hinduism. In modern India the Hindu prohibitions about who might eat with whom, discussed in Chapter 7, extended into rules about who might eat what items within the scheme of pollution. By no means were all Hindus vegetarians. At the bottom of the caste hierarchy, the sweeper, the only person who could eat the leftovers of other castes, could eat pork as well as beef (Mayer, 1960: 44–5). Those nearer the middle of the scheme were distinguished by castes who might eat mutton, goat, wild pig, and other game meat, as against those who could eat none of meat, fish, or eggs. Arguments were advanced that Hinduism had always seen meat-eating as demeaning.

However, the push toward a ruling vegetarianism in post-imperial India had to confront the notion that meat-eating was a vital element in modernization and something to be desired among the rising middle-classes (Khare, 1992). Indeed, early in his career Gandhi renounced vegetarianism and encouraged Indians to believe they could overcome their colonial masters by adopting the British flesh diet. He lived to regret this aberration and returned to an advocacy of ethical vegetarianism. Opposition to beef-eating, rooted in Hindu thought, took on new meaning in the struggle against British colonialism, a conflict in which the British were cast as enthusiastic beef-eaters.

Historically, some regions of India, most of them located in the south, have been vegetarian as a whole. At the beginning of the twenty-first century, approximately 30 percent of the country's population is (lacto) vegetarian (Alsdorf 2010: 2). However, a majority of these vegetarians is female, whereas Hindu men frequently eat fish, chicken, and mutton, claiming it is necessary to enable them to perform heavy labor. In spite of these variations, and in spite of the growth of meat-eating among the more prosperous classes, the proportion of vegetarians is considerably larger in India than in most other countries.

Although vegetarianism in its various forms is gaining adherents in the West, high-end estimates for Europe show only about 7 percent claiming vegetarianism, 5 percent in Australia (about 2 percent actually following a vegetarian diet), and in North America no more than 3 percent. In East Asia the proportions are smaller still. In China, Korea, and Japan, vegetarianism is confined almost entirely to the rural poor, and uncommon even among the Buddhist priesthood (Preece, 2008: 2–4). Something similar is true of Africa and Latin America (and Spain and Portugal), where vegetarians and vegetarian movements are rare.

Ironically, perhaps, vegetarianism can prosper in the midst of dedicated meat-eating populations. At the same time, animists are rarely vegetarians. And rejection of a vegetarian ethic does not necessarily go together with the substantial consumption of flesh and other animal products. Thus, for example, the non-vegetarian Chinese have always eaten meat in small quantities and until recently rejected milk and dairy altogether. In 2000 average daily consumption of animal products made up only about 17 percent of daily calories in China, compared to 27 percent in the United States, 31 percent in the United Kingdom, 38 percent in France and New Zealand, and 44 percent

in Mongolia. Examples at the lower end of the scale include India (7 percent), Iraq (4), and Bangladesh (3). Poverty in combination with ideology proves highly successful in the limitation of meat-eating, whereas prosperity with ideology proves less successful than historical poverty without an ethical ideology.

REFERENCES

A'Hearn, B. (2003) Anthropometric evidence on living standards in northern Italy, 1730–1860. *Journal of Economic History* 63: 351–81.

Alsdorf, L. (2010) *The History of Vegetarianism and Cow-Veneration in India*. London: Routledge.

Aronson, N. (1982) Nutrition as a social problem: A case study of entrepreneurial strategy in science. *Social Problems* 29: 474–87.

Bell, R.M. (1985) *Holy Anorexia*. Chicago: University of Chicago Press.

Bleich, S., Cutler, D., Murray, C. and Adams, A. (2007) Why is the developed world obese? *NBER Working Paper No. 12954*.

Bogin, B. and Keep, R. (1999) Eight thousand years of economic and political history in Latin America revealed by anthropometry. *Annals of Human Biology* 26: 333–51.

Bollinger, B., Leslie, P. and Sorensen, A. (2010) Calorie posting in Chain restaurants. *NBER Working Paper No. 15648*.

Brumberg, J.J. (1988) *Fasting Girls: The Emergence of Anorexia Nervosa as a Modern Disease*. Cambridge, MA: Harvard University Press.

Bynum, C.W. (1987) *Holy Feast and Holy Fast: The Religious Significance of Food to Medieval Women*. Berkeley, CA: University of California Press.

Cinnirella, F. (2008) Optimists or pessimists? A reconsideration of nutritional status in Britain, 1740–1865. *European Review of Economic History* 12: 325–54.

Conner, M. and Armitage, C.J. (2002) *The Social Psychology of Food*. Buckingham, UK: Open University Press.

Counihan, C.M. (1999) *The Anthropology of Food and Body: Gender, Meaning, and Power*. New York: Routledge.

Cullather, N. (2007) The foreign policy of the calorie. *American Historical Review* 112: 337–64.

Curtin, P.D. (1992) The slavery hypothesis for hypertension among African Americans: The historical evidence. *American Journal of Public Health* 82: 1681–6.

Floud, R., Wachter, K.W. and Gregory, A. (1990) *Height, Health and History: Nutritional Status in the United Kingdom, 1750–1980*. Cambridge: Cambridge University Press.

Fogel, R.W. (2004) *The Escape from Hunger and Premature Death, 1700–2100*. Cambridge: Cambridge University Press.

Galal, O.M. (2002) The nutrition transition in Egypt: Obesity, undernutrition and the food consumption context. *Public Health Nutrition* 5: 141–8.

Gard, M. and Wright, J. (2005) *The Obesity Epidemic: Science, Morality and Ideology*. London: Routledge.

Garnsey, P. (1999) *Food and Society in Classical Antiquity*. Cambridge: Cambridge University Press.

Geissler, C. (1993) Stature and other indicators of development: comparisons in Thailand and the Philippines, Korea and Iran. In C. Geissler and D.J. Oddy (eds) *Food, Diet and Economic Change Past and Present*, pp. 207–23. Leicester, UK: Leicester University Press.

Gifford, K. (2002) Dietary fats, eating guides, and public policy: History, critique, and recommendations. *American Journal of Medicine* 113 (9B): 89S–106S.

Gilman, S.L. (2008a) *Fat: A Cultural History of Obesity*. Cambridge,: Polity.

Gilman, S.L. (2008b) *Diets and Dieting: A Cultural Encyclopedia*. New York: Routledge.

Griffith, R.M. (2004) *Born Again Bodies: Flesh and Spirit in American Christianity*. Berkeley, CA: University of California Press.

Haines, M.R., Craig, L.A. and Weiss, T. (2003) The short and the dead: Nutrition, mortality, and the "Antebellum Puzzle" in the United States. *Journal of Economic History* 63: 382–413.

Hatton, T.J. and Bray, B.E. (2010) Long run trends in the heights of European men, 19th–20th centuries. *Economics and Human Biology* 8: 405–13.

Herndon, A.M. (2008) Taking the devil into your mouth: Ritualized American weight-loss narratives of morality, pain, and betrayal. *Perspectives in Biology and Medicine* 51: 207–19.

Higman, B.W. (1979) Growth in Afro-Caribbean slave populations. *American Journal of Physical Anthropology* 50: 373–86.

Hoverd, W.J., and Sibley, C.G. (2007) Immoral bodies: The implicit association between moral discourse and the body. *Journal for the Scientific Study of Religion* 46: 391–403.

Inwood, K., Oxley, L. and Roberts, E. (2010) Physical stature in nineteenth-century New Zealand: A preliminary interpretation. *Australian Economic History Review* 50: 262–83.

Jongman, W.M. (2007) The early Roman empire: Consumption. In W. Scheidel, I. Morris and R. Saller (eds) *The Cambridge Economic History of the Greco-Roman World*, pp. 592–618. Cambridge: Cambridge University Press.

Joshel, S.R. (2010) *Slavery in the Roman World*. Cambridge: Cambridge University Press.

Kamminga, H. and Cunningham, A. (eds) (1995) *The Science and Culture of Nutrition, 1840–1940*. Amsterdam: Editions Rodopi.

Khare, R.S. (ed.) (1992) *The Eternal Food: Gastronomic Ideas and Experiences of Hindus and Buddhists*. New York: State University of New York Press.

Klimentidis, Y.C., Beasley, T.M., Lin, H.-Y. *et al.* (2010) Canaries in the coal mine: A cross-species analysis of the plurality of obesity epidemics. *Proceedings of the Royal Society B* (published online before print 24 November).

Komlos, J. (1998) Shrinking in a growing economy? The mystery of physical stature during the Industrial Revolution. *Journal of Economic History* 58: 779–802.

Komlos, J. (2010) The recent decline in the height of African-American women. *Economics and Human Biology* 8: 58–66.

Komlos, J. and Lauderdale, B.E. (2007) The mysterious trend in American heights in the 20th century. *Annals of Human Biology* 34: 206–15.

Laidlaw, J. (1995) *Riches and Renunciation: Religion, Economy, and Society among the Jains*. Oxford: Clarendon Press.

Mayer, A.C. (1960) *Caste and Kinship in Central India: A Village and Its Region*. Berkeley, CA: University of California Press.

McCollum, E.V. (1957) *A History of Nutrition: The Sequence of Ideas in Nutrition Investigation*. Boston: Houghton Mifflin Company.

McGowan, A. (1999) *Ascetic Eucharists: Food and Drink in Early Christian Ritual Meals*. Oxford: Clarendon Press.

Monaghan, L.F. (2008) *Men and the War on Obesity: A Sociological Study*. London: Routledge.

Morgan, S.L. (2000) Richer and taller: Stature and living standards in China, 1979–1995. *China Journal* 44: 1–39.

Popkin, B.M. and Gordon-Larsen, P. (2004) The nutrition transition: Worldwide obesity dynamics and their determinants. *International Journal of Obesity* 28: S2–S9.

Preece, R. (2008) *Sins of the Flesh: A History of Ethical Vegetarian Thought*. Vancouver: UBC Press.

Rowlands, M. (2007) *Animal Rights: Moral Theory and Practice*. London: Palgrave Macmillan.

Semproli, S. and Gualdi-Russo, E. (2007) Childhood malnutrition and growth in a rural area of western Kenya. *American Journal of Physical Anthropology* 132: 463–9.

Smil, V. (2008) *Energy in Nature and Society: General Energetics of Complex Systems*. Cambridge, MA: MIT Press.

Sobo, E.J. (1994) The sweetness of fat: Health, procreation, and sociability in rural Jamaica. In N. Sault (ed.) *Many Mirrors: Body Image and Social Relations*, pp. 132–54. New Brunswick, NJ: Rutgers University Press.

Steckel, R.H. and Rose, J.C. (2002) Patterns of health in the Western Hemisphere. In R.H. Steckel and J.C. Rose (eds) *The Backbone of History: Health and Nutrition in the Western Hemisphere*, pp. 563–79. Cambridge: Cambridge University Press.

Stuart, T. (2006) *The Bloodless Revolution: A Cultural History of Vegetarianism from 1600 to Modern Times*. New York: W.W. Norton.

Ulrich, K.E. (2007) Food fights: Buddhist, Hindu, and Jain dietary polemics in South India. *History of Religions* 46: 229–61.

Vallely, A. (2009) Jainism. In P.B. Clarke and P. Beyer (eds) *The World's Religions: Continuities and Transformations*, pp. 325–37. London: Routledge.

Vester, K. (2010) Regime change: Gender, class, and the invention of dieting in post-bellum America. *Journal of Social History* 44: 39–70.

Viner, R.M., Roche, E., Maguire, S.A. and Nicholls, D.E. (2010) Childhood protection and obesity: Framework for practice. *British Medical Journal* 341: 3074.

Wansink, B. (2007) *Mindless Eating: Why We Eat More Than We Think*. New York: Bantam Books.

Wilkins, J.M. and Hill, S. (eds) (2006) *Food in the Ancient World*. Oxford: Blackwell Publishing.

Wilks, R., McFarlane-Anderson, N., Bennett, F. *et al.* (1996) Obesity in peoples of the African diaspora. In D.J. Chadwick and G. Cardew (eds) *The Origins and Consequences of Obesity*, pp. 37–48. Chichester, UK: John Wiley & Sons/Ciba Foundation Symposium 201.

Worboys, M. (1988) The discovery of colonial malnutrition between the wars. In D. Arnold (ed.) *Imperial Medicine and Indigenous Societies*, pp. 208–25. Manchester: Manchester University Press.

Zakrzewski, S.R. (2003) Variation in Ancient Egyptian stature and body proportions. *American Journal of Physical Anthropology* 121: 219–229.

CHAPTER TEN

Starving

In spite of global plenty, starvation persists. In 2010 the total number of hungry, or food insecure, people in the world was more than one billion or one-in-seven (Figure 10.1). Their hunger was not the result of technological inadequacy but rather evidence of a lack of will to redistribute resources and reserves, a failure of global government and politics. This imbalance represented a new form of subsistence crisis because of its global scale but also reflected long-existing failures to cope with regional and local crises.

The significance and impact of subsistence crises always depended largely on their predictability and duration. The easiest variety to cope with was the seasonal shortage, controlled by weather and climate, which was relatively predictable and brief. In some climatic regimes, the crisis occurred at just about the same time every year, meaning that each year had its "hungry time" when resources were at their minimum. In hunter-gatherer societies, this was the time of the year that people turned to inferior food types and temporarily lost weight and condition. For agrarian people, this was the period between the exhaustion of current food supplies and the bringing in of the new harvest. In medieval and early modern Europe, it is generally agreed, the poor suffered chronic undernutrition and lived under the constant threat of starvation. The inevitability of annual periods of near starvation was overcome only in the eighteenth century, in large part because of the introduction from the New World of maize and potatoes. The same was true of much of Asia.

Other crises were frequent but less predictable, the consequence of drought, flood, hurricane, fire, or pestilence. Although these had a strong element of seasonality, and occurred often enough to encourage people to make preparations, the extent of the crisis and the level of security required was less

How Food Made History, First Edition. B. W. Higman.

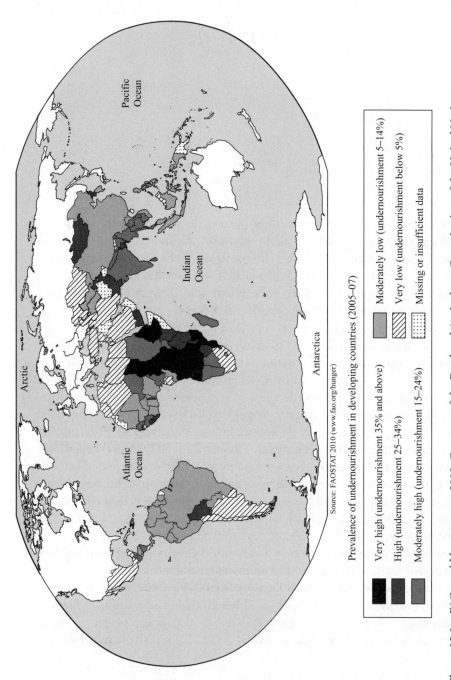

Source: FAOSTAT 2010 (www.fao.org/hunger)

Prevalence of undernourishment in developing countries (2005–07)

Very high (undernourishment 35% and above)

High (undernourishment 25–34%)

Moderately high (undernourishment 15–24%)

Moderately low (undernourishment 5–14%)

Very low (undernourishment below 5%)

Missing or insufficient data

Figure 10.1 FAO world hunger map 2010. Courtesy of the Food and Agriculture Organization of the United Nations: http://www.fao.org/economic/ess/food-security-statistics/faohunger-map/en/.

certain. Drought had a further element of unpredictability in terms of duration. Whereas droughts and plagues were completely negative, floods did bring water and fresh soil; hurricanes opened up new niches in the environment, and sometimes delivered new species, and wildfire similarly transformed and renewed landscapes in positive ways.

Earthquake and volcanic eruption were more dramatic but generally infrequent, so much so that many communities developed no memory of their destructive presence. Even when accompanied by tsunamis, these spectacular events were more likely to destroy urban structures than to create general agricultural havoc and widespread starvation. War and pillage also contributed unpredictably to the history of subsistence crises, as did the demands of local lords and the social-planning of states. An army passing through the countryside could be as bad as a plague of locusts.

Famine

The most extreme variety of subsistence crisis is famine, an event distinguished from other varieties of food shortage or malnutrition by excess mortality. Major famines are sufficiently rare to give them a central role in the collective memory, and enable their use as chronological markers, much like natural disasters such as volcanic eruptions and tsunamis. They also are sometimes given names, often similar to the style of naming wars, and referring to an implied cause. Thus, the Irish Potato Famine of 1846–51 is also known as the Great Famine, and the Chinese famine of 1959–61 (sometimes dated 1958–62) is often called the Great Leap Forward Famine or Mao's Great Famine.

Although "famine" is typically understood as a failure of food supply, the nature of such failure has changed significantly. Rather than being seen as an independent event with implications for society and polity, famine is now generally understood as the outcome of fundamental failures of social organization. Rather than simply blaming a lack of rainfall or a plague or plant disease, in which human cultures are seen as mere passive victims, famine is thought to be the product of multiple causes. Thus, although famine was typically the immediate product of natural disaster, most often drought, it may equally be seen as the outcome of risk-taking behavior, part of an interactive process in which political and class failures created the context and controlled the distribution of available supplies. If not quite punishment for moral failure or representing the wrath of gods, famine is now typically interpreted as the product of failures of government.

Reassessment of the historical record mirrors change in the pattern of famine since about 1900. Excess mortality resulting from simple crop failure virtually disappeared in the twentieth century but at the same time the century witnessed some of the world's worst ever famines, all of them the result of civil conflict, warfare, or mistaken central planning (Ó Gráda, 2008: 5). This recent experience has helped throw light on the long-term historical record, suggesting the determining role played by policy and decision-making, and diminishing the notion that suffering represents divine retribution or the inevitable consequence of population dynamics.

However, failure of supply cannot always be explained in terms of hoarding or market manipulation and, in all periods, the role of ecological variability was not insignificant. In the long term, the correlation between drought and famine is strong. Both drought and famine differ from other kinds of disasters in developing slowly, sometimes almost imperceptibly, but famines caused by drought are frequently of greater extent and longer duration than other varieties of famine, with more severe effects (Lee and Zhang, 2010: 251). Naturally arid regions, and places where rainfall variability is substantial, tend to suffer most heavily. It is therefore particularly significant that climatic fluctuation is greater in Africa and Australia than it is in most of the temperate northern hemisphere; a seasonal drought is quite a different challenge from a drought that persists for a decade. It is also important to notice that large-scale El Niño/Southern Oscillation events have brought drought and reduced yields across extensive regions of the globe. The event of 1972, for example, created a shortfall in the production of rice, wheat, and other grains equal to almost one-tenth of world consumption. The sudden disappearance of the world's market in rice was frightening, followed as it was in 1973 by the "energy crisis" that saw oil prices dramatically elevated, though both of these alarms were temporary and soon enough forgotten (Timmer, 2010: 2).

It is true that famine can occur in the absence of a real decline in food availability. In these cases, in the model argued by Sen (1981: 154), famine results from social and political inability or unwillingness to accept the entitlements of particular classes or groups of people, whether on a national or a local scale. The most obvious example here is the hoarding of supplies and the trading of scarce resources for profit. Such acts are not necessarily induced by shortage but may also be systemic. For example, colonial rule in Indonesia in the nineteenth century was founded on aggressive land taxes which, in times of reduced crops, forced farmers to surrender a large proportion of their harvest, and to sell some of their working cattle and land (Fernando, 2010). Starvation and depopulation followed, people searching for edible roots to survive, while rice stockpiles, to which they had contributed, were not opened to them.

Modern famines have often occurred in the midst of local and international political instability, particularly warfare and associated trade blockades. At worst, famine deaths in the midst of plenty constitute a form of genocide, through self-conscious neglect or the harsh application of market price mechanisms. The modern world, and some of its more respected leaders, learned to turn a blind eye, just as occurred in cases of unmitigated genocide and ethnic cleansing. Doing so paralleled the global coexistence of hunger and obesity, scarcity and abundance. Famine was no longer a shared experience.

In the long-term historical record, only famines which caused extreme mortality stand out. It is impossible to reconstruct a complete list or to determine certainly whether the frequency of occurrence has changed significantly over time. The scale of mortality naturally tends to be greater in recent times, simply because total populations have become much larger. On these terms, looking at absolute numbers of famine deaths, the greatest ever is often said to be the Chinese Great Leap Forward Famine of 1959–61 (or 1958–62), in which perhaps 35 million people died, or even 45 million for the longer period (Dikötter, 2010: 324–34). The crude death rate approached 50 per thousand in 1960, the worst year of the famine, and overall it killed one in every twenty. In the villages and communities at the center of the famine, deaths exceeded 300 per thousand, almost one in three (Chen, 2010: 161; Kane, 1988: 84–8). Other famines occurred in China in the twentieth century but that of 1959–61 accounted for roughly one-half of all the world's famine deaths over the hundred years. The Great Leap Forward Famine in China is attributed directly to human failure, the implementation of mistaken public policy, rather than having anything to do with natural disaster. The same applies to the 1932–4 famine in the Soviet Union, associated with Stalin's collectivization of agriculture, in which tragically the objective was to greatly increase the availability of food not to curtail it.

Other major famines of the twentieth century typically killed smaller pro- portions of the world's populations than the one in twenty ratio in China 1959–61. Bengal did experience a similar rate in the famine of 1943 that accounted for at least three million deaths, but (as in the case of China) the number varies with definitions of the duration of the event. The Bangladesh famine of 1974 killed about 1.5 million people, approximately one in 45 of the population. This event was largely rural in its impact but even in the most affected villages the death rate was only about 60 per thousand. The Russian famine of 1921–2 killed a similar proportion, about one in 40 of the European portion of the state, but more in the grain-growing Volga region where the event was concentrated (Kane, 1988: 19–22).

In terms of ratios of famine deaths to total populations, the Irish famine of 1845–9 comes close to the top of the list, killing about one million, or one in eight. This catastrophe was the direct consequence of the potato blight that wiped out the staple crop but equally the product of ideology (Kinealy, 1997). Ireland's colonial masters, the British, looked on while the laws of free-trade political economy cut their swathe, interpreting willful neglect as the providential working out of market principles necessary to the achievement of Malthusian equilibrium.

The shipment of food supplies out of deficit markets, in the midst of famine, was in some cases an act of political vindictiveness or simply selfish, profiteering policy. It might also serve wider political ambitions. For example, in order to fulfill ideological Cold War objectives, China sent large shipments of the country's rice and maize, as well as some of its scarce doctors, to frontline African states such as Guinea and the Sudan in the early 1960s, in spite of shortage at home in the later years of the Great Leap Forward Famine. Somewhat similar, in late-nineteenth-century Iran, it was the neglect of irrigation systems and a shift from food cropping to opium cultivation, at the same time as the country was being opened up to external influences and heavily taxed, that led to the Great Famine of 1870–1872. The ratio of famine deaths in Iran is uncertain but as many as three million died and it is probable that the proportion was even greater than that experienced in Ireland (Seyf, 2010: 296–8).

Although the twentieth century witnessed some of the largest and best-publicized famines of all time, in Asia and Africa, the broad tendency was downward. The exceptions of the twentieth century were spectacular, but exceptions all the same. Thus China recorded close to a famine a year over the past two millennia, and suffered the dramatic trauma of 1959–61, but thereafter proved able to restrict deaths from starvation to a minimum. In India the capacity of famine to cause mass deaths virtually disappeared by the beginning of the twentieth century. In most of Europe this was true by the early eighteenth century. Similarly, although Africa came to prominence as a center of famine in the late twentieth century, the long-term trend was positive. Food shortages ceased to kill great numbers in Africa during the twentieth century as a result of reductions in poverty, improvements in government, better transport and superior access to markets. However, at the same time as famine deaths declined in Africa, hunger continued to stalk the land, and, writes John Iliffe (1987: 6), "epidemic starvation for all but the rich gave way to endemic undernutrition for the very poor."

Ireland's Great Famine came almost at the end of Western Europe's famine history. In the thousand years before the eighteenth century, Western Europe and the Mediterranean had been one of the world's most important famine regions. Over this long period, both Britain and France reported famines about once every decade. Before about AD 500, the Greco-Roman world similarly reported a significant history of famine, though it appears less common than in medieval and early modern Europe. Examples of much earlier famines come from the regions of the first agricultural and urban revolutions, the Fertile Crescent.

Crop failure was common in the ancient world. In fertile Babylonia, around 200 BC, famine followed when the typically volatile grain price reached extraordinary highs. This volatility resulted from the absence of an integrated market, caused by the heavy cost of moving bulky goods by sea and the virtual impossibility of overland transportation. This meant that when grain yields were high in Babylonia little of the surplus was shipped out of the region and when yields were poor there was little chance of making good the need (van der Spek, 2007: 419–22).

Things were different where regional variations in supply and demand could be balanced by trade or requisition, as in the classical Greco-Roman world. In the Mediterranean, the wheat crop failed probably once every four years and two successive drought years might be enough to create a subsistence crisis. However, when famine did occur, it was usually the product of abnormal conditions, such as the combination of a series of poor harvests and prolonged warfare. The Romans ensured the provision of Rome by taxing the crops of the provinces, resulting in the shipping of product from Sicily, Sardinia, and northern Africa to such an extent that it created or exacerbated shortages in those places. Compulsory purchases were also made in Sicily, on top of the tithe. But, whereas farmers could see out hard times by consuming more of what they produced or benefiting by high prices, city-dwellers were particularly vulnerable to erratic and extreme price variability.

Even in Rome, people died of starvation when supplies were temporarily cut off, for example during the civil war of the Late Republic (Harris, 2007: 530–531). In addition, the city's numerous inhabitants were less able to shift to famine foods than their rural fellow citizens. The city could only survive if its food security was guaranteed and this necessitated the exercise of strong public authority, something the imperial system was capable of delivering. Outside Rome and Athens, however, food supply was relatively unregulated, left in the hands of private enterprise rather than committed to state traders or fleets (Gallant, 1991: 5–7; Garnsey, 1988: 271–2). The effect was to give substantial power to local aristocracies, who fulfilled their moral duty to avert disaster by means of a public generosity that worked to underpin their honor and prestige.

It is striking that all of the famines discussed thus far occurred in Eurasia and Africa. Elsewhere around the world, societal famine was rare. The great demographic disaster that followed in the wake of Columbus in the Americas certainly had something to do with food supplies but the rapidity of the decimation is generally taken to indicate that epidemic disease was the major cause. On the islands of the Caribbean, where the destruction began, the introduction of large mammals quickly degraded the carefully tended gardens of the indigenous peoples, but disease and demographic collapse marched on ahead, taking their heavy toll even before the agricultural base had been undermined. Once the process was set in motion, the people debilitated by disease lacked the energy needed to tend their crops and process their cassava and maize, thus reducing food supplies and making the communities more vulnerable to epidemics. On the other hand, depopulation reduced the demand for food while extending the area available for agriculture. In general, it seems right to conclude that famine was not a common feature of life in sixteenth-century Spanish America, for either the indigenous or the colonizing peoples (Super, 1988: 53).

For colonizing European settlers one of the great attractions of the Americas was the prospect of living without hunger. They found there a land of plenty, with its own abundance of species and a soil that enabled the productive cultivation and grazing of introduced plants and animals. Some of the earliest European settlements, notably the English colony at Jamestown, Virginia, founded in 1607, did suffer initial periods of privation and deaths by starvation. They did so because they depended on supplies brought with them across the Atlantic, preferring these to local foods, or followed a nutrition-deficient diet based on corn which led to pellagra and scurvy, anorexia and apathy. Some refused to eat corn because they thought it toxic, the food of savages. These colonists starved in the midst of abundance (Kupperman, 1979). Those who tried to make good the deficiency by stealing from stores and ships did no better. A Jamestown colonist who stole two pints of oatmeal had a needle stuck through his tongue before being chained to a tree and left to starve to death (Eden, 2008: 73).

Such events affected small numbers of people and served chiefly to encourage the wider use of local commodities, beyond cassava and maize, and to promote the cultivation of plants introduced from the Old World. Settlers and their dependents quickly discovered what was good to eat in this new environment, and were astounded by the bounty of fish, fowl, and fruit.

Throughout the Americas, the rapid spread of European exploitation and settlement was founded on the abundant food supply. It was essential not simply for the subsistence or immediate consumption of the settler communities but also for the extraction of other kinds of wealth, from silver and gold to dyewoods, sugar, and cocoa. The vast toiling slave labor force of the tropical plantations depended on the fruitfulness of forest and provision ground and equally the bounty of field and fishery that underpinned regional trading networks. Extreme hunger occurred only when these systems broke down. For example, famine deaths, enough to double the death rate of the enslaved, occurred in Jamaica during the American Revolution, when food supplies normally traded south were blocked and hurricanes uprooted plantain walks. Overall, however, the colonial populations of the Americas suffered little by way of hunger. Even the enslaved populations, though exploited severely and regularly undernourished, were more likely to die of malnutrition than starvation. When famine did rear its head, as for example in Mexico 1785–6, the outcome paled into insignificance compared to the experience of Eurasia.

Before Columbus, few major instances of famine are known for the Americas. The most dramatic collapse of a civilization, that of the Maya, had something to do with the declining productivity of the agricultural system but did not spring fully formed from extreme famine. Rather, the "collapse" was a process prolonged over centuries of political turmoil and aggressive leadership. In some regions this led to militarized settlement patterns, in which reduced populations lived in fortified sites, exhausting the soils within their defensive limits rather than following the Classic Maya model in which biodiversity and dispersed field systems had proved a successful subsistence strategy. But the breakdown of this ecological adaptation was long and drawn out, a process in which few individuals actually starved to death (Demarest, 2004: 254–5, 274–6). In Mexico a combination of droughts and frosts created a deadly famine in the middle of the fifteenth century. Elsewhere, throughout the Americas, the indigenous peoples developed food systems that ensured the exploitation of different resources in different seasons and stored or preserved enough to get through the coldest winters and longest droughts. They did not inhabit a paradise and the most extreme weather events were capable of wiping out the best-planned reserves, requiring resort to famine foods and causing the premature deaths of the oldest and weakest, but large-scale famine seems to have been uncommon.

The experience of the Americas was repeated, with minor variations, in Australia, New Zealand, and the Pacific. There, indigenous populations certainly knew the meaning of hunger, but as an episodic or seasonal event rather than as regular near starvation or famine. They learned to live within the resources of localized environments, sometimes moving plants and animals from place to place, as in the diffusion of the breadfruit through the Pacific, but rarely trading food in significant amounts. Seasonal availability was key. Thus, indigenous peoples sometimes divided the year into as few as two named seasons and sometimes as many as six, defined partly by weather events but partly also by the availability of particular foods or the opportunity for particular activities such as fishing and hunting. Extreme weather conditions, particularly extended droughts, resulted in food shortages for desert-dwelling groups and communities, but millennia of close observation and experimentation meant that almost always something could be found to eat. Thus, the mere presence and extended duration of drought was not necessarily sufficient to cause famine, especially where population densities were low.

In contrast to their experience in North America, the Europeans who came to live in Australia less often perceived a native abundance of food resources, but they quickly associated the land with plenty, particularly cheap meat. To an even greater extent than in North America, this abundance came to be found in the products of introduced plants and animals rather than any indigenous species. Kangaroo was eaten at first, of necessity, but quickly replaced in the European Australian diet by lamb and beef. The barbecue and the meat pie came as close to national foods as could be achieved by such a society. Whatever they ate, famine was unheard of.

Famine foods

In societies built on differences in wealth, class, and caste, the famine foods of the better off often looked very much like the normal fare of the poor. In ancient China, a first response to shortage was to shift to inferior varieties, notably a substitution of wheat and beans, considered coarser grains, for the much-favored millet. When the cereals ran out, the people turned to roots and tubers or, in extremis, mudcakes seasoned with weeds (Schafer, 1977: 107–8). By around AD 1000, the necessities of Chinese life were said to be firewood, rice, salt, oil, soybean sauce, and tea. Those with a little more wealth could not get by without soup and *tshai* to accompany their meals of rice. When the rice ran out, and where it was impossible to migrate or to obtain supplies from outside a region, then peasant farmers had to forage, turning to roots and making flour from the seeds of unusual plants or even using their husks and hulls. More than 400 famine-food plants were known in China, around this time, half of them herbs, the others divided between trees, cereals, fruit, and vegetables. All of these were plants not normally eaten but known to be edible. Knowledge was passed on efficiently, partly because the frequency of crises made it easy and necessary to learn.

In places where famine was less common, flours were sometimes made from little-understood husks and nuts which actively increased the risk of gastric illnesses and death. In the ancient Mediterranean, the shoots of trees and bushes were cooked and eaten, along with fresh grass, and the roots and tubers of indigestible plants (Garnsey, 1999: 37). Such alternatives were normally the fodder of animals. In China, eating bark and grass always suggested desperation.

A new range of famine foods was recognized in China at the end of the sixteenth century, namely plants introduced from the Americas such as maize and sweet potatoes, which had to serve time on the margins of the food system before being accepted as items of regular diet (Chaudhuri, 1990: 169–70). But basic food preparation and cooking techniques were much the same in times of stress and plenty. It was just a matter of applying these skills to "inferior" ingredients during famine, often in ways that expanded rather than narrowed the cuisine.

In the Americas, pre-Columbian peoples survived the barren periods by eating whatever roots, herbs, fruits, nuts, and seeds they could find, turning to species they normally did not prefer. Sixteenth-century Spanish explorers of the Mexican desert reported people in famine eating spiders, the eggs of ants, worms, lizards, snakes, wood and earth, and the dung of deer. Similarly, in Australia survival through the hardest times depended on a willingness to eat any and everything. In times of plenty, on the other hand, the same people happily surrendered most of these foods, for a diet rich in the meat of kangaroos, wallabies, waterbirds, and crocodiles.

In Ireland, during the Potato Famine of 1846–52, people turned to cheaper less palatable foods like maize, but when such substitutes were exhausted ate fungi, seaweed, berries, nettles, frogs, and rats. Ironically, in Ethiopia in 1888–92 it was the extremity of the famine that finally induced the people in desperation to begin eating potatoes which had been introduced to the country several decades earlier but, as in many other places, had not been well received (Pankhurst, 1966: 120–121). It was in comparison to the dung of camels and mules, and the corpses of donkeys, hyenas, and jackals, that the foreign taste of the potato first came to seem appealing.

Perhaps the hardest choices about what to eat occurred during wartime, especially sieges. It was in these extreme circumstances that people ate what was normally rejected, both for reasons of taste and moral repugnance. Rats, horses and pet cats and dogs might be consumed, or even fellow human beings. Cannibalism is reported from ancient China, for example, and occurred during famines in peace as well as war. In the Egyptian famine of AD 1065 people ate cats and dogs, if they could find them, and one another (Garnsey, 1999: 37). In Iran in 1870–1872 it was grass and carrion, the blood that could be got at the abattoir, and cannibalism (Seyf, 2010: 297). In the great Ethiopian famine of 1888–92, says Pankhurst (1966: 120), the extent of social disintegration was seen in "the emergence all over the country of various 'unnatural practices,' including the eating of traditionally forbidden food, the abandonment or sale of children by their parents, self-enslavement, suicide, murder, and cannibalism." In the siege of Leningrad, 1941–42, almost any animal, from pigeon to pet, was eaten despite reluctance and shame, and chunks of nondescript human flesh were offered in markets, cut from the buttocks of corpses that lay in the streets (Goldstein, 2005: 151).

The logistics of food supply in wartime was always a mighty challenge. Prolonged campaigns routinely led to attacks on whatever was to hand, whether it was the property of friend or foe. In the Mfecane wars in southern Africa, as elsewhere, plunder of household stores and killing of cattle was regarded as appropriate provisioning. Shaka permitted the eating of meat during campaigns, though his troops were in peacetime more restricted in their diets. Other African leaders organized groups of farmers to produce supplies.

In the twentieth century, nutritionists found in wartime examples of deprivation they otherwise could study only in colonial settings. In part, this situation was new, a product of the great dependence on an integrated global market that had built up by the early twentieth century when food accounted for more than one-quarter of the world's exports. World War I brought shortages and fears of famine, regulation, and a renewed protectionism in search of food security. The impact of World War II was even more direct in Europe, with the totalitarian Third Reich plundering fields and storehouses both to feed expansion and to sustain the German people.

Survival strategies

Broadly, responses to food shortage take three main forms. The first is the modification of diet, by eating "famine foods." The second response involves efforts to increase the productivity of existing resources by technological, social, or even ideological means, by inventing or adopting new tools or introducing irrigation, for example, or by surrendering taboos that prohibited the eating of particular things (including cannibalism in the worst case) or praying for rain or manna from heaven. Third, demand can be dampened, by reducing the total population and its density, through the shifting of people to less-affected regions, changing the age structure (by infanticide, in extremis), or lowering fertility.

The outcome of these three responses is often complicated, however, because in most complex societies elite groups have responsibility for making vital decisions, and may choose to favor practices and ideologies that increase rather than reduce societal vulnerability, for example systems of tribute or the forcible acquisition of resources. Further, wealthy elites often had an interest in practices such as deforestation, monocultural agriculture, and overgrazing, that had long-term deleterious effects on natural resources. Negative outcomes also were common where the extended duration of drought and famine was not predicted or predictable.

In the long term, populations had little choice but to adjust to short-term, annual variations in food availability. The immediate solution to limited supplies in the harshest season of the year was of course to invent or adopt technologies of preservation or to trade. It is no surprise that the reduced impact of seasonality observed in the world food system over the past two centuries matches the period in which preservation technologies became sophisticated and trade in basic commodities common and relatively cheap. Before this period, and including hunter-gatherers as well as agriculturists and pastoralists, the expectation of seasonal shortage was common. Where little could be preserved or exchanged, there the population had little hope of growth, entering an uneasy equilibrium of people and natural productivity.

In the worst case, the population of a small isolated island might be wiped out completely but replaced quite quickly by new migrants. On the other hand, where populations were effectively small, a balance could be achieved by living in the midst of great plenty in normal times and consuming only what was necessary, so that in hard times there was enough to go around except in the most extreme circumstances. In terms of the long-term impact of shortage on demographic development the effect was typically minor. Indeed, the same applies to much larger demographic disasters, the outcome of major famines, for example, in which seemingly substantial losses can be caught up rapidly.

For more than two thousand years, the Chinese employed a system of public granaries, established by the central state, independent of local rulers and of the commercial market, stocked with reserves sufficient to see out several bad years (Will and Bin Wong, 1991: 1–8). The importance of ensuring food supplies in this way was not merely a matter of charity but seen also as essential to the moral authority and stability of the state. Further, in geographically large states such as China, there was a need to attempt to respond to regional imbalances. Importantly, the development of large cities in China expanded the notion of state responsibility, to ensure the urban populations did not starve while the rural people retained what they produced, but also went together with a need to provision the military in times of stress and potential unrest. In many towns and cities, kitchens were set up for the free distribution of rice gruel, to help those who lacked the resources or energy to cook.

Something similar occurred in ancient Rome, with public allocations of grain largely confined to the city, drawing heavily on other regions of the empire for its food supplies. The Byzantine state maintained the tradition but narrowed distributions to a form of urban poor relief rather than general public munificence. The rulers of the Ottoman Empire similarly applied the Muslim belief that government should play a central role in bringing stability to food supplies, though once again with a focus on urban centers, notably Constantinople.

Again, the state stored much of the food produced by the Incas in a decentralized system spread across the rugged highland terrain of the Andes centered on Cuzco (LeVine, 1992). The system was a vital element in the expansion and consolidation of the empire, beginning around 3500 BP. The Inca storehouses were filled by means of taxation and tied labor, and contained substantial reserves of textiles and manufactured items as well as food. Separate storehouses were built for potatoes and other tubers, using specialized technologies of ventilation and floor construction, varied to deal with local weather conditions; and for maize, which was stored in large jars placed in windowless chambers.

In Christian Europe, public granaries were rarely built, though the French did consider the possibility, as an emergency response, in the eighteenth century. Generally, the church was given the task of caring for the poor, while the state looked after the provisioning of cities, and the market was allowed a much greater role. This contrast with China forms part of the basis for the "great divergence" but equally demonstrates the earlier success of the Chinese in stabilizing their agrarian state (Will and Bin Wong 1991: 507–25).

The threat of shortage and famine was a vital driver in the planned storage of food. The importance of these foods being available and nutritious whenever called on determined in turn the kinds of crops that were chosen for cultivation. Grains had much in their favor. The necessity of preparing for the worst ensured their availability more generally and they remained a primary normal resource rather than a designated famine food. Governments of all sorts had an immediate interest in ensuring food security for their people, because insecurity meant instability, with the possibility of food riots, violence, and looting as well as the threat of migration and disease. In modern times, famine migration has often been directed at movement into cities, resulting in pressure on resources and the addition of refugee populations to already growing marginal, shantytown settlements.

Responses to famine have varied with public policy and notions of universal responsibility. Doctrinaire free trade and laissez-faire models, which gained dominance in the nineteenth century, were often used to justify neglect and support a belief that the market was the best mechanism for resolving issues of supply and demand. Thus, the British state remained a distant observer in the initial phases of the Irish famine, which began in 1846, the year free trade in grain was established as a mantra, on the grounds that state intervention was something best avoided.

This was a piece of political economy that fitted neatly with the influential ideas of Thomas Robert Malthus, expressed in his *Essay on the Principle of Population*, first published in 1798, in which he argues that the potential for population growth follows a geometric rate whereas an arithmetic rule applies to increases in the world's food supplies. Malthus believed that population growth would always run ahead of the world's ability to produce more food and that increases in the supply of food would be quickly made up by natural increase, thus placing fresh pressure on resources. Famine was inevitable. Politicians used this dismal Malthusian scenario to turn a blind eye. Doing so was easy enough, as famine became a thing of the past, something that happened somewhere else, in most of peacetime Western Europe and North America. Further, what Malthus did not predict was the great increase in world food production that followed the application of industrial technologies to agriculture and fisheries. These twentieth-century developments enabled food supply to keep up with rapid and substantial population growth, on a global scale, and even witnessed an increase in calories available per capita (Howe, 2010: 34–6). The global catastrophe that might have been expected under Malthusian conditions was avoided (or at least delayed), though the voices of doomsayers remained loud.

Food aid

Attitudes to subsistence crises changed after World War II but in complex and sometimes contradictory ways. It was in this period that the notion of "food aid" came to the fore as public policy, both as an activity of nation-states and of international organizations. The FAO (Food and Agriculture Organization) of the United Nations played a leading role, though its brief was to improve long-term nutrition generally not merely to respond to crises. In spite of the existence of the FAO, famines remained a constant, as noticed already, in Asia and Africa. Toward the end of the twentieth century, Africa became the focus of concern. The World Food Program of the United Nations, set up in 1963, had major responsibility for food aid but also invested in grass-roots improvement of food resources and distribution. From the 1980s, however, proliferating emergencies forced an emphasis on aid. A range of nongovernmental agencies, particularly church-based organizations, also became active. More prominent in the public eye were independent efforts at famine relief, such as Band Aid promoted by the singer Bob Geldof, in response to the 1984 famine in Ethiopia, and followed by a series of Live Aid concerts. These efforts contributed to the emergence of a larger campaign to "make poverty history." Although these enterprises were criticized for their capitalist cast, there is no doubt they saved many lives.

Food aid can, however, have unexpected and negative effects. In the midst of extreme food shortage, the setting up of feeding centers often draws masses of hungry people to relief sites, exceeding the capacity to satisfy need (Howe, 2010: 41–3). The refugees are cut off from any famine foods they might have exploited in their home places. Crowded camps develop, and sanitation and hygiene become difficult to maintain. Disease breaks out and the overall result can be elevated mortality. Indeed, it has been argued that in the 1984 famine in the Darfur region of Sudan, more people died from communicable diseases prevalent in camps than from starvation. Much the same occurred in the Ethiopian famine of 1999–2000, where outbreaks of measles following humanitarian intervention rapidly increased the level of mortality, particularly among young children.

National contributions to food aid were regularly criticized for being self-interested and even inimical in their long-term effects on food security and production in the very developing countries that suffered famine. In many ways, these programs followed general principles laid down in the Great Depression of the 1930s, when the United States government first legislated to provide food aid to low-income individuals. This initiative permitted the Department of Agriculture, through the Federal Surplus Commodities Corporation, to purchase farm products for distribution to the needy or to contribute to school meal systems. From the beginning the primary objective was to support prices, benefiting farmers. This scheme was replaced by a food stamps program in 1939, continuing until 1943, following a dual system: orange stamps, which had to be purchased and were meant to be equivalent to the normal food expenditure of a family, and free blue stamps, which could be used only to purchase items on a monthly list of surplus foods. In the

1950s most of the US agricultural surplus was disposed of abroad, though large numbers of poor Americans received distributions.

A revived food stamp program was initiated in 1961, one of the first acts of the government of President John F. Kennedy, using this time a single stamp that could be applied to the purchase of almost any item, excluding some imported foods, thus allowing considerable choice. Income was the sole qualification for eligibility and interest now began to be shown in the nutritional consequences of the scheme, so that welfare considerations came to balance the support of farmers. The objective was to end hunger in the United States, as part of the War on Poverty commenced in 1965, and to end demeaning distributions (MacDonald, 1977). However, the numbers of people receiving food stamps increased to more than four million by 1970 (one in 50 of the population) and to 30 million by 2010 (about one in 10). When obesity became prominent as a problem in the 1980s, it was observed that the most vulnerable individuals tended to be poor, recipients of food stamps, and female (Zagorsky and Smith, 2009). By the beginning of the twenty-first century, changes to the program were proposed to encourage low-calorie, high-nutrient food choices by, for instance, differential pricing for the food-insecure to shift them from fatty foods to fresh fruit and vegetables.

An unusual example of state control of food resources in the late twentieth century, outside the socialist realm, occurred in the Dominican Republic, where from the 1960s the food economy became increasingly dependent on imports. When a left-leaning government was elected in 1962, following the assassination of the dictator Rafael Trujillo, it established a nationwide network of storage facilities, silos, vehicles to collect and distribute food, and stores, and markets. The state also supported a system of school breakfasts and low-price restaurants. This system subsidized basic commodities, distributed food baskets at Christmas, and cared for people affected by flood and hurricane, in order to bestow political patronage and attract support for the regime. When the Dominican Republic needed aid in the 1990s to reinforce its economy, the IMF sought the end of the state food system, but it survived and at the presidential election of 2008 food handouts were important in the competition for votes. Although by then this statist food system seemed an anachronism, it played a significant role not only in political democratization but also in the defense of the Dominican Republic's forest against agricultural advance (Mitchell, 2009). It was an outcome in strong contrast to that in its island neighbor, Haiti, where the degradation of the environment went hand in hand with starvation and food-price riots.

From the 1960s, world output was sufficient to ensure enough food for everyone. The impediments to achieving this goal were essentially barriers to trade and aid that prevented flow from regions of surplus to regions of need. As discussed in Chapter 6, particularly in relation to the flow of grain, these impediments are essentially political. They derive from the use of policy to shore up domestic political power and to influence and intervene in the political systems of other countries. This was particularly true of the United States, where a vast surplus was produced in 1961 and the government looked for ways to support hard-pressed grain farmers, whose votes were wanted. Very large food-aid grain shipments began to be made to countries afflicted by famine, such as India. Such aid saved many lives but the impetus came from domestic political needs rather than any humanitarian impulse. Further, it is argued that food aid helped change tastes and provide an entry for imports into new markets, particularly in poor countries in Asia, Africa, and parts of Latin America.

The long-term effect of these policies has been the reduction or even destruction of local food producers who are unable to compete successfully with cheap (often subsidized) imports. In Ethiopia, where massive food aid continued for almost three decades with hardly a pause, food production was less in 2010 than it had been in 1984, and its subsistence farmers poorer (Bishop and Hilhorst, 2010: 181–2). In the case of Haiti, conditions attached to foreign loans, notably a 1994 IMF package, required the country to liberalize its market as part of the assistance deal. The result was that cheap US rice, made cheap in part by means of subsidies, overwhelmed the market and effectively wiped out local Haitian farmers.

The policy underlying these developments, promoted by the IMF and the World Bank and the developed economies of the North, was directed at creating a new international division of labor and export specialization, in which the developing countries would benefit by focussing on products other than grains. They were also expected to surrender state systems, mostly established after decolonization, used to direct the distribution of food at controlled prices, particularly grains. On the other hand, they were to accept cereals and dairy products from the developed countries burdened by surpluses and able to sell cheaply (Patnaik, 2009: 71).

Inflation-adjusted prices for rice, corn, and wheat have all fallen since 1900. Ironically, the outcome is to make poor economies increasingly vulnerable to the vagaries of international market prices and therefore vulnerable both to local food shortages created by natural disasters and to shortages elsewhere. Thus the crisis of 2008, which saw steep increases in the prices of basic foods such as rice, resulted in riots in Haiti, Egypt, and many other African nations (Timmer, 2010). As always, it was a sharp increase in prices that brought on these riots rather than absolute poverty and hunger, neither of which is a potent source of protest.

Food riots often originate in inflated prices, caused by shortage of supply of one kind or another, and are therefore often directed at particular stores thought to be profiteering, whether retail or public (Bentley, 2001). In early modern Europe, this sometimes meant the seizure and sale at a just price of foods overpriced by a retailer, together with the perhaps surprising payment of the proceeds to the delinquent merchant, honoring the "moral economy" of tradition while using the food riot as a pre-industrial way of showing their anger at social and economic injustice. Second, food riots have taken the form of blockades, attempting to prevent the shipment of grain or other foods from one town or region to another. Third, market riots consist of the simple looting of retail shops and storage depots, in order to protest shortages and high prices, and the deliberate destruction of the property of the perpetrators. Fourth, riots with a greater degree of symbolic political action may consist simply of dumping samples of the food on the grounds of, for example, government officials purportedly in charge of distribution.

Boycotts were more common in the twentieth century, as consumers became able to pick and choose substitutes more freely in the midst of plenty. In this case, a single food item such as milk or bread could be boycotted, often with dramatic effect, or a single manufacturer such as Nestlé might be singled out for protest. Women played a large role in such boycotts, as they had done in most other forms of food riot. Over time, the varied types of riot and styles of protest often slipped from one kind to another or contained more than one element. The Boston Tea Party, for example, in which colonists tipped Indian tea into Boston harbor in 1773, was a protest at British customs duties and imperial power, picking out a single symbolic commodity, the quintessential ceremonial commodity in the development of eighteenth-century consumer society, and destroying it.

Contemporaneous bread rioters in France singled out bakers but also directed their anger at government marketing controls and gave vent to anger at individual bakers. Liberty and rights, nationalism and patriotism, and wider questions of identity, all found their way into the pattern of protest. Little of this had to do with hunger, yet just as the Americas were largely free of famine so did food protests flourish among twentieth-century Americans, the people of plenty. Thus, for example there were protests in the United States in the 1930s over the destruction of grain and pork, as a means of supporting prices, and Civil Rights protests frequently used the denial of service at a lunch counter as a symbol of the denial of full citizenship.

Impact

The demographic consequences of famine have always been stark. The immediate image is one of skeletal bodies piled up or spilled into common graves, much like pictures of the victims of mass killings and plagues. As in these cases, famine deaths were selective and therefore had significant effects on the structure of populations and on their future prospects of growth. In particular, famines tended to kill first the most vulnerable individuals of a community, targeting the old and the weak, the infants, and parentless. The wealthy did better, being able to afford food at any price and possessing the resources to build up their own personal stocks. They might die of disease but they were unlikely to starve to death. The poor and the weak, on the other hand, were most vulnerable in epidemics, with most to fear from coincident cholera and the like.

Premature births and stillbirths were common during famine. Mothers gave birth to underweight babies, and had difficulty breastfeeding. Infant mortality was also typically very high, as was the mortality of all children under ten. This created a changed age structure, so that the cohort of adult workers was reduced not immediately but beginning about ten years after the end of a famine. The imbalance was less significant than it might have been, however, because famine mortality was also high among adults over 45 years of age, so that the population of older people requiring support was reduced. At its worst, infanticide increased when mothers could not bear the suffering of their children. In the midst of the worst famines to affect Africa, vulnerable individuals, including kin, might be sold into slavery to relieve the burden on a community's resources. Some of these people were trafficked down to the coast and entered the Atlantic slave trade (Curtin, 1983: 379–81). The proportion is impossible to estimate but spikes in the slave trade often matched periods of famine, making hunger a contributor to this forced migration.

Famine affected fertility as well as mortality. This resulted partly from the death of fertile women, potential mothers, but also derived from the effect of starvation on the potential for successful pregnancies and child-birth. Amenorrhea, the absence of menstruation, resulted from inadequate food, especially for those women required to perform hard manual work. Reduced fertility also resulted where young adult males, potential fathers, left famine regions to seek work elsewhere. Once again, these effects were closely related to wealth. In the Bangladesh famine of 1974, for example, the wealthiest social groups continued to marry and their fertility rates declined less than half as much as those of the poor (Kane, 1988: 19). Selective mortality, the desertion of wives by husbands, and the wandering of orphans searching for food, led inevitably to family breakdown. It often also led to migration from rural to urban areas where food supplies were superior, as in movement to Calcutta in the Bengal famine of 1943, for example. In some cases, however, the effect was merely to spread the famine wider, with disease in its wake.

Children born during famine or growing up in its shadow experienced stunting, the common effect of extreme undernutrition. For example, children born in China in 1959 achieved heights as adults 1 in. (3 cm) shorter than they would have done in the absence of famine (Chen and Zhou, 2007). They were more likely to suffer from hypertension. Similar outcomes have been identified for the Dutch Potato Famine of 1846–7, occurring relatively late in life (Lindeboom, Portrait and van den Berg, 2010). Among those who lived beyond 50 years of age, males born during this famine lost 5.0 years of life and females 2.5 years. The Dutch famine of 1944–5 also had a delayed impact on health, affecting people in adulthood even when their weights were normal at birth (Roseboom *et al.*, 2001).

Down to the eighteenth century, hunger, disease, and climatic variability all contributed to the relatively slow growth of population. Extreme hunger often resulted in migration to urban centers, as noticed earlier, but much of this was temporary. More significant was the permanent movement of large populations from famine-stricken regions to other countries. The Irish famine of 1846–52 saw about one million people leave Ireland for the United States and the United Kingdom. Nineteenth-century famines in Asia contributed to the flow of indentured workers to many plantation economies, as far away as Africa and the Americas. Recent famines in northeastern Brazil impelled migration into the Amazon rainforest. In these examples, famine played a role in the imperial project of colonization.

Persistent shortage, and the onset of climatic change also worked to stimulate trade by providing the natural basis for exchange. For example, the climatic crisis that affected Africa around 3700 BP led communities in the increasingly arid Sahara to turn to the mining of salt and the development of metallurgical enterprises, in order to trade these products with their southern neighbors in return for food (Hassan, 2002: 21–3). Severe droughts in this period similarly stimulated the appearance of cultivation in West Africa and of pastoral economies in East Africa, in much the same way that climatic shocks had stimulated the first farmers.

Two claims

An important claim is that famine is the product of human – governmental and moral – failure rather than the direct consequence of unmanageable natural disasters. Droughts and floods serve as triggers but it is the failure to plan and act, in the past as well as the present, that matters most.

Second, as noted in Chapter 8, it can be claimed that persistent shortages together with frequent but intermittent dependence on famine foods lead to innovations, both in terms of the development of trades in food and in the use of ingredients in specific culinary styles.

REFERENCES

Bentley, A. (2001) Reading food riots: Scarcity, abundance and national identity. In P. Scholliers (ed.) *Food, Drink and Identity: Cooking, Eating and Drinking in Europe Since the Middle Ages*, pp. 179–93. Oxford: Berg.

Bishop, C. and Hilhorst, D. (2010) From food aid to food security: The case of the safety net policy in Ethiopia. *Journal of Modern African Studies* 48: 181–202.

Chaudhuri, K.N. (1990) *Asia before Europe: Economy and Civilisation of the Indian Ocean from the Rise of Islam to 1750*. Cambridge: Cambridge University Press.

Chen, Y. (2010) When food became scarce: Life and death in Chinese villages during the Great Leap Forward famine. *Journal of the Historical Society* 10: 117–65.

Chen, Y. and Zhou, L.-A. (2007) The long-term health and economic consequences of the 1959–61 famine in China. *Journal of Health Economics* 26: 659–81.

Curtin, P.D. (1983) Nutrition in African history. *Journal of Interdisciplinary History* 14: 371–82.

Demarest, A.(2004) *Ancient Maya: The Rise and Fall of a Rainforest Civilization*. Cambridge: Cambridge University Press.

Dikötter, F. (2010) *Mao's Great Famine: The History of China's Most Devastating Catastrophe, 1958–62*. London: Bloomsbury.

Eden, T. (2008) *The Early American Table: Food and Society in the New World*. DeKalb, IL: Northern Illinois University Press.

Fernando, M.R. (2010) Famine in a land of plenty: Plight of a rice-growing community in Java, 1883–84. *Journal of Southeast Asian Studies* 41: 291–320.

Gallant, T.W. (1991) *Risk and Survival in Ancient Greece: Reconstructing the Rural Domestic Economy*. Stanford, CA: Stanford University Press.

Garnsey, P. (1988) *Famine and Food Supply in the Greco-Roman World: Responses to Risk and Crisis*. Cambridge: Cambridge University Press.

Garnsey, P. (1999) *Food and Society in Classical Antiquity*. Cambridge: Cambridge University Press.

Goldstein, D. (2005) Women under siege: Leningrad 1941–1942. In A.V. Avakian and B. Haber (eds) *From Betty Crocker to Feminist Food Studies: Critical Perspectives on Women and Food*, pp. 143–60. Amherst, MA: University of Massachusetts Press.

Harris, W.V. (2007) The late republic. In W. Scheidel, I. Morris and R. Saller (eds) *The Cambridge Economic History of the Greco-Roman World*, pp. 511–39. Cambridge: Cambridge University Press.

Hassan, F.A. (2002) Palaeoclimate, food and culture change in Africa: An overview. In F.A. Hassan (ed.) *Droughts, Food and Culture: Ecological Change and Food Security in Africa's Later Prehistory*, pp. 11–26. New York: Kluwer Academic.

Howe, P. (2010) Archetypes of famine and response. *Disasters* 34: 30–54.

Iliffe, J. (1987) *The African Poor: A History*. Cambridge: Cambridge University Press.

Kane, P. (1988) *Famine in China, 1959–61: Demographic and Social Implications*. Basingstoke, UK: Macmillan Press.

Kinealy, C. (1997) *A Death-Dealing Famine: The Great Hunger in Ireland*. London: Pluto Press.

Kupperman, K.O. (1979) Apathy and death in early Jamestown. *Journal of American History* 66: 24–40.

Lee, H.F. and Zhang, D.D. (2010) Natural disasters in northwestern China, AD 1270–1949. *Climate Research* 41: 245–57.

LeVine, T.Y. (ed.) (1992) *Inka Storage Systems*. Norman, OK: University of Oklahoma Press.

Lindeboom, M., Portrait, F. and van den Berg, G.J. (2010) Long-run effects on longevity of a nutritional shock early in life: The Dutch Potato Famine of 1846–47. *Journal of Health Economics* 29: 617–29.

MacDonald, M. (1977) Food stamps: An analytical history. *Social Service Review* 51: 642–58.

Mitchell, K. (2009) Democratisation, external exposure and state food distribution in the Dominican Republic. *Bulletin of Latin American Research* 28: 204–26.

Ó Gráda, C. (2008) The ripple that drowns? Twentieth-century famines in China and India as economic history. *Economic History Review* 61: 5–37.

Pankhurst, R. (1966) The great Ethiopian famine of 1888–1892: A new assessment. *Journal of the History of Medicine and Allied Sciences* 21: 95–124.

Patnaik, U. (2009) Origins of the food crisis in India and developing countries. *Monthly Review* 61: 63–77.

Roseboom, T.J., van der Meulen, J.H., Ravelli, A.C. *et al.* (2001) Effects of prenatal exposure to the Dutch famine on adult disease in later life: An overview. *Molecular and Cellular Endocrinology* 185: 93–98.

Schafer, E.H. (1977) T'ang. In K.C. Chang (ed.) *Food in Chinese Culture: Anthropological and Historical Perspectives*, pp. 87–140. New Haven, CT: Yale University Press.

Sen, A. (1981) *Poverty and Famines: An Essay on Entitlement and Deprivation*. Oxford: Clarendon Press.

Seyf, A. (2010) Iran and the Great Famine, 1870–72. *Middle Eastern Studies* 46: 289–306.

van der Spek, R.J. (2007) The Hellenistic Near East. In W. Scheidel, I. Morris and R. Saller (eds) *The Cambridge Economic History of the Greco-Roman World*, pp. 409–33.

Super, J.C. (1988) *Food, Conquest, and Colonization in Sixteenth-Century Spanish America*. Albuquerque, NM: University of New Mexico Press.

Timmer, C.P. (2010) Reflections on food crises past. *Food Policy* 35: 1–11.

Will, P.-É. and Bin Wong, R. (1991) *Nourish the People: The State Civilian Granary System in China, 1650–1850*. Ann Arbor: Center for Chinese Studies, University of Michigan.

Zagorsky, J.L. and Smith, P.K. (2009) Does the U.S. Food Stamp Program contribute to adult weight gain? *Economics and Human Biology* 7: 246–58.

Conclusion: Cornucopia or Pandora's Box?

The global supermarket exists as a concrete representation of cornucopia, every imaginable food seemingly within reach in any season. The modern food court offers a similar seductive image, freshly cooked foods from myriad cultures on offer, all in one place. But the tantalizing offerings of both supermarket and food court are also seen by consumers as potential traps, leading them down the path of obesity and ill health, rousing concerns about waste of resources and materials, and worries about the impact of the system on the environment. At the social level, those who live on the fat of the land also fear a future in which food crises create widespread political unrest, conflict over essential food-producing resources, and systemic failure in the global supply chain. Such fears, prospering in the midst of apparent plenty, are often apocalyptic in their predictions of catastrophe and cataclysm.

At the same time, in the same world, starvation and undernourishment remain very real specters for too many. Wondering where the next meal will come from and wondering whether it might be one's last are fears both ancient and modern in their immediacy and potency. It is the coexistence of the extremes that gives current concerns their peculiar flavor.

The period in which we live, emerging from the embers of World War II but having its real beginning in about 1960, is unlike any other in world history. It stands out because of the rapidity and scale of change, and because of the way in which it represents a new relationship between humans and the earth from which they drew their being (McNeill, 2010: 423–34). Food has a fundamental place in this changed relationship and this new world.

The complexity and global character of the modern world food system reflects its overwhelming dependence on agriculture, particularly

How Food Made History, First Edition. B. W. Higman.
© 2012 B. W. Higman. Published 2012 by Blackwell Publishing Ltd.

industrialized agriculture and to a lesser extent industrialized fishing. It is a highly productive system, but founded on an astoundingly small range of primary food sources, dominated by products obtained from the domesticated grains maize, wheat, and rice, and the animals pig, cow, and chicken. The world's population more than doubled between 1960 and 2010, to reach almost seven billion, a number and density of people who found enough to eat by increasing the productivity of an extended area of cropland, through irrigation, the application of fertilizers, and genetic modification. The catch of marine fish was massively increased, as was production of the meat of chickens, pigs, and cattle. These increases in the output of food depended on a balancing reduction in the world's forests and grasslands, and changes in the composition of maritime fish stocks. Essential to all of these components of growth was a much more spectacular increase in the use of energy, notably coal and even more oil, which contributed also to the growth of cities and urban population concentrations, as well as an increasingly wide range of non-food industrial enterprises.

Although the origins of these immense changes in world population and product were several, food was at the core. In the furnace of the Cold War, governments of all persuasions, including those of new states, anxious to confirm their viability, came quickly to see that political success depended on the capacity to feed their people. In the immediate postwar period, food shortages persisted in much of Europe, the Soviet Union, and China, as well as in colonial Asia and Africa. Pressure on resources built rapidly from the growth of population. Perception of a global food problem, something well remembered from the decades before World War II, translated in the West into something seen as a Malthusian problem of population and hence of national security. The most important response to these threats was the Green Revolution of the 1950s, discussed in Chapter 3, which contributed to massive increases in productivity without dramatically increasing cropland, but through its dependence on irrigation and chemicals and pesticides brought its own particular pattern of dire ecological consequences, both on earth and in the atmosphere. The production of meat in particular came to be condemned for its contribution to climate change.

Of the many contrasts between the modern world food system and that which dominated the earth five thousand years ago, the most obvious is the reduction of the forest and the tenuous survival of hunter-gatherer economies. The balance between these two fundamentally different modes has been reversed, with immense consequences for the use of the planet's resources and its landscapes. It must therefore be asked why the transition occurred and why hunter-gatherer peoples resisted the change, many of them for very long periods, in the presence of expanding agricultural communities. These are some of the most enduring puzzles in history and archeology.

Before the superabundance of the modern world food system, it was commonplace for historians to laud the agricultural technologies that supported urbanization and enabled the development of "civilized" cultures. In more recent times, historians and anthropologists, doing their shopping at the global supermarket, have become critical of this interpretation (Garnsey, 1999: 2). It is now almost orthodoxy to emphasize the many negative features associated with agriculture, including limited diets and biodiversity, poor health, and increased exposure to famine and under-nourishment, and to find much to like about hunting and gathering, and less complex societies. The conclusion is advocated as strongly for the Americas as for Eurasia (Manning, 2004; Steckel and Rose, 2002: 575). Thus, writing under threat of nuclear annihilation, Lee and DeVore (1968: 3) observed that *Homo sapiens* had lived happily without agriculture for many millennia, indeed the greater part of human history, and argued that "the hunting way of life has been the most successful and persistent adaptation man has ever achieved."

In spite of advocacy of this perspective, continuing changes in the world's landscape have placed great pressure on surviving forest hunter-gatherer societies. For example, the Batwa Pygmies of the East African Great Lakes region were ejected from their homelands in the late twentieth century and forced to watch their forests destroyed to make way for crop farming under colonialism, then turned into game reserves for the benefit of tourists (Lewis, 2000). These indigenous peoples had experienced an extended process of colonization, first by agricultural peoples, then by pastoralists backed by the powerful expansionist kingdoms of the region, and Europeans who sought to clear the forest in order to cultivate commercial crops. The forest that had provided their food was severely depleted by each of these invaders, while the closure of forest to appeal to latter-day ecotourists forced many of the Batwa to attempt unwanted lifestyles and diets.

The agrarian, urbanized world, developing as well as developed, continues its progress in spite of the protests of these minority peoples. Although they may be questioned, the outcomes of agricultural systems are widely recognized to include food surpluses and food security, disease and poor nutrition, arts and crafts, hierarchies (both social and religious), writing, scholarship, the political state, imperialism, and large-scale conflict. It is a mixed bag but, once part of this world, few choose to abandon it for the benefits of hunter-gatherer lifestyles. Indeed, some have questioned the extent of those benefits, declaring the idea that tropical forest ecosystems offered a "cornucopia of foods" is false (Headland, 1987: 464). The argument is that many of the potential foods available in forest plants required processing technologies (such as metal tools) not available to early peoples and that for such hunter-gatherer groups the forest provided only a meager food resource. In the past, many hunter-gatherer societies reached high levels of complexity comparable to early farming peoples. The richly resourced habitats in which these outcomes were achieved have, however, generally been occupied and transformed by cultivators. To maintain existing world population densities there is little choice but to persist with the agricultural model in its most sophisticated forms.

The view that the origins of modern food problems can be traced to agriculture has deep roots. First farmers observed their neighbor hunter-gatherers securing their food without bending their backs or raising a sweat, and, indeed, the farmers enjoyed an inferior diet and were probably the less healthy of the two groups. In myth, in many different traditions, agriculture became a punishment for offending the gods, a symbol of failures of human obedience and the seduction of forbidden fruit.

The reasons for coming to depend on agriculture and a limited range of domesticated plants and animals, on an increasingly global scale, have little to do with improvements in diet or nutrition but stem rather from the food security that could support larger and denser populations, and complex societies, brought within the fold of government and hierarchy (Wells, 2010). Only in recent decades have the benefits of the system, measured in longevity and wellbeing and the abundance of food, become really substantial. This development may be seen as the result of an acceleration of the pace at which human beings have exploited the earth's energy, the clocking up of a vast debt to nature that will have to be paid off in the future. Stepping away from the natural limits to the exploitation of the food resources of a particular habitat that encouraged hunter-gatherers to move on to new sites had many benefits, but the spread of human beings into almost every ecological niche the world has to offer seems to place the entire enterprise at risk.

Although the breeding of crop plants and farm animals has been central to improvement in food supply over the long term, from the very beginning of self-conscious selection and domestication, the techniques of genetic modification that dominated the Green Revolution retain much active energy (Olmstead and Rhode, 2008). The process is highly dynamic and the world will have to wait to see how well it works out. So far so good, from the point of view of the ability of the earth to feed a large population, but if it is to fail the outcome will be known much sooner (Vasey, 1992). Rather as in the interpretation of the impact of the Industrial Revolution on health and wellbeing, expert opinion is divided between optimists and pessimists, those who believe genetic engineering and human creativity can conquer all and those who see technology as the root cause of the problem. As discussed in Chapter 10, the view that all that is needed is to increase food production in order to keep up with growing demand is flawed. The prevention of food crises and "the coming famine" (Cribb, 2010) is much more a matter of good global governance, the removal of market distortions (Lang, 2010), averting the great waste which occurs in the global supermarket system (Stuart, 2009), and recognition of the necessity of ensuring sustainability.

The impact of population growth and urbanization on the world's food resources extends beyond agriculture, most obviously in the great demand for fish and meat that saw the application of industrial technologies to the hunting of wild species, increasingly leading to the depletion of stocks and to extinctions (Garcia and Grainger, 2005). As noted earlier, it is rare for domesticated species to become extinct, though particular varieties may in fact drop out of sight. The potato is a good example of the latter and became an object of attempts to preserve rare varieties in Peru in the late twentieth century. Here the cause of extinction or potential extinction is not so much overconsumption as neglect and the overwhelming popularity of relatively small numbers of varieties. In view of the species survival of domesticated animals used for food, it has been argued in recent times that the most effective way to ensure survival is to domesticate and eat wild animals. Further, the hunting of animals has been advocated as a means of managing numbers and ensuring their place in the food chain and the conservation of their habitats. Rather than exterminating specific animals as vermin, it may be best to make them food, with an economic and environmental value. Something similar could be argued for maritime resources, though in this case part of the solution may be simply eating a wider variety of what is caught rather than favoring a small number of desirable fishes.

These seemingly overwhelming contemporary fears of famine and food crisis, ecological disaster and imminent extinctions occur alongside a separate stream of fears stirred up by the onslaught of globalization on national and regional cuisines. Here the fear is cultural as well as economic, but no less a matter of survival. Not surprisingly, the French have demonstrated particular distress, seeing the assault as central to the viability of a complete culture, as discussed in Chapter 8. But these are examples of remembered loss rather than any enthusiasm for the food world of hunting and gathering or even for self-sufficient peasant agriculture. They seem trivial compared to the more fundamental fears that surround our food.

REFERENCES

Cribb, J. (2010) *The Coming Famine: The Global Food Crisis and What We Can Do To Avoid It*. Berkeley, CA: University of California Press.

Garcia, S.M., and Grainger, R.J.R. (2005) Gloom and doom? The future of marine capture fisheries. *Philosophical Transactions of the Royal Society B* 360: 21–46.

Garnsey, P. (1999) *Food and Society in Classical Antiquity*. Cambridge: Cambridge University Press.

Headland, T.N. (1987) The wild yam question: How well could independent hunter-gatherers live in a tropical rain forest ecosystem? *Human Ecology* 15: 463–91.

Lang, T. (2010) Crisis? What crisis? The normality of the current food crisis. *Journal of Agrarian Change* 10: 87–97.

Lee, R.B., and DeVore, I. (eds) (1968) *Man the Hunter.* Chicago: Aldine Publishing Company.

Lewis, J. (2000) *The Batwa Pygmies of the Great Lakes Region.* London: Minority Rights Group International.

Manning, R. (2004) *Against the Grain: How Agriculture Has Hijacked Civilization.* New York: North Point Press.

McNeill, J.R. (2010) The biosphere and the Cold War. In M.P. Leffler and O.A. Westad (eds) *The Cambridge History of the Cold War*, Vol. 3, pp. 422–44. Cambridge: Cambridge University Press.

Olmstead, A.L. and Rhode, P.W. (2008) *Creating Abundance: Biological Innovation and American Agricultural Development.* Cambridge: Cambridge University Press.

Steckel, R.H. and Rose, J.C. (2002) Patterns of health in the Western Hemisphere. In R.H. Steckel and J.C. Rose (eds) *The Backbone of History: Health and Nutrition in the Western Hemisphere*, pp. 563–79. Cambridge: Cambridge University Press.

Stuart, T. (2009) *Waste: Uncovering the Global Food Scandal.* London: Penguin Books.

Vasey, D.E. (1992) *An Ecological History of Agriculture: 10,000 b.c. – a.d. 10,000.* Ames, IA: Iowa State University Press.

Wells, S. (2010) *Pandora's Seed: The Unforeseen Cost of Civilization.* New York: Random House.

Suggested Further Reading

Theoretical analysis remains relatively scarce in food history. Probably the most thoughtful contributions, written by anthropologists rather than historians, remain Jack Goody (1982) *Cooking, Cuisine and Class: A Study in Comparative Sociology* (Cambridge: Cambridge University Press) and Sidney W. Mintz (1996) *Tasting Food, Tasting Freedom* (Boston: Beacon). Strong interpretations occur in general histories such as Felipe Fernández-Armesto (2002) *Food: A History* (London: Pan Books), Jeffrey M. Pilcher (2006) *Food in World History* (New York: Routledge), and Paul Freedman (ed.) (2007) *Food: The History of Taste* (Los Angeles: University of California Press). Also useful are Raymond Grew (ed.) (1999) *Food in Global History* (Boulder, CO: Westview Press) and Charles B. Heiser Jr. (1990) *Seed to Civilization: The Story of Food* (Cambridge, MA: Harvard University Press). The most comprehensive systematic account of world food history is found in the two massive volumes of Kenneth F. Kiple and Kriemhild C. Ornelas (eds) (2000) *Cambridge World History of Food* (Cambridge: Cambridge University Press).

For the chemical and physiological background of food and nutrition, see Harald Brüssow (2007) *The Quest for Food: A Natural History of Eating* (New York: Springer), Harold McGee (1984) *On Food and Cooking: The Science and Lore of the Kitchen* (London: Unwin Hyman), and Vaclav Smil (2008) *Energy in Nature and Society: General Energetics of Complex Systems* (Cambridge, MA: MIT Press).

Anthropological approaches to questions of choice are introduced well in E.N. Anderson (2005) *Everyone Eats: Understanding Food and Culture* (New York: New York University Press), Elizabeth D. Capaldi (ed.) (1996) *Why We Eat What We Eat: The Psychology of Eating* (Washington: American Psycho-

How Food Made History, First Edition. B. W. Higman.
© 2012 B. W. Higman. Published 2012 by Blackwell Publishing Ltd.

logical Association), and Richard Shepherd and Monique Raats (eds) (2006) *The Psychology of Food Choice* (Cambridge, MA: CABI Publications). The best discussions of taboos and prohibitions are Marvin Harris (1985) *Good to Eat: Riddles of Food and Culture* (New York: Simon & Schuster) and Frederick J. Simoons (1994) *Eat Not This Flesh: Food Avoidances from Prehistory to the Present* (Madison, WI: University of Wisconsin Press). The best recent account of vegetarianism is Tristram Stuart (2007) *The Bloodless Revolution: A Cultural History of Vegetarianism from 1600 to Modern Times* (New York: W.W. Norton). The consequences of choice are treated philosophically and ethically in Peter Singer and Jim Mason (2006) *The Way We Eat: Why Our Food Choices Matter* (New York: Holtzbrinck Publishers).

Early diet is reconstructed in Craig B. Stanford and Henry T. Bunn (eds) (2001) *Meat-Eating and Human Evolution* (Oxford: Oxford University Press), Peter S. Ungar and Mark F. Teaford (eds) (2002) *Human Diet: Its Origin and Evolution* (Westport, CT: Bergin and Garvey), and Peter S. Ungar (ed.) (2007) *Evolution of the Human Diet: The Known, the Unknown, and the Unknowable* (Oxford: Oxford University Press). The relationship between food and other aspects of early human history is treated systematically in Ivan Crowe (2000) *The Quest for Food: Its Role in Human Evolution and Migration* (Stroud, UK: Tempus).

The classic work on the Neolithic Revolution is V. Gordon Childe (1936) *Man Makes Himself* (London: Watts and Co.). Recent reconsiderations include Graeme Barker (2006) *The Agricultural Revolution in Prehistory: Why did Foragers become Farmers?* (Oxford: Oxford University Press) and Peter Bellwood (2005) *First Farmers: The Origins of Agricultural Societies* (Oxford: Blackwell Publishing, 2005). Ancient Africa is covered well in Thurstan Shaw, Paul Sinclair, Bassey Andah and Alex Okpoko (eds) (1993) *The Archaeology of Africa: Food, Metals and Towns* (London: Routledge) and J. Desmond Clark and Steve A. Brandt (eds) (1984) *From Hunters to Farmers: The Causes and Consequences of Food Production in Africa* (Berkeley: University of California Press). For Eurasia, see David R. Harris (ed.) (1996) *The Origins and Spread of Agriculture and Pastoralism in Eurasia* (London: UCL Press), John M. Wilkins and Shaun Hill (2006) *Food in the Ancient World* (Oxford: Blackwell), H.E.M. Cool (2006) *Eating and Drinking in Roman Britain* (Cambridge: Cambridge University Press), and Peter Garnsey (1999) *Food and Society in Classical Antiquity* (Cambridge: Cambridge University Press). A valuable trilogy on the Americas before Columbus is William M. Denevan (2001) *Cultivated Landscapes of Native Amazonia and the Andes* (Oxford: Oxford University Press), William E. Doolittle (2000) *Cultivated Landscapes of Native North America* (Oxford: Oxford University Press), and Thomas M. Whitmore and B.L. Turner II (2001) *Cultivated Landscapes of Middle America on the Eve of Conquest* (Oxford: Oxford University Press).

The global spread and redistribution of plants and animals is treated broadly by Alfred W. Crosby Jr. (1972) *The Columbian Exchange: Biological and Cultural Consequences of 1492* (Westport, CT: Greenwood) and Jared Diamond (1997) *Guns, Germs and Steel: A Short History of Everybody for the Last 13,000 years* (New York: W.W. Norton). Jack R. Harlan (1975) *Crops and Man* (Madison, WI: American Society of Agronomy) is the classic work on plants. For the Americas generally, see William W. Dunmire (2004) *Gardens of New Spain: How Mediterranean Plants and Foods Changed America* (Austin, TX: University of Texas Press) and Nelson Foster and Linda S. Cordell (eds) (1992) *Chilies to Chocolate: Food the Americas gave the World* (Tucson, AZ: University of Arizona Press). Also useful are Henry Hobhouse (1987) *Seeds of Change: Five Plants that Transformed Mankind* (New York: Harper & Row) and Denis J. Murphy (2007) *People, Plants, and Genes: The Story of Crops and Humanity* (Oxford: Oxford University Press). Although not up to date, Jack Ralph Kloppenburg (1988) *First the Seed: The Political Economy of Plant Biotechnology 1492–2000* (Cambridge: Cambridge University Press) remains important.

Specialized works, dealing with particular plants, include Betty Fussell (1992) *The Story of Corn* (Albuquerque, NM: University of New Mexico Press), Judith A. Carney (2001) *Black Rice: The African Origins of Rice Cultivation in the Americas* (Cambridge, MA: Harvard University Press), Chris Ballard, Paula Brown, R. Michael Bourke, and Tracy Harwood (eds) (2005) *The Sweet Potato in Oceania: A Reappraisal* (Sydney, Australia: University of Sydney, Oceania Monographs no. 56), Lucien Degras (1983) *The Yam: A Tropical Root Crop* (Oxford: Macmillan, 1983), William O. Jones (1959) *Manioc in Africa* (Stanford, CA: Stanford University Press), James C. McCann (2005) *Maize and Grace: Africa's Encounter with a New World Crop, 1500–2000* (Cambridge, MA: Harvard University Press), and John Reader (2008) *Propitious Esculent: The Potato in World History* (London: William Heinemann). Although its style now seems out of date, the seminal work in commodity history is Redcliffe N. Salaman's (1949) *The History and Social Influence of the Potato* (Cambridge: Cambridge University Press). An influential extension of the model is Sidney W. Mintz (1985) *Sweetness and Power: The Place of Sugar in Modern History* (New York: Viking).

Agricultural history is given a large context in Daniel E. Vasey (1992) *An Ecological History of Agriculture: 10,000 b.c.–a.d. 10,000* (Ames, IA: Iowa State University Press). Aspects of modern agriculture are considered in Giovanni Federico (2005) *Feeding the World: An Economic History of Agriculture 1800–2000* (Princeton: Princeton University Press), Deborah Fitzgerald (2003) *Every Farm a Factory: The Industrial Ideal in American Agriculture* (New Haven, CT: Yale University Press), and Nick Cullather (2010) *The Hungry World: America's Cold War Battle Against Poverty in Asia* (Cambridge, MA: Harvard University Press). For a broad survey of contemporary patterns, see Alfred R. Conklin Jr. and Thomas Stilwell (2007) *World Food: Production and Use* (Hoboken, NJ:

John Wiley & Sons). Animal foods are considered in Umberto Albarella, Keith Dobney, Anton Ervynck and Peter Rowley-Conwy (eds) (2007) *Pigs and Humans: 10,000 years of Interaction* (Oxford: Oxford University Press), Richard Perren (2006) *Taste, Trade and Technology: The Development of the International Meat Industry since 1840* (Aldershot, UK: Ashgate), and Richard W. Bulliet (2005) *Hunters, Herders, and Hamburgers: The Past and Future of Human–Animals Relationships* (New York: Columbia University Press). The extraordinary rise of the chicken is discussed in Jane Dixon (2002) *The Changing Chicken: Chooks, Cooks and Culinary Culture* (Sydney, Australia: UNSW Press).

A valuable guide to the world of hunting and gathering is Richard B. Lee and Richard Daly (eds) (1999) *The Cambridge Encyclopedia of Hunters and Gatherers* (Cambridge: Cambridge University Press). For pastoralism, see John G. Galaty and Douglas L. Johnson (eds) (1990) *The World of Pastoralism: Herding Systems in Comparative Perspective* (New York: Guilford Press) and Tim Ingold (1980) *Hunters, Pastoralists and Ranchers: Reindeer Economies and Their Transformations* (Cambridge: Cambridge University Press). The best general histories of fishing are D.H. Cushing (1988) *The Provident Sea* (Cambridge: Cambridge University Press) and Callum Roberts (2007) *The Unnatural History of the Sea: The Past and Future of Humanity and Fishing* (London: Gaia).

Salt is covered well by S.A.M. Adshead (1992) *Salt and Civilization* (New York: St Martin's Press) and Mark Kurlansky (2003) *Salt: A World History* (New York: Penguin). The best source on ancient methods of preservation is Robert I. Curtis (2001) *Ancient Food Technology* (Leiden, The Netherlands: Brill). Ancient trades, other than salt, are discussed in John Keay (2006) *The Spice Route: A History* (Berkeley: University of California Press), while modern trade and distribution patterns are considered in Tim Lang and Michael Heasman (2004) *Food Wars: The Global Battle for Mouths, Minds and Markets* (London: Earthscan), Peter J. Atkins, Peter Lummel and Derek J. Oddy (eds) (2007) *Food and the City in Europe since 1800* (Aldershot, UK: Ashgate), Beverley Kingston (1994) *Basket, Bag and Trolley: A History of Shopping in Australia* (Melbourne: Oxford University Press), and Warren Belasco and Roger Horowitz (eds) (2009) *Food Chains: From Farmyard to Shopping Cart* (Philadelphia: University of Pennsylvania Press). The intimate relationship between trade and aid is discussed in Robert Paalberg (2010) *Food Politics: What Everyone Needs to Know* (Oxford: Oxford University Press), and Christopher B. Barrett and Daniel G. Maxwell (2005) *Food Aid after Fifty Years: Recasting Its Role* (London: Routledge). Gunilla Andrae and Björn Beckman's (1985) *The Wheat Trap: Bread and Underdevelopment in Nigeria* (London: Zed Books) provides a critical assessment of the impact of nutritional doctrine and trade imperatives. A broader critique of recent trade policy trends is found in Jennifer Clapp and Doris Fuchs (eds) (2009) *Corporate Power and Global Agrifood Governance* (Cambridge, MA: MIT Press).

Among drinks, the best studied are coffee and cocoa: Mark Prendergrast (1999) *Uncommon Grounds: The History of Coffee and How It Transformed Our World* (New York: Basic Books), Brian William Cowan (2005) *The Social Life of Coffee: The Emergence of the British Coffeehouse* (New Haven, CT: Yale University Press), Taylor Clark (2007) *Starbucked: A Double Tall Tale of Caffeine, Commerce and Culture* (New York: Little, Brown), William Gervase Clarence-Smith (2000) *Cocoa and Chocolate, 1765–1914* (London: Routledge), and Sophie D. Coe and Michael D. Coe (1996) *The True History of Chocolate* (London: Thames and Hudson). See also Di Wang (2008) *The Teahouse: Small Business, Everyday Culture, and Public Politics in Chengdu, 1900–1950* (Stanford, CA: Stanford University Press), and Robert John Foster (2008) *Coca-Globalization: Following Soft Drinks from New York to New Guinea* (New York: Palgrave Macmillan).

Styles of cooking are the subject of Lizzie Collingham (2005) *Curry: A Biography* (London: Chatto & Windus), John A. Jakle and Keith A. Sculle (1999) *Fast Food: Roadside Restaurants in the Automobile Age* (Baltimore: Johns Hopkins University Press), John K. Walton (1992) *Fish and Chips and the British Working Class 1870–1940* (Leicester, UK: Leicester University Press), and Ruth Oldenziel and Karin Zachmann (eds) (2009) *Cold War Kitchen: Americanization, Technology, and European Users* (Cambridge, MA: MIT Press).

Works on particular culinary styles or cuisines are numerous. For French, see Jean-Robert Pitte (2002) *French Gastronomy: The History and Geography of a Passion* (New York: Columbia University Press), Priscilla Parkhurst Ferguson (2004) *Accounting for Taste: The Triumph of French Cuisine* (Cambridge: Cambridge University Press), and Rebecca L. Spang (2000) *The Invention of the Restaurant: Paris and Modern Gastronomic Culture* (Cambridge, MA: Harvard University Press). For Chinese, the classic work edited by K.C. Chang (1977) *Food in Chinese Culture: Anthropological and Historical Perspectives* (New Haven, CT: Yale University Press), Roel Sterckx (2005) *Of Tripod and Palate: Food, Politics and Religion in Traditional China* (New York: Palgrave Macmillan), E.N. Anderson (1988) *The Food of China* (New Haven, CT: Yale University Press), and Seung-Joon Lee (2011) *Gourmets in the Land of Famine: The Culture and Politics of Rice in Modern Canton* (Stanford, CA: Stanford University Press). For Japanese, Naomichi Ishige (2001) *The History and Culture of Japanese Food* (London: Kegan Paul) and Katarzyna J. Cwiertka (2006) *Modern Japanese Cuisine: Food, Power and National Identity* (London: Reaktion Books). For African, James C. McCann (2009) *Stirring the Pot: A History of African Cuisine* (Athens, OH: Ohio University Press). For Pacific Islander, Nancy J. Pollock (1992) *These Roots Remain: Food Habits in Islands of the Central and Eastern Pacific since Western Contact* (Honolulu, HI: University of Hawaii Press), and Deborah Gewertz and Frederick Errington (2010) *Cheap*

Meat: Flap Food Nations of the Pacific Islands (Berkeley: University of California Press). For Italian, Alberto Capatti and Massimo Montanari (2003) *Italian Cuisine: A Cultural History* (New York: Columbia University Press) and Carol Helstosky (2004) *Garlic and Oil: Food and Politics in Italy* (Oxford: Berg). For Russian, R.E.F. Smith and David Christian (1984) *Bread and Salt: A Social and Economic History of Food and Drink in Russia* (Cambridge: Cambridge University Press). For Jamaican, B.W. Higman (2008) *Jamaican Food: History, Biology, Culture* (Mona, Jamaica: University of the West Indies Press). For Australian, Michael Symons (2007) *One Continuous Picnic: A Gastronomic History of Australia* (Melbourne: Melbourne University Press). For British, Joan Thirsk (2007) *Food in Early Modern England: Phases, Fads, Fashions, 1500–1760* (London: Hambledon Continuum) and Kate Colquhoun (2007) *Taste: The Story of Britain Through Its Cooking* (London: Bloomsbury).

An important comparison is found in Stephen Mennell (1985) *All Manners of Food: Eating and Taste in England and France from the Middle Ages to the Present* (Oxford: Blackwell). For a larger region, see Ken Albala (2003) *Food in Early Modern Europe* (Westport, CT: Greenwood Press) and Joan Fitzpatrick (ed.) (2010) *Renaissance Food from Rabelais to Shakespeare: Culinary Readings and Culinary Histories* (Farnham, Surrey, UK: Ashgate).

Gender is at the center of Arlene Voski Avakian and Barbara Haber (eds) (2005) *From Betty Crocker to Feminist Food Studies: Critical Perspectives on Women and Food* (Amherst, MA: University of Massachusetts Press). Interesting studies of ethnic and regional food identities in the United States include Linda Keller Brown and Kay Mussell (eds) (1984) *Ethnic and Regional Foodways in the United States: The Performance of Group Identity* (Knoxville, TN: University of Tennessee Press), Anne L. Bower (ed.) (2007) *African American Foodways: Explorations of History and Culture* (Urbana, IL: University of Illinois Press), Hasia R. Diner (2001) *Hungering for America: Italian, Irish, and Jewish Foodways in the Age of Migration* (Cambridge, MA: Harvard University Press), and Barbara G. Shortridge and James R. Shortridge (eds) (1998) *The Taste of American Place: A Reader on Regional and Ethnic Foods* (Lanham, MD: Rowman & Littlefield). Also useful is David Bell and Gill Valentine (1997) *Consuming Geographies: We Are Where We Eat* (London: Routledge).

Globalization has produced a large literature. Among the more important contributions are: Alexander Nützenadel and Frank Trentmann (eds) (2008) *Food and Globalization: Consumption, Markets and Politics in the Modern World* (Oxford: Berg), Carol Helsotsky (2008) *Pizza: A Global History* (London: Reaktion), Silvano Serventi (2002) *Pasta: The Story of a Universal Food* (New York: Columbia University Press), J.A.G. Roberts (2002) *China to Chinatown: Chinese Food in the West* (London: Reaktion Books), and David Y.H. Wu and

Sidney C.H. Cheung (eds) (2002) *The Globalization of Chinese Food* (Honolulu, HI: University of Hawaii Press).

Recent work on the history of nutrition includes: Walter Gratzer (2005) *Terrors of the Table: The Curious History of Nutrition* (Oxford: Oxford University Press), Harmke Kamminga and Andrew Cunningham (eds) (1995) *The Science and Culture of Nutrition, 1840–1940* (Amsterdam: Editions Rodopi), and Richard H. Steckel and Jerome C. Rose (eds) (2002) *The Backbone of History: Health and Nutrition in the Western Hemisphere* (Cambridge: Cambridge University Press). Interesting studies of its impact on voyagers are found in J. Watt, E.J. Freeman and W.F. Bynum (eds) (1981) *Starving Sailors: The Influence of Nutrition upon Naval and Maritime History* (Greenwich, UK: National Maritime Museum). Obesity is studied in Michael Gard and Jan Wright (2005) *The Obesity Epidemic: Science, Morality and Ideology* (London: Routledge) and Sander L. Gilman (2008) *Fat: A Cultural History of Obesity* (Cambridge: Polity). Gilman's (2008) *Diets and Dieting: A Cultural Encyclopedia* (New York: Routledge) provides a wide-ranging treatment of ideas and models. For general studies of famine history, see Cormac Ó Gráda (2009) *Famine: A Short History* (Princeton: Princeton University Press) and James Vernon (2007) *Hunger: A Modern History*. Cambridge, MA: Harvard University Press).

Current fears for the future are argued strongly in Julian Cribb (2010) *The Coming Famine: The Global Food Crisis and What We Can Do to Avoid It* (Berkeley: University of California Press) and Paul Roberts (2008) *The End of Food: The Coming Crisis in the World Food Industry* (Boston: Houghton Mifflin). A longer-term critique is Spencer Wells (2010) *Pandora's Seed: The Unforeseen Cost of Civilization* (New York: Random House). Earlier viewpoints are expressed in Julian Morris and Roger Bate (eds) (1999) *Fearing Food: Risk, Health and Environment* (Oxford: Butterworth Heinemann), Harvey Levenstein (1993) *Paradox of Plenty: A Social History of Eating in Modern America* (New York: Oxford University Press), and David Grigg (1985) *The World Food Problem 1950–1980* (Oxford: Blackwell). See also Warren Belasco (2006) *Meals to Come: A History of the Future of Food* (Berkeley: University of California Press).

Atlases that provide a useful view of select recent trends include: Thomas J. Bassett and Alex Winter-Nelson (2010) *The Atlas of World Hunger* (Chicago: University of Chicago Press) and Erik Millstone and Tim Lang (2003) *The Atlas of Food: Who Eats What, Where and Why* (London: Earthscan).

Of the easily accessible statistical databases, the most comprehensive for the period since 1960 is that supported by the Food and Agriculture Organization (United Nations): http://faostat.fao.org.

Index

How Food Made History, First Edition. B. W. Higman.
© 2012 B. W. Higman. Published 2012 by Blackwell Publishing Ltd.